Rational Extremism

The Political Economy of Radicalism

Extremists are people whose ideas or tactics are viewed as outside the mainstream. Looked at this way, extremists are not necessarily twisted or evil. But they can be, especially when they are intolerant and violent. What makes extremists turn violent? This book assumes that extremists are rational: given their ends, they choose the best means to achieve them. The analysis explains why extremist leaders use the tactics they do and why they are often insensitive to punishment and to loss of life. It also explains how rational people can be motivated to die for a cause. The book covers different aspects of extremism, including nationalism, revolution, suicide terrorism, and global *jihad*. The arguments are illustrated with important episodes of extremism, including the French Revolution, the rise of nationalism in Yugoslavia under Milosevic, and the emergence of suicide terror and Al Qaeda today.

Ronald Wintrobe is Professor of Economics at the University of Western Ontario, where he also codirects the Political Economy Research Group. Professor Wintrobe is the author of *The Political Economy of Dictatorship* (1998) and coauthor (with Albert Breton) of *The Logic of Bureaucratic Conduct* (1982). He is also coeditor (with Albert Breton, Gianluigi Galeotti, and Pierre Salmon) of *Rational Foundations of Democratic Politics* (2003), *Political Extremism and Rationality* (2002), *Understanding Democracy: Economic and Political Perspectives* (1997), and *Nationalism and Rationality* (1995). All of these titles were published by Cambridge University Press. He is also author or coauthor of many book chapters and articles in leading professional journals, and he has written and narrated two radio programs (on dictatorship and on extremism) for the Canadian Broadcasting Corporation's *Ideas* series.

Rational Extremism

The Political Economy of Radicalism

RONALD WINTROBE

University of Western Ontario

CAMBRIDGE
UNIVERSITY PRESS

CAMBRIDGE UNIVERSITY PRESS
Cambridge, New York, Melbourne, Madrid, Cape Town, Singapore, São Paulo

Cambridge University Press
32 Avenue of the Americas, New York, NY 10013-2473, USA

www.cambridge.org
Information on this title: www.cambridge.org/9780521859646

First published 2006

Printed in the United States of America

A catalog record for this publication is available from the British Library.

Library of Congress Cataloging in Publication Data
Wintrobe, Ronald.
Rational extremism : the political economy of radicalism / Ronald Wintrobe.
p. cm.
ISBN 0-521-85964-6 (hardcover : alk. paper)
1. Radicalism. 2. Political violence. 3. Terrorism. 4. Group identity. I. Title.
HN49.R3W56 2006
320.53–dc22   2005031821

ISBN-13 978-0-521-85964-6 hardback
ISBN-10 0-521-85964-6 hardback

To the memory of my mother and father

Contents

Acknowledgments   *page* ix

PART 1.   INTRODUCTION

1   The Problem of Extremism   3

PART 2.   GROUPS

2   Social Interactions, Trust, and Group Solidarity   21
3   Some Illustrations and a General Framework   53

PART 3.   EXTREMISM

4   The Calculus of Discontent   75
5   Can Suicide Bombers Be Rational?   108
6   Religion and Suicide Terror   144

PART 4.   REVOLUTIONS, NATIONALISM, AND *JIHAD*

7   Rational Revolutions   161
8   Slobodan Milosevic and the Fire of Nationalism   190
9   *Jihad vs. McWorld* Revisited   215

PART 5.   CONCLUSION

10   Summary of Propositions and Policy Implications   245

References   261
Index   275

Acknowledgments

I am grateful to Tim Besley, Geoffrey Brennan, Albert Breton, Giorgio Brosio, Morris Coats, Isaac Ehrlich, Silvia Fedeli, Mario Ferrero, Tom Flanagan, Joel Fried, Gianluigi Galeotti, Martin Gervais, David Hojman, Louis Imbeau, Phil Keefer, Murray Klippenstein, Jenna Jordan, Peter Kurrild-Klitgaard, Jean-Dominique Lafay, David Laibson, Adria Lawrence, Carla Marchese, Isidoro Mazza, Clark McCauley, Juan Mendoza, Sid Noel, Guido Ortona, Bob Pape, Peter Rosenthal, Charles Rowley, Pierre Salmon, Susan Stokes, Peter Streufert, Janez Sustersic, Maria Laura Di Tomasso, George Tridimas, Richard Vernon, Sara Wolch, Bob Young, and Ekkart Zimmermann for their sometimes detailed and always helpful comments and discussions of various chapters of the book. I would also like to thank Mario Ferrero for encouraging me to write on the subjects of revolution and religion, subjects that are now included in this book.

Parts of the book have been presented at various meetings of the American Economic Association, the Canadian Economic Association, the Canadian Political Science Association, the Public Choice Society, and the European Public Choice Society, as well as at meetings sponsored by the George Mason Faculty of Law, the German Institute for Economic Research (DIW), the Slovenian Institute of Macroeconomic Analysis and Development, the Nationalism and Ethnic Conflict Research Group at the University of Western Ontario, and the Villa Colombella Group. Chapters have also been presented at seminars at the universities of Buffalo, Catania, Chicago, Eastern Piedmont, Pennsylvania, Turin, and Western Ontario. I am indebted to the organizers of those seminars for being interested in my work and to participants for helpful comments. Any remaining errors are my own.

I am grateful to the Social Sciences and Humanities Research Council of Canada for financial support. Without its help I could not have written this book. I also would like to thank Enrico Colombatto for inviting me to the International Centre for Economic Research (ICER), Turin, Italy, which provided a most pleasant and stimulating environment and support; during this time chapter 4 was initially drafted and many other chapters were rewritten. I wish to thank Miana Plesca for able research assistance. Leslie Farrant and Paula Nopper provided superb secretarial support, and I want to extend a special acknowledgment to them. Finally, heartfelt thanks to my wife Diana for her support and her patience and affection during the years it has taken to write this book.

PART ONE

INTRODUCTION

ONE

The Problem of Extremism

1.1 Introduction

Extremist movements often appear mysterious, frightening, and irrational. Extremists like Osama bin Laden are said to be different from us: they are twisted, deviant, fanatical, or simply "evil." One reason, of course, is the extraordinary destruction of which they are sometimes capable, as symbolized by the events of 9/11. Another reason is the apparently single-minded passion of their leaders. And while the leaders of these movements often appear dogmatic, perhaps even more frightening is the oft-observed fanatical loyalty of their followers.

But extremism is not new. While the means of terror used by Al Qaeda were never used before, in many respects the phenomena associated with 9/11 are not new at all. Europe in particular has a long history of extremism. Perhaps the first modern example of extremism in power was the "Terror" (the word was invented then) associated with the Jacobin ascendancy during the French Revolution. In the twentieth century, extremist movements continued to take power in Europe with the rise of fascism in Italy, Nazism in Germany, and communism in the former Soviet Union and Eastern Europe. More recently, extremist groups in Europe have remained much smaller and have never risen to power but have been important and destructive. Movements included those involving the Red Brigades on the left and Propaganda Due on the right in Italy in the 1970s, the Baader-Meinhof Gang of the 1970s in Germany, and the antiimmigration National Front of Le Pen in France, which continues today.

North America has also had its share of extremist activity – for example, the Ku Klux Klan, the John Birch Society, the Weathermen, McCarthyism, and the right-wing militias in the United States and the Front de Liberation de Quebec in Canada. Of course, at one time the label "extremist" was often attached to people in the (now entirely mainstream) civil rights, women's, and gay and lesbian movements in the United States. Fringe movements continue to be important there; for example, in late 2004 the American National Rifle Association successfully opposed extending the ban on assault weapons such as AK-47s and Uzi submachine guns, thus making it easier to purchase them and leading its opponents to suggest that the group's initials actually stand for "No Rational Argument."

In other countries, anticolonialism was an important source of extremism in the twentieth century. Even Nelson Mandela, head of the group "Spirit of the Nation" in his early days, planned and participated in violent activities, although the group did not cause any deaths. However, extremism is not necessarily violent: the classic example of a nonviolent extremist is Gandhi, who invented the idea of nonviolence as a force with his concept of *satyagraha*. Recently, Mark Juergensmeyer has suggested in his book *Gandhi's Way* (1992) that Gandhi's methods have a place in resolving many important conflicts in the world today.

At the other (philosophical) end of the violent-nonviolent spectrum in anticolonialism there is possibly Franz Fanon, whose book *The Wretched of the Earth* (1963) developed a psychology of extremism, centered on the pleasure and rejuvenation to be experienced in the struggle for a just cause. Only by a process of violent overthrow, he argued, was it possible for the colonized person to develop for the first time as an individual and to get rid of colonialism and domination.

The Middle East has been an important source of extremism since the Second World War. This includes the activities of the Jewish Irgun against the British, the Hezbollah in Lebanon (which invented modern suicide bombing as a terrorist tactic), and the activities of Palestinian organizations like Hamas as well as Jewish extremists associated with the fundamentalists in the settler movement.

The first point about this list of examples is that extremists are not all bad people; the list includes heroes as well as demons. Indeed, extremists are often both, though in the eyes of different people.

The second point is that there is a certain sense in which all these groups appear to be part of the same phenomenon. Hannah Arendt (1951, 1973) pointed out that Soviet communism and Nazi fascism were similar in so many respects that they could be called by the same name: "totalitarian." Clifford Geertz (2003) refers to the "totalitarian" nature of Islamic fundamentalist organizations, and Christopher Hitchens calls the contemporary Islamic terrorists "Islamofascists." Of course, not all of the movements listed fit these labels. However, there is no entry for "extremism" in the *Oxford Companion to the Politics of the World* (Krieger 1993). Nor is there an entry for "radicalism." Of course, there are entries for communism, anti-Semitism, fascism, and so on. This reflects the fact that, while there is lots of work on individual extremist movements, there is little or none on the problem in general. Yet, when one listens to or reads about extremists even with completely opposite points of view, they often seem to be, at one level, basically the same. For example, the Jewish fundamentalists in Israel and the extremists of Hamas have nothing whatsoever in common except:

- Both are against any compromise with the other side.
- Both want the entire land of Palestine for their group.
- Both are entirely sure of their position.
- Both advocate and sometimes use violence to achieve their ends.
- Both are nationalistic.
- Both are intolerant of dissent within their group.
- Both demonize the other side, so that the members of Hamas, as viewed by the Israeli fundamentalists, sometimes sound exactly like the Israeli fundamentalists as viewed by Hamas.

To pursue the last point, one common element in extremism is that it either arises in response to, or spawns an enemy that is fundamentally opposed to it. Thus the threat from the left in Europe in the late 1960s spawned the rise of the extreme right in the 1990s (Kitschelt 1997). Sometimes there is even a sense in which the opposite ends of the spectrum seem to be collaborating, if only implicitly. After all, they typically do have one objective in common – both wish to undermine the center. The 1970s in Italy was known as "the years of lead" because so many violent incidents occurred there, on both the right and the left. After every major terrorist incident, the question always seemed to be, Was the extreme right or the extreme left responsible?[1] And many on the extreme right and left in Italy were pleased at the incident that culminated the period – the kidnapping and murder of Italy's leading politician, Aldo Moro, in 1978. This destroyed

---

[1] The period of terror in Italy began with the bombing of the Piazza Fontana in 1969. Sixteen people died, and eighty-eight were wounded. The police immediately arrested an anarchist named Giuseppe Pinelli. Three days later, while in police custody, Penelli mysteriously died. His death was later ruled "accidental," but the explanations given by the police were so incredible and contradictory that few people believed them. Later, the playwright Dario Fo wrote a farce about the whole affair called *Accidental Death of an Anarchist* (2003). Initially the act was attributed to the left. No one was ever convicted of the Piazza Fontana bombing, but it's now accepted that it was actually the work of neofascists on the right, rather than extremists on the left (Ginsborg 2003). It was part of the so-called Strategy of Tension. This is a term coined to describe a devious plan of the right: to plant bombs and then blame the carnage on the left. The point was to sow panic and build support for a hard-line authoritarian regime, which would then put a stop to the violence.

the "historic compromise" whereby the Communist left and the Christian Democratic right would both move to the center (Drake 1995) and the Communist Party would formally enter the government. This would have been the first time in history that communism would take power via the democratic process instead of a revolution. People on both extremes hated the idea, the extreme right because they hated the idea of Communists in power, and the extreme left because it would destroy its hopes for a genuine Marxist revolution. Indeed, it was difficult to figure out which group killed him, and a succession of trials was held to uncover the truth, aspects of which are still not certain. In the same way, elements in both Hamas and the Jewish extremist groups were pleased when the Oslo peace process was torpedoed by the murder of Israel's Prime Minister Yitzhak Rabin.

The starting point of this book is that the similarities among extremist movements make it worthwhile to investigate them as a single phenomenon. So the problem to which this book is addressed is the problem of the origins, behavior, consequences, and (where desirable) control of extremism.

The simplest way to think of an extremist is someone whose views are outside the mainstream on some issue or dimension. In the twentieth century, extremists were typically persons on the extreme right or the extreme left. But the dimension could also be nationalism, religion, security, or any other politically important dimension.

In addition, the word "extremist" is also used to refer to a person or group that uses extremist *methods,* such as violence or terrorism, to achieve its goals. And extremism can refer to other things as well. For example, as we have suggested, extremists are typically against any compromise, they are entirely sure of their position, and they are intolerant of dissent within their group.

So persons or movements may be called extreme because their views are far out of the mainstream on some issue, or because they use violence to further their goals, or because they are rigid and intolerant of other points of view. A group can be extremist if it has only one of these features. Some movements – Al Qaeda is a good example – have all of them. Indeed, this is not surprising, because, as we will show, the latter two characteristics, the predilection for violence and the tendency toward rigidity and intolerance, can be derived from the first characteristic.

1.2 The Approach – Rationality

We will look at the phenomena of extremism from the point of view of modern political economy. This means that we will assume that extremist groups and the individuals who join them are *rational*. That is, given their goals, they try to adopt the best means to achieve them. The idea that extremists are rational is not new. For example, a recent study of all suicide terrorist attacks worldwide from 1980 to 2001 showed that suicide attacks are typically organized in coherent campaigns that are started and stopped by the group's leadership, directed at targets that are thought to be vulnerable to this pressure, and always conducted for a specific purpose – that of gaining control over what the terrorists see as their national territory (Pape 2003). In a similar vein, Enders and Sandler (2003) provide some evidence that terrorists behave rationally when they select attacks, substituting less protected targets after protection has been increased at other targets. For example, the tightening of security measures at government embassies and government buildings provoked terrorists to turn to aircraft hijacking. When airports installed metal detectors, terrorists selected civilian targets that were less protected.[2]

With respect to terrorists, too often the media just report their actions, especially when they are violent and even repulsive. But the repulsiveness can be deliberately designed to frighten people and to provoke their governments into overreacting. The hope is this will backfire and ultimately advance the aims of the extremists. It's a kind of "judo politics."

Extremism often involves dissent and demonstrations against the existing situation. In a review of the early literature on political extremism, Knoke (1990) points out that psychological explanations often dominated discussions of extremism in the past. Thus, for example, it was often argued that individuals who experienced intolerable psychological stresses in their daily lives and joined in mob actions were accessing a safety valve that let off steam but accomplished little in the way of solving their problems. Accordingly, participants in extremist movements were often marginal to society or dispossessed by economic change.

Empirical evidence has now accumulated that contradicts these explanations, at least as applied to social movements in general. The evidence drawn from such classic social movements as the black civil rights movement in the U.S. South, the women's movement, Three Mile Island protests, poor peoples movements, and social protest under Weimar consistently suggests that collective actions generally attract participants of higher social economic status who are more integrated and better connected to societal institutions than are nonparticipants.

---

[2] More recently, of course, they have also found new ways to get at the old targets.

Instead, the modern approach tends to see social movements, including extremist movements, as the main vehicle for marginal and excluded people to gain access to and influence within an established political system. It follows that extremism can be modeled as a form of political competition.

I assume extremists are rational. This does not mean that they are necessarily selfish, cold, or that they calculate everything. It means only that, given their goals, they try to achieve them as fully as possible and this means choosing the best method to achieve them. Nor does it mean they are the same as you and I because their goals are different. For example, the goals of Al Qaeda are obviously not shared by most people in the West. But the point of the assumption of rationality is to understand their behavior, not to exonerate them or judge them. When we understand what they are about, we make them human and that enables us to put ourselves in their place. This helps us to understand why they do what they do and, where their actions are threatening and warrant measures to be taken against them, to combat them.

The assumption that extremists are rational means it is important to understand the goals of the extremist movement in question. Although these movements differ wildly, they often have one thing in common – a particular structure of "all or nothing" or indivisibility or utopianism. Yet, although the nature of the goals of extremist groups plays an important role in determining the choice of extremist methods by group leaders, "the cause" of extremist groups is not necessarily "the cause" of the extremism of their *members*.[3] We look at what makes people join (or support) extremist groups; why extremist groups sometimes adopt beliefs that, to an outsider, are patently false; and what conditions are conducive to the flourishing of extremism and terrorism, especially suicide terrorism.

The rational approach to political behavior is associated with public choice theory. In that theory, extremism has an obvious interpretation because the central question in public choice theory is whether there is "convergence" of the political parties at the median in left-right space.[4] Extremism would mean that a group would locate toward one of the extremes of left or right. However, there is no real theory of extremism in the standard model because either there is convergence at the median or, as a result of the well-known Arrow problem, there is simply no equilibrium and "anything can happen." In Wittman-Hibbs-Alesina-Alesina-Rosenthal models, in which

---

[3] Any more than the goals of a firm (profits, say) or a government (reelection) explain the actions of individual subordinates within that firm or government bureau.

[4] The standard survey of public choice theory is Mueller (2003).

parties are, in part, ideologically motivated, convergence is not complete, and the parties may become polarized to a greater or lesser degree, but again there is no real theory of extremist behavior.

One reason for this state of affairs is that extremism is a complex phenomenon that typically involves more than the simple left-right dimension. For example, extremism is often associated with other phenomena, including utopianism, nationalism, revolutionary activity, *jihad* (struggle), or terrorism. To understand these aspects of extremism, I provide chapters on each of these subjects. Each chapter is illustrated with a detailed example or with several examples: utopianism with communism, the Palestinian conflict, and Islam; nationalism with the rise of Slobodan Milosevic; revolution with the great French Revolution; and *jihad* and terrorism with contemporary Islamic Radicalism.

Another reason that extremism is difficult to understand, which is implicit in each of the phenomena just mentioned, is that there is something left out of the standard rational choice picture. Perhaps the simplest way to describe what is left out is to begin by observing that, in the traditional rational choice approach, there are only two kinds of actors – individuals and the state. Here, we change this to include groups and social interactions. People have a preference for social interaction or for solidarity, or they prefer to live in societies with larger stocks of social capital, or they wish to be members of groups. The next section expands on this idea.

1.3 Rationality with a Twist: The Importance of Groups and Solidarity

Solidarity denotes "unity" or "oneness of purpose." Sometimes solidarity is motivated by empathy or identification,[5] as when we feel for others who have experienced a misfortune that could have happened to us, and we may contribute time or money to help them.

The desire for group identification seems to be a fundamental characteristic of human beings (D. Brown 1991). This preference has been demonstrated in very simple experiments, such as one in which people were sorted by their teacher into groups with brown eyes and those with blue eyes, and the individuals within each group immediately began distinguishing between "insiders" and "outsiders," based on eye color.[6] The nature of the

---

[5] "What did the Dalai Lama say to the hot dog vendor? Make me ONE with Everything" (joke told by Anthony Downs in his Presidential Address to the Public Choice Society).

[6] Huddy (2003), reviews these experiments and subsequent work.

group with which one identifies appears to be subject to wide variation and can include the family, the workplace, religion, political party, sporting clubs, ethnicity, and the nation-state.

However, working against solidarity within any group is the well-known "free-rider" problem: even though individuals within the group are better off when the group prospers as a whole, any individual can always gain through the pursuit of individual advantage even when that conflicts with the interests of the group. In biology, this destroys the possibility of group selection (Williams 1966). In society, the pursuit of individual advantage can have the same destructive effect on solidarity within groups. But groups find ways to deal with the free-rider problem, and an interesting literature has developed on this point, which we review in the next chapter.

Solidarity may also be motivated by pure self-interest. For example, if a person's rewards are greater if he remains with a group, solidarity with the group may be a totally self-interested choice. Business firms, unions, armies, political parties, and other organizations often find it in their interest to structure incentives within their organization to reward loyalty, and so employees and participants may choose solidarity with others in the organization without any motivation other than their own welfare.

Whatever the motivation,[7] the more solidarity there is among the members of a group, the more they are capable of making exchanges with one another, or cooperating as a group toward some common goal. For this reason, solidarity is like social capital or trust and is often classed with it. These concepts are closely related to each other (I provide precise definitions of them in the next chapter).

What is the connection between solidarity and extremism? Extremism is normally seen as the essence of individualism, but political extremism in some ways is actually its opposite. Thus the conformity often observed *within* extremist movements is remarkable, and often greater and more disconcerting than the conformity within the wider society to which such movements set themselves up in opposition.[8] Thus, in some ways, conformity and extremism are opposites; in other ways, they are simply different aspects of the same phenomenon.

---

[7] It would be interesting to find evidence or to design an experiment that would distinguish the two motivations.

[8] To see this point in the context of spatial models, observe that a person whose preferences are located near the center of the political distribution usually has the option of shifting his allegiance to a party on either the right or left and thus retains his individualism. But a person at the extreme tends to be stuck with the extremist group, the more so the more extreme he gets.

The connection between extremism and group solidarity can be seen in many extremist groups. It is no accident that "organic" or "group" concepts are typically more central to the extremist vision, as was the case with fascism (the word itself indicates the strength of a group compared to the assorted individuals within it), Nazism, and, of course, communism. Other, lesser-known movements such as the radical Hindus in the 1920s or the Japanese Tokkotai (Special Attack Forces or kamikazes) have a similar structure (Buruma and Margalit 2004). Even right-wing militants who celebrate "individualism" and independence from the state exhibit a remarkable internal conformity, as shown in the classic study of right-wing American extremism by Lipset and Rabb (1978). Ba'athism, the ideology of the Syrian and former Iraqi governments, is, according to Buruma and Margalit, a "synthesis, forged in the 1930s and 1940s, of fascism and romantic nostalgia for an 'organic' community of Arabs" One of its key thinkers, Sati' Husri, used the idea of *asabiyya*, or Arab blood solidarity, developed in the fourteenth century by Ibn Khaldun, and this is still the official ideology of Ba'athists today (Buruma and Margalit 2004, pp. 145–146).

It has been observed that Islam is the most communitarian of the three monotheisms (Black 2001, p. 309). Radical Islam is based on the idea that the world is in a state of *jahiliyya* (barbarism or idolatry), which emerges from the West. So the conflict between radical Islam and the West is not just religious but is about fundamentally different kinds of community, between that based on individuals, pursuing their own interests, and the idea of a community based on pure faith (Buruma and Margalit 2004, p. 119).

To anticipate some of our conclusions, the role of social capital or solidarity in society can be summed up as follows. On the one hand, membership in a cohesive group or life in a community with abundant social capital is to many people a deep source of satisfaction. Social capital is said to contribute to happiness not only because of the pleasures of living in a society where people are more cohesive, but also because of its many indirect benefits, including lower crime rates, more education, and faster economic development.

On the other hand, an important implication of the standard economic approach to social capital is that behavior can be highly unstable when the stock of social capital is large (as we will see in more detail in Chapter 2). Further, as the rest of this book is devoted to showing, there is a deep connection between social capital or solidarity and all of the manifestations of extremism just discussed: terrorism (particularly suicide terrorism), nationalism, revolutionary activity, and *jihad*. The result is that the world is a more unstable, violent, and extremist place than would be predicted by models that do not incorporate social interactions. Whether one likes this world better than the typical rational choice universe of individual rational actors and the state depends on one's point of view. But, beyond this question, there is a more important point: to the extent that economic theory or social science does not take social interactions or the desire for solidarity into account in its analyses and policy predictions and implications, it may make wrong analyses, utter false predictions, and prescribe bad policies.

1.4 Outline of the Book

The next chapter looks at social interactions. I consider a number of problems, the answers to which have traditionally vexed social scientists. The standard way of looking at these problems in rational choice theory is individualistic. It does not take account of group relations or the social interactions among the participants, or their desire for solidarity. By social interactions I refer to the idea that what one person does depends on what other people do: either positively (the more they do it, the more you want to do it, as in conformist behavior or religious participation or network externalities) or negatively (the more they do it, the less you want to do it, as in snobbery or status). It has long been known that social interactions can play havoc with traditional economic models: for example, bandwagon effects can cause demand curves to slope upward. But such effects remain little understood. In Chapter 2, I summarize some of the literature on social interactions and suggest that understanding and incorporating social relations into rational choice theory are key to understanding a number of otherwise seemingly unrelated puzzles in economics and politics.

Chapter 3 applies this perspective to three diverse puzzles, which are important but are unrelated to extremist activity, in order to explain the approach further and to demonstrate its power. The applications include crime prevention, the 1997–1998 Asian economic crisis, and the microfinance revolution as a way of combating poverty. The basic notion is that, in each case, considering social interactions illuminates the problem, shows what is wrong with the standard way of thinking, and suggests a different policy prescription than would be considered otherwise. In addition, a preliminary attempt is made to integrate the diverse contributions that have been made to each of these problems into a simple yet general picture.

Part 2 begins the analysis of extremism from this same perspective. Chapter 4 looks at the demand for extremist actions and asks what would make the leader of a political group choose terror and violence as a method of political competition. I assume that extremist leaders are rational; therefore, given their goals, they choose the best methods to achieve them. It follows that knowing their goals is important to understand their behavior. I show that, under certain circumstances, groups that have extreme *goals* – that is, they take extremist positions on issues – tend also to use extremist *methods,* such as terrorism and violence, to pursue those goals. That is, extremist thoughts and ideas tend to produce extremist violence.

In particular, extremists in position adopt extremist methods when there is an indivisibility that characterizes the relationship between the intermediate goal of the group and its ultimate goal. In Chapter 4 I look at three examples: communism (control over the means of production is an intermediate goal to the achievement of a communist society), nationalism (control over territory is an intermediate goal to the achievement of nationhood), and Islamic fundamentalism (ridding the Muslim nations of foreign and secular influences is an intermediate goal to the achievement of an Islamic society). In turn, conflict between each of these and opposing groups (respectively, capitalism, other groups with the same territorial ambition, secularism), is, in a sense, inevitable as it results from the conflict between their ultimate goals.

If correct, the argument of this chapter would appear to raise a troubling challenge to liberal theory. Freedom of thought is central to liberal theory, provided that democratic methods are used to pursue that goal. If there tends to be a correlation between extremist positions and extremist methods, then it may be difficult for the state to combat the latter without imposing controls on the former.

Here is an illustration: Eric Hobsbawm begins *The Age of Extremes: The Short Twentieth Century, 1914–1991* with a section called "The Century: A Bird's Eye View," in which twelve distinguished people, including three Nobel laureates, give a one-paragraph summation of the twentieth century. It is fair to say that comments such as "the most violent century in human history" (William Golding) or "the most terrible century in Western history" (Isaiah Berlin) are not unrepresentative. The musician Yehudi Menuhin says that "If I had to sum up the twentieth century, I would say that it raised the greatest hopes ever conceived by humanity, and destroyed all illusions and ideals."[9] My point in this chapter is that perhaps these two observations are connected: it was *because* the ideas or goals promulgated in the century were so grand that so much violence occurred.

---

[9] Hobsbawm (1994), pp. 1–2, taken from Paolo Agosti and Giovanna Borgese, *Mi Pare un secolo: Ritratti e parole di centosei protagonisti del Novecento* (Turin, 1992).

The most important policy implication of the chapter is that one should look at the goals of extremist groups in order to understand their actions. The reason is that it is the indivisibility of the goal that explains the extremism of the actions, and if one can unbundle the goal or make the indivisible divisible, then there may be ways to provide these goals in a way that satisfies some of the members of the group and thus dries up support for the grander ambitions of the leaders of extremist groups.

Chapter 5 turns to the supply side of suicide terrorism. I ask how it is possible for a person to rationally commit suicide to further the goals of a group. I begin with the desire for solidarity. Individuals get solidarity in part by conformity to the goals of the group, that is, they "trade" their own autonomy for solidarity. The central result is the "solidarity multiplier." This concept shows why people who join a group to get solidarity find that, once in, they tend to go further in the direction of giving up their autonomy in order to get solidarity than they originally wanted. Small trades of this type are common, but under certain conditions there is a "multiplier" effect in which the desire for solidarity feeds on itself in a self-reinforcing process. Under certain conditions this self-reinforcing process of choosing more solidarity implies a corner solution where solidarity is maximal and the individual's values are entirely that of the group. Near to or at a corner, rational suicide for the group is possible.

I then look at the structure of Al Qaeda to see whether it possesses features that favor this solution. Two properties of Al Qaeda make this model of organizational control particularly appropriate: its cellular structure and its version of Islam, which is more capable of generating the intense social cohesion involved in such sacrifices than other religions.

Chapter 6 considers the popular idea that individuals may become suicide martyrs in exchange for the rewards of heaven (the famous "seventy-two virgins" explanation). I use an analogy here between God and the monarchy (the One God was indeed initially conceived of as "The Absolute Monarch"). I build on the North-Weingast theory of the monarchy sometimes called the "Irony of Absolutism." I conclude that exchanges with God are unenforceable, and suicide martyrdom as an exchange for an afterlife is not rational. This does not mean that people may not *believe* that they are committing the ultimate sacrifice in exchange for the rewards of heaven. But the reason for holding the belief may not lie in its being true or logical, but in the fact that others hold it. As suggested in Chapter 5, individuals may be willing to adopt the beliefs of a group in exchange for solidarity or the feeling of belonging to the group. Religious behavior may represent this kind of implicit "contract." It is not a contract with God but with a religious group that professes a particular set of beliefs, and which claims to represent God. In that case, a person may end up at or near a corner solution, in which rational suicide for the cause is possible. In the "solidarity" model the individuals concerned have high discount rates (the feeling of solidarity is experienced prior to and while the act of martyrdom is committed), whereas in the after-life model a low discount rate is implied. Evidence on the typical "profile" of suicide martyrs could be used to estimate this discount rate.

In brief, the second part of the book describes how leaders and followers in a typical group behave and what makes them behave in an extreme fashion. Leaders are extreme when they demand fundamental changes, or resort to the ordering of violent and terrorist operations to provide those goals. Followers are extreme when they are willing to sacrifice so much for the cause.

The third part of the book deals with macrophenomena of extremism – revolutions, nationalism, and the effects of "globalization" on extremism. Chapter 7 begins by asking if a rational choice explanation of revolution is possible. I note first and analyze critically the interesting recent literature on revolution developed mainly by sociologists with reference to the East German, Iranian, and other contemporary revolutions. I then propose my own approach to this question, which starts by distinguishing between indi-vidual and what could be called "collective" rationality. In analyzing revo-lutions (as distinct from riots, strikes, or other forms of collective action), I have argued that the second type is logically prior to the first, that is, one cannot look at the incentives facing an individual potential leader or fol-lower of a revolutionary movement without considering what type of state is being faced and whether it is strong or weak. The basic condition under which a (collectively) rational revolution can occur is if the state has been weakened, so that the mechanisms that have sustained the ruler in office no longer function effectively. If the state is weak, then leadership of revolu-tionary movements will tend to occur spontaneously. This, in turn, tends to make individual participation in revolutionary activity rational, as dynamic collective processes (cascades or bandwagon effects) may be set in motion by the prospect of success in overthrowing the government. I illustrate these arguments with the great French Revolution.

One implication of this approach is that group action is necessary to secure individual human rights. Individuals are not free to acquire more human rights by themselves; this requires group support and sometimes revolutionary action. This paradox is precisely expressed in the French Revolution, which is why we will illustrate Chapter 7 with it. Normally the French Revolution is associated with the Rights of Man and is seen as the foundation of democratic politics. But in order to obtain human rights, group action and group power were necessary, in this case to overthrow the government. But then, once the regime is overthrown, what guarantees that a democracy guaranteeing human rights will necessarily take its place?

This leads logically to ask if revolution can be collectively rational, not only in the sense that the current state's ability to function is severely impaired, but in the sense that the regime that replaces it is expected to represent an improvement. I consider various criteria here and ultimately suggest that one criterion may be sufficient (though not necessary): that the revolution results in more democracy. The chapter ends with a sketch of some possible revolutionary dynamics. These show some of the possibilities inherent in any revolutionary situation, and why revolutions sometimes turn extreme, as the French Revolution did.

Chapter 8 focuses on nationalism, ethnic cleansing, and war, with special reference to the Milosevic regime in Serbia. The question addressed is, Why did nationalism spread so quickly in Yugoslavia after the fall of communism? The basic argument is simple: first, like any dictator, Milosevic needed support in order to survive in office. His provocative and warlike actions toward other groups are best understood not as the latest round in a centuries-old tradition of ethnic fighting, but as the attempts of a competitive politician trying to survive in a situation where the old basis of power had collapsed. Second, in attempting to survive the wave of democratization that swept Eastern Europe after 1989, Milosevic played a wild card – the nationalist card. Nationalism can be wild because, under some circumstances, it is contagious. Especially when combined with the security dilemma, it can spread uncontrollably. Ethnic cleansing and war are explained in this light as neither deliberate, coldly planned strategies of brutal repression, nor the results of complete miscalculation, but the results of a process in which the leadership of the regime was reacting to events that it may have set in motion, but did not entirely control.

The starting point of Chapter 9 is Benjamin Barber's analysis of globalization in his 1995 book, *Jihad vs. McWorld.* Barber seemed to foresee the current world situation better than many others, and so this chapter tries to see if one can interpret his vision in rational choice terms. In this context, globalization, identified by Barber as the forces of McWorld, is pitted against another powerful force, *jihad.* But Barber also asserted that *McWorld stimulates jihad.* I provide a simple explanation of how this happens in terms of rational choice. I focus specifically on the economic system of production for concreteness and suggest that one can identify two broad systems, the shareholder (in North America and Britain) and stakeholder (variants of which are common in Europe and Asia) systems; whereas the shareholder system is superior in terms of transparency, the stakeholder system is better at generating and promoting solidarity and thus holding the forces of *jihad* in check. However, it is often suggested that the solidarity system is inimical to economic growth and prone to corruption. I present some evidence and commentary on this point, particularly with respect to the Korean and Chinese systems, in which there has been spectacular growth along with substantial corruption.

In Chapter 10 I summarize some of the important points in the book in eighteen propositions. I also present a simple table that shows the common logical structure to problems involving group interactions and, as well, pulls together the implications of the argument in each case for public policy.

PART TWO

GROUPS

TWO

Social Interactions, Trust, and Group Solidarity

2.1 Basic Ideas

The starting point of this book is that to understand extremism, one has to look not only at individuals but at the interactions between them and between the individual and the group. In this chapter and the next, I consider a number of social problems, the solutions to which have traditionally vexed social scientists. The standard way of looking at these problems is individualistic. I change this by incorporating social interactions,[1] which means incorporating the actions of others directly into the utility functions of individuals. In my view, this leads to a deeper understanding of these problems, and it sometimes changes the policy prescriptions used to deal with these phenomena. To illustrate this last point, consider some of the policy questions that have attracted attention in Canada, the United States, and the world over the past few years. Such a list might include the problem of crime, the Asian crisis of 1997–1998, and the persistence of poverty. There are, of course, other important problems such as terrorism, but we will deal with that in Chapters 4, 5, 6, and 9.

In each case, an individualistic approach leads to one set of prescriptions to solve the problem, usually involving prices. Consider the problem of crime. The standard approach in economics looks at an individual who might be contemplating a crime, and assumes he makes his decision based on the expected return (monetary or psychic) from the crime on the one hand and the probability of being caught and the size of the penalty if caught and convicted on the other. To prevent crime, it is obvious that in this framework one should raise its "price": either raise the level of policing, and thus the

---

[1] In this respect I am following the advice of Van Winden (1999), who advocates this shift in viewpoint and develops it himself for interest groups and political behavior.

probability that an offender will be caught, p, or the size of the punishment, f. Now, social interactions play no role here. But if they were admitted, then this conclusion might not seem so obvious. Some of the social interactions ignored include:

1. A great deal of crime in Canada and especially the United States is committed by young people who are part of gangs. As Levitt and Venkatesh (2000) have shown, it is difficult to explain gang participation on simple economic grounds.
2. Punishment in the form of jail terms automatically exposes the criminal to opportunities to socialize and form networks with criminals.
3. Punishment carries stigma, and as a result of being punished, individuals may find it harder to get a job than before, thus again increasing the relative gains to illegal activity.
4. The most serious form of crime is often organized crime, which is typically neglected in this framework.
5. We would expect to see more crime wherever there is not much social capital. Indeed, on one reading, this is the basis of the "broken windows" approach, discussed further in Chapter 3.

Finally, two further social interactions complicate the task of policy:

6. In communities where gangs are dominant, the sociologist Jankowski (1991) found that people in the community typically have to choose whether to side with the gang and help gang members avoid capture by the police, or to help the police. The help of the community is often crucial to the apprehension of gang members who have committed crimes. If the penalties are "too high" so that community members think them unfair, that may cause them to switch from being on the side of the police to siding with the gang. As a result, excessive penalties may have a counterproductive effect so that the probability of a criminal getting caught may actually fall, possibly increasing the crime rate on balance, as Akerlof and Yellen (1994) show.
7. As Andreoni (1995) has demonstrated, in jurisdictions where capital punishment is used, juries typically (and rationally) become less willing to vote for conviction if they have any doubt about guilt or innocence. They are obviously more afraid of making an error when the judge might sentence the offender to death than when life imprisonment is the maximum penalty. In that case, the increase in the penalty lowers the probability of conviction.

It is worth noting that all of these social interactions appear to invalidate the standard policy prescription that crime can be reduced through the implementation of higher penalties. Now look at another example. In the Asian crisis, the standard approach used by the International Monetary Fund (IMF) to deal with the crisis looked at Asian firms as if they were no different from firms in Latin America or in the United States, and proposed a standardized "structural adjustment" remedy for the emerging crisis. But Asian firms are different: they are embedded in a network of social relations, including relations with banks and sometimes with governments. The systems differ from country to country but all of them were collectively referred to as "alliance" capitalism and subsequently earned the title of "crony" capitalism because of the importance of networks of social relations involved compared with their importance to an American firm. One implication is that, because of the close relations between the firm and the bank, the ratio of debt to equity is usually much higher than that typical of American firms. So when the IMF imposed an adjustment package of raising prices (interest rates) to restore the confidence of investors, this had the immediate effect of threatening many firms with bankruptcy (Wade and Veneroso 1998). Again, social relations do make a difference and should be taken into account in formulating policy.

This chapter reviews some of the literature on social interactions. I focus specifically on accounts – mainly from economics, but also from political science and history – that deal with the creation and destruction of solidarity, trust, and social capital. The next section provides an overview of some of the most important general models of social interactions. The third section then turns to the basic concept used in this book, group solidarity, and elucidates it by means of four examples of different kinds of groups: the family, as it has been described in economics since the work of Becker (1974); the behavior of individuals in the army, as described by the historian John Keegan in his book, *The Face of Battle* (1976); religious groups, as described by Iannacconne (1992) and Berman (2003); and classical extremist movements, namely communism and fascism, perhaps the most important examples of solidarity in politics. Section 4 turns to social capital, with special reference to Putnam's account of it in politics in his books *Making Democracy Work* (1993) and *Bowling Alone* (2000). Section 5 turns to the question of how assets like production of trust and social capital are produced. Sections 6 describes one property that solidarity, social capital, and trust all share: contagion. An appendix provides a simple set of mathematical definitions of solidarity, social capital, and other, related concepts such as reputation and general trust, and shows the close relationships among them. In this way I try to make the concepts, often used loosely, precise.

2.2 Social Interactions

To begin with, we can distinguish at least four types of social interactions:

1. In *social or preference interdependencies*, what I do depends on what you (other people) do. For example, in herd behavior in financial markets, creditors act on the basis of the actions of other creditors, not on the basis of the debtor's fundamentals as perceived by the individual investors. Or, in conformist behavior, I may do the same thing as other people (watch a "hit" TV program, for example) simply because my utility depends positively on doing what others are doing. Or I may buy a Hummer vehicle for the opposite reason – because few others can afford to do it.

2. In *social capital, trust,* or *networks*,[2] what I do depends on the degree of confidence or *trust* I have that you will fulfill an obligation.

3. With the *emotions*[3] – for example, sympathy, antipathy toward others – what I do depends on whether I am positively or negatively inclined toward you.

4. One important class of behavior that is sometimes classified with the other categories is described by the term "solidarity." Solidarity denotes "unity" or "oneness of purpose." Sometimes solidarity is motivated by empathy or identification, as when we feel for others who have experienced a misfortune that could have happened to us and contribute something to ameliorate their situation. At other times, it may be motivated by self-interest. Either way, the more solidarity there is among the members of a group, the more they are capable of cooperating as a group toward some common goal.[4] For this reason solidarity is like social capital and is often classed with it. For example, Putnam's (1993) "horizontal social capital" would seem to be the same thing as solidarity.

---

[2] As described by Coleman (1990) or, in the context of bureaucracy, by Breton and Wintrobe (1982).

[3] See Frank (1988) and Elster (1999).

[4] A formal proof of a related proposition – that the more "divided" or further apart the members of a community are, the less the community is capable of action – can be found in Wintrobe (1998a), chap. 11.

General theories of social interactions in modern economics probably begin with Becker's (1974) paper, discussed in detail in the next section. Becker has also made important subsequent contributions to the subject, especially the essays collected in Becker (1996) and the book by Becker and Murphy (2000). Although the term "social capital" is usually attributed to Glenn Loury (1977), it was widely introduced into economics by a sociologist, James Coleman, in his magisterial *Foundations of Social Theory* (1990).The economist George Akerlof has also made many important contributions to social economics, including his work on gift exchange, the rat race,[5] and obedience (1991). In an early contribution, Margolis (1982) tries to reconcile group-oriented and selfish behavior. More recently, Fehr (2004) argues that a propensity to punish norm violations may be an evolutionary adaptation, even though such behavior is not individually rational (because the individual has to incur a cost to do so). Other recent general studies include Bernheim's (1994) on conformity and Banerjee's (1992) on herd behavior.

Much interesting work has also been done in recent years incorporating some form of social relation into the consideration of a specific problem. For example, Glaeser, Sacerdote, and Scheinkman's (1996) empirical work shows the importance of social interactions in explaining crime rates; Iannacconne (e.g., 1992) and Berman (2000) analyze religion; Diamond and Dybvig (1983) model financial panics; and Chong (1991), Morton (1991), Uhlaner (1989) and Shachar and Nalebuff (1999) use social interactions to explain political participation.

The simplest form of social interaction is probably interdependent preferences. Thus, characteristics of others, for example, what clothes they are wearing or what restaurants they eat at, enter one's utility function. Equivalently, one can follow Becker's (1974) formulation on social interactions, in which the "relevant characteristics of others" enter as part of an individual's "social income" rather than as his utility function. One commonly modeled type of independent preferences is conformism.[6] For example, Jones (1984, p. 42), in an early contribution, modeled the utility function of employees deciding on the level of effort. He argues that, because of workplace pressures, workers dislike supplying a level of effort that is far from the output levels of other members of the working group.

---

[5] See the essays collected in Akerlof (1984).
[6] While I cannot survey all of the rational choice literature on conformity here, Sunstein's (2003) book appears to give a fairly comprehensive survey.

Alternatively, as in Bernheim's (1994) model, it may be that individuals care about esteem (status or popularity). Esteem depends on how one is perceived and, in Bernheim's formulation, is determined by public perceptions of an individual's type. However, an individual's type is not directly observable, and so others must infer his type from his choices or actions. The key variable in his model is the effect of an individual's actions on the esteem she is held in by others versus their effect on the individual's direct utility. The larger the first (status) relative to the second (direct utility), for example, the more it is likely that an individual's behavior will be governed by some norm of social behavior.

One application of the notion of conformity to political behavior is Kuran's (1995) theory of "preference falsification." In this theory, people present "public" preferences that differ from their private preferences. Thus, they conform, but only on the surface. Kuran develops many implications of this idea – how it inhibits change, hides racism, and, perhaps most interestingly, makes it very difficult to understand when a society is ripe for revolution, so that, when revolutions do occur, they are invariably unforeseen. Chapter 7 on revolutions reconsiders some aspects of this idea.

One thing that is common to revolutionary movements is solidarity. This topic is discussed next.

2.3 Solidarity

As mentioned already, solidarity denotes "unity" or "oneness of purpose." The more solidarity there is among the members of a group, the more they are capable of cooperating as a group toward some common goal.[7] A desire for group identification seems to be a fundamental characteristic of human beings.[8] This preference has been demonstrated in very simple experiments, such as the one where people were sorted by their teacher into groups with brown eyes and those with blue eyes, and the individuals within each group immediately began distinguishing between "insiders" and "outsiders," based on eye color.[9] The nature of the group identified with appears to be subject to wide variation. A wide variety of groups with which individuals identify can be listed, including the family, workplace, religion, political party, sporting clubs, ethnicity, and the nation-state. However, working against solidarity within any group is the well-known "free-rider" problem: even

---

[7] A formal proof of this proposition can be found in Wintrobe (1998a), chap. 11.

[8] D. Brown (1991).

[9] See Huddy (2003) who reviews these experiments and subsequent work.

though individuals within the group are better off when the group prospers as a whole, any individual can always gain through the pursuit of individual advantage, even when that conflicts with the interests of the group. In biology, this problem destroys the possibility of group selection (Williams 1966). In society, the pursuit of individual advantage can have the same destructive effect on solidarity within groups.

The classic sociological treatise on solidarity is Durkheim's *Division of Labor in Society* (1893). Perhaps the most important recent work on this topic from the rational choice point of view is Michael Hechter's *Principles of Group Solidarity*. Hechter suggests that solidarity can be best understood as "compliance in the absence of compensation or a quid pro quo" (1987, p. 10). His theory of solidarity emphasizes two variables in particular: the individual's dependence on the group, and the group's capacity to use formal controls to sanction deviance from its prescriptions. The result is that the greater the degree of dependence, and the greater the group's control capacity, the greater the solidarity of the group (1987, p. 52).

In economics, perhaps the best account of solidarity, and the best way to see the meaning of the concept as it is used here, is Becker's (1974) theory of the family.

2.3.1 The Family

Becker's account of the family is a special case of his (1974) general theory of social interactions. In this theory, a person's "social income" is the sum of his personal income plus the value to him or her of the "relevant characteristics of others." These could be very general, for example, the "esteem" in which he is held by others, or any other aspect of the individual's social (or physical) environment. Using his notation, let the individual's utility function be

$$U = Z(x, R) \tag{2.1}$$

where a single commodity, R, is produced with a single good, x. For example, R may be the distinction or the "esteem" in which the person is held. Then

$$R = D_i + h \tag{2.2}$$

where D_i = the social environment inherited by i (e.g., by the distinction of his family) and h = the amount he contributes to augment it.

The family is a special case of this general concept. Suppose that the family has a "head" (i) who is defined not by sex or age but by the fact that he cares sufficiently about the other family members to make transfers to them. Then the "head"'s social income is

$$S_i = I_i + p_R D_i = p_x x + p_R R \tag{2.3}$$

where p_R is the price of a unit of R (e.g., the cost of making transfers to other members of the family).

If it is costless to make transfers within the family, then $p_R = 1$. Suppose that $D_i = I_j$, where I_j = the income of some other family member j whom the head cares about. Then the head's social income is just

$$S_i = I_i + I_j = I_{ij}. \tag{2.4}$$

The head's social income is just "the family's income" – the sum of his own income plus the income of the other family members whom he cares about. It immediately follows that if the head could take an action that would raise his own income (I_i) by some amount b, but lower that of another family member (I_j) by more than that, c, he would not take that action, because it would lower his own (social) income (I_{ij}). Thus, as is obvious from equation 2.4, so far as the head is concerned, the family is a solidary unit, that is, the family is *one*. As Becker (1974, p. 1079) says, "A family with a head can be said to maximize 'its' consistent and transitive utility function of the consumption of different members subject to a budget constraint defined on family variables. The 'family's' utility function is identical with that of one member, the head, because his concern for the welfare of other members, so to speak, integrates all of the members' utility functions into one consistent 'family' function."

More remarkably, other family members are also motivated to care only for the income of the family as a whole, even if they are completely selfish, so long as the head cares sufficiently about them that he (or she) redistributes income among them. Consider a selfish ("rotten" in Becker's original terminology) kid, s, who could take some action that would raise his income by b but lower that of another family member by some larger amount, c. If, as a result of his action, family income is lower, the head will redistribute income among the members of the family so that each has the same share as before, so the result will be that s's income is lower than before. So s will not take that action. This is the famous "rotten kid theorem."[10] It implies that even utterly selfish members will act to maximize the income of the family as a

---

[10] Further work on this subject by Bergstrom (1989) and others suggests that certain restrictions apply for the theorem to hold. However, the broad logic of solidarity discussed here remains.

whole. Thus for them, too, the family is *one*, that is, the individual members will display perfect solidarity with the family. Alternatively, in the language of economics, they maximize the objective of the group, family income, not their own income.

This is solidarity in its purest form. What produces it? Sometimes it is asserted that it is the magical power of love that implies this result. But this is only partially true. What is necessary is that there is a preset distribution of assets among the family, and that income is redistributed to the various members so that this distribution is maintained. In Becker's family, this is done by the head out of love. But this is not necessary: *any* motive that results in the same set of actions with the same level of automaticity would have the same effect. Thus, suppose that the head does not love anyone in the family at all, but feels for reasons of justice, say, that the shares of the various family members should be maintained in a certain proportion. Then each member of the family will have the same motivation to maximize the welfare of the family as a whole (family income) that they have when the head cares for them. Other possible motives that lead to the same behavior might be a respect for tradition or even the head's own desire for a feeling of power. Alternatively, let us suppose a purely "democratic" family, in which all members are required to have the same equal share of the total income of the family. Then this democratic rule effectively substitutes for Becker's head in motivating all members to maximize family income.

This point immediately suggests that the theory has applications outside the family, where love may not rule (or even in families where love is not sufficiently strong). So the theory might apply to a cult, youth gang, religious group, political organization, business firm, or community where the leader has the power and the motivation to create solidarity among the members of the group. Of course, if the group is very large, the free-rider problem will arise. And disincentives from giving itself, for example, the so-called Samaritan's dilemma (Buchanan 1977) – the tendency for giving to create an unhealthy dependence – might also occur, as they could of course within the family itself. But, even in these cases, if the head of the group has the information and the power to ensure that the individual who does not cooperate simply makes himself worse off (along with the group as a whole), the theorem will continue to apply.

However, the rule of equality among family members would have to be enforced by some outside body (or perhaps by the members themselves, say, by a periodic "vote" among family members, and some designated method of enforcement). On the other hand, the "rule" of Becker's head is self-enforcing, so long as the head controls enough of the family's income to sustain positive gift giving.[11]

To summarize, what *does* seem to be required for the theory to apply is the existence of a leader with sufficient power to make the necessary redistributions so that no one feels that he can profit by taking actions that yield selfish benefits at the expense of the welfare of the whole. Now, there is an authoritarian element here, even though the head does not exercise power over the members in any way except by giving to them. What if other members prefer a different distribution of income? What if it is the head who is "rotten"? How can he be removed and replaced by a different, perhaps less selfish head? So it appears to be the combination of authoritarianism and altruism that is central to the rotten-kid theorem. Is this always necessary for solidarity? Let us consider another example.

2.3.2 The Army

Another place where solidarity appears to be vital is in battle. What motivates soldiers to kill and to be willing to participate in battles at the possible cost of their own lives? I do not know of anyone who knows the answer to this question, but certainly one of the most celebrated accounts of possible answers to it is John Keegan's *The Face of Battle* (1976), which synthesizes and analyzes a large number of historical accounts of the nature of battle, often as experienced by the protagonists. According to Keegan, solidarity is central to understanding the experience of battle:

What battles have in common is human: the behaviour of men struggling to reconcile their instinct for self-preservation, their sense of honour and the achievement of some aim over which other men are ready to kill them. The study of battle is therefore always a study of fear and usually of courage; always of leadership, usually of obedience; always of compulsion, sometimes of insubordination; always of anxiety, sometimes of elation or catharsis; always of uncertainty and doubt, misinformation and misapprehension, usually also of faith and sometimes of vision; always of violence, sometimes also of cruelty, self-sacrifice, compassion; *above all, it is always a study of solidarity and usually also of disintegration – for it is towards the disintegration of human groups that battle is directed.* (1976, p. 298; emphasis added)

In Keegan's account, the army that retains its solidarity triumphs over its adversary, which disintegrates. What produces the solidarity necessary to

---

[11] Thus a movement to greater equality among family members could reduce the power of the head, and destroy the theorem, if after the move family incomes were sufficiently equal that the head no longer wished to give to his spouse.

win? Early in the book there is a striking revelation, drawn from the writings of the nineteenth-century French officer Ardant du Picq:

[S]oldiers die in largest numbers when they run, because it is when they turn their backs to the enemy that they are least able to defend themselves. It is their rational acceptance of the danger of running that makes civilized soldiers so formidable, he [du Picq] says, that and the discipline which has them in its bonds. And by discipline he does not mean the operation of an abstract principle but the example and sanctions exercised by the officers of an organized force. *Men fight, he says, in short, from fear; fear of the consequences first of not fighting (i.e., punishment), then of not fighting well (i.e., slaughter).* (Keegan 1976, p. 71; emphasis added)

The battlefield is in this view "a place of terror," and "suppression of fear [is seen] chiefly as the officer's task" (p. 72). On this account, it is fear, or more precisely the desire to overcome fear, that produces solidarity. But fear could obviously result in the desire to escape as well. So some other ingredient is required.

When the United States entered the Second World War, it assembled a team of historians to record its war effort in detail, and this group decided from the outset to use du Picq's approach, focusing not on grand strategy or logistics but on the experiences of common soldiers. The guiding theme of their approach would be an examination of how the American soldier overcame his fears to do his duty (Keegan 1976, p. 73), and they conducted thousands of interviews with individuals and groups fresh from combat. The conclusions of the American Historical Teams were publicized in pungent capsule form by the leading historian of the European theater, General S. L. A. Marshall in his book, *Men against Fire*. Like the American historians, Marshall came to a radically different idea of how the soldier's fear should be overcome: "fear is general among men, but . . . men are commonly loath that their fear will be expressed in specific acts that their comrades will recognize as cowardice. The majority are unwilling to take extraordinary risks and do not aspire to a hero's role, but they are equally unwilling that they should be considered the least worthy among those present." It is therefore vital, in Marshall's view, that an army should foster the closest acquaintance among its soldiers, that it should seek to create groups of friends, centered if possible on someone identified as a "natural" fighter, because it is their mutual acquaintanceship that will ensure no one flinches or shirks. "When a soldier is . . . known to the men who are around him, he . . . has reason to fear the one thing he is likely to value more highly than life – his reputation as a man among other men."[12]

---

[12] S. L. A. Marshall, *Men against Fire* (New York: William Morrow, 1947), p. 73.

Indeed, fear is not just felt by the soldiers but by the officers as well:

Inside every army is a crowd struggling to get out, and the strongest fear with which every commander lives – stronger than his fear of defeat or even mutiny – is that of an army reverting to a crowd through some error of his making. For a crowd is the antithesis of an army, a human assembly animated not by discipline but by mood, by the play of inconstant and potentially infectious emotion which, if it spreads, is fatal to an army's subordination. Hence it is that the bitterest of military insults contain the accusation of crowdlike conduct – rabble, riff-raff, scum, *canaille, Pobel* – and the deepest contempt soldiers can harbour is reserved for leaders whose armies dissolved between their fingers – Cadorna, Kerensky, Gough, Gamelin, Perceval. (Keegan 1976, p. 174)

With respect to the line infantrymen in the Battle of Waterloo, who had "the unspectacular duty of standing to be shot at," Keegan asks the simple question (repeated later for soldiers in other battles such as the Battle of the Somme in 1916): "What sustained him?" Various possibilities are considered, including the prospect of loot (looting appears to have been a universal activity, energetically practiced even during the battle itself), drink (many had drunk spirits before the battle, and continued to drink while it was in progress), and the simple mechanism of coercion. But the two elements that appeared to be most important in sustaining the will to combat in his view are group solidarity and individual leadership (pp. 181–183). Moreover, the leadership of the officers is crucial in creating solidarity. But how? There is no single account of how this happens in Keegan, but one thing that is emphasized is the capacity of leaders to show their own solidarity with their men, as demonstrated by their willingness to undertake the same sacrifices demanded of their men in a brave fashion: "It was the receipt of wounds, not the infliction of death, which demonstrated an officer's courage; that demonstration was reinforced by his refusal to leave his post even when wounded, or by his insistence on returning as soon as his wounds have been dressed; and it was by a punctiliousness in obeying orders which made wounds or death inevitable that an officer's honour was consummated" (p. 189).

As to how solidarity itself is created, Keegan's account is a bit more mysterious. One obvious point is that it is not created overnight. The soldiers are continually marching, and in other ways experiencing things together under the unified command of the leader. Keegan also suggests that the leaders are, in turn, motivated by the figure they cut in their fellow officers' eyes. "Honour was paramount, and it was by establishing one's honourableness with one's fellows that leadership was exerted indirectly over the common soldiers." Hence the truth in the oft-repeated saying that "the Battle of Waterloo was won on the playing fields of Eton" (Keegan 1976, p. 192).

Stepping back from the details of these accounts, it would seem that the battlefield can be represented as a prisoners' dilemma game. The soldier is tempted to run, and if he and only he escapes, he will be better off. But if all run, that is the worst possible outcome for each one as an individual and for all. And there is also the possibility of a bandwagon effect: if one person panics, this may cause others in the unit to panic and run away, and the result is that many more people are killed than when they stand firm.

It immediately follows that a "rotten" soldier is much more dangerous to the unit of an army than a "rotten" kid is to the family. The reason is that the former's behavior may result, via the triggering of a bandwagon effect, in the utter destruction of the unit. Thus, in order to win, the army (and each unit within it) must act as *one*. Either the unit remains solidary, and the army wins, or it disintegrates, and the army loses. "Rotten" behavior in the family would not seem as likely to have this dynamic implication.

Although no formal summary can do justice to these historical accounts or Keegan's synthesis of them, the following propositions may be abstracted from them:

1. Fear is the central problem in battle.
2. Both the officers and the soldiers experience it.
3. The officer's duty is to cause the soldiers under his command to overcome their fear.
4. Solidarity is the means to do this.
5. The officers, or the informal leader among the soldiers within the unit create this solidarity by showing by example that he is not afraid.
6. In a battle, one unit remains solidary while the opposing unit disintegrates. The unit that succeeds in remaining solidary, other things equal, wins the battle over the unit that does not.

It follows that we can write a production function for a unit of the army engaged in battle, with solidarity as an "input." We will see that this idea that solidarity as a determinant of success applies in many other contexts as well. Of course, the likelihood of victory does not depend solely on solidarity. Other factors – the army's size, its level of capital equipment, the ability of its generals and officers, and the strategies used – are important. But from our point of view Keegan's central point can be represented by the inclusion of solidarity in the production function:

$$P = P(S, K, L) \tag{2.5}$$

where P = the probability that the army wins the battle, as a function of S = the level of solidarity in the unit, where a unit is defined as the group engaged in a battle, K = the unit's capital equipment, and L = the unit's size.

The army and the family are not the only spheres of life in which solidarity is important. Some other examples include nationalism, based on the idea of *one* nation; monotheistic religion, which is dominated by the idea of *one* God; democracy, in the Rousseauian sense of it as a system that implements *one* will (the will of the people or the General Will). There can be no presumption that the mechanism for creating solidarity can be analyzed in the same way in all of these cases. But it is worthwhile to have a look at them.

2.3.3 Religious Groups

The desire for solidarity itself can sometimes be met as a side benefit from groups formed for other reasons. Religious participation is one example. Alternatively, it may be the other way round, namely, that people join religious groups as a result of the desire for social interaction (Sacerdote and Glaeser 2001).

In economic models of religious participation, an externality arises from the fact that the utility of participation depends positively on the participation of others (it can be painful to sing hymns in an otherwise empty church). Various forms of organized religion (churches, synagogues) and unorganized ones (cults) arise to internalize this externality and therefore to develop the capacity for religious participation. For example, in Iannacconne's (1992) model, a cult requires sacrifices on the part of would-be participants, or it stigmatizes them in one way or another. The idea is to limit participation to those who are most committed, or to stigmatize relations with nonparticipants, thus reducing the free-rider problem and stimulating the average level of participation of members.

Here an individual has the choice between working and earning the wage w, the earnings from which can be spent on secular commodities s, or religious participation, which has its own rewards, and which also contributes to the production of the club good A. The optimality condition is

$$w/p = MRS_{RS} + MRS_{AS} \qquad (2.6)$$

However, the members of the club would ordinarily tend to ignore the externality represented by the second term. Ideally, a tax on consumption should be set in order to internalize this externality. The club is not a government and is not capable of implementing a tax. Instead, it can implement *prohibitions* on various forms of secular activity, which have the same effect as a tax on it. Or it can attempt to *screen* out high-wage individuals who would be particularly likely to free-ride on the contributions of others. Religious sects (and possibly other groups, such as ethnic groups) are particularly capable of solving this problem because they possess mechanisms that tend to exclude free riders. One of these is sacrifice: for example, the requirement that years of study in a madras or yeshiva are necessary for entry and continuation in the community. Another is "prohibitions" (such as peculiar dress codes or dietary or Sabbath restrictions) that act as a "tax" on secular consumption, and thus dispose members to increase their association with group members and their contributions to the club good.

This assumes the technology of production of the club good is such that the value of the good is the average of the individual contributions, that is,

$$C(R_i) = C(\bar{R}) \tag{2.7}$$

where R_i is the religious activity of the individual members, $R_i = 0$ (free-riding) or $R_i = 1$, (loyalty), which contributes to the production of the public good A. Another type of technology is where the value of the good is multiplicative:

$$C(R_i) = C(\Pi R_i). \tag{2.8}$$

This technology, which Berman (2003) argues is characteristic of many activities of militias, for example, securing a trade route, or of terrorist activity, is particularly sensitive to defection. The reason is that if any one person defects, the value of the good produced falls to zero. Consequently, loyalty is particularly important in this case.

This explains why groups like Hamas that provide social services such as schools and mutual insurance to their members are also so effective at terrorism. In these activities, one disloyal person can destroy the whole operation. Groups that have mechanisms such as sacrifice and prohibitions that eliminate free-riding can thus be particularly effective at these activities. At the same time, counterterrorist activities like those practiced by the Israelis, which attempt to compromise select individuals within the terrorist network, can also be particularly effective.

2.3.4 Solidarity and Classical Extremism: The French Revolution, Fascism, and Communism

To Rousseau, sometimes referred to as "the philosopher of the French revolution,"[13] the role of an external enemy was central in creating solidarity (see,

---

[13] For example, by Taylor (1980).

e.g., Rousseau 1997). Rousseau thought democracy meant the implementation of the General Will. But how does the General Will emerge instead of individual interests? His solution was that the external enemy existed *within each person*, that is, in his particular interest.[14] Hannah Arendt summarizes his thought on this question:

In Rousseau's construction the nation need not wait for an enemy to threaten its borders in order to rise "like one man" and to bring about the *union sacree:* the oneness of the nation is guaranteed in so far as each citizen carries within himself the common enemy as well as the general interest which the common enemy brings into existence; for the common enemy is the particular interest or the particular will of each man. If only each particular man rises against himself in his own particularity,

---

[14] Runciman and Sen (1965) suggest that one way to provide a modern interpretation of Rousseau is to employ the prisoners' dilemma game. They interpret the general will as the cooperative solution to the game. Of course, this solution often differs from the equilibrium outcome, since people have a tendency to defect. They suggest that the equilibrium or defection solution may be likened to Rousseau's "will of all," while the cooperative solution represents the "general will." They also argue that this supplies a meaning to the phrase "forced to be free": in the case of the two prisoners in the prisoners' dilemma game, they would both be ready to appoint an agent who would see to it that neither of them confessed. From their arguments and many other examples, it is apparent that the notion of democracy in Rousseau's sense (as opposed to the Schumpeter-Downs conception of it as essentially meaning electoral competition) continues to appeal to many scholars of politics. On these accounts, democracy is a system that somehow implements the "will" of the people – that is, it is a means to collective ends, rather than just a method for aggregating narrow interests (see, e.g., Arblaster 1987 or Grofman and Feld 1988. Normally, in such accounts, it seems to be accepted that, as Grofman and Feld put it, "democracy works better when individuals try to see beyond their narrow self-interests to see the collective good" (p. 572). This point is elaborated by Grofman and Feld (1988) who interpret Rousseau's general will as meaning the same thing that Condorcet asserted in his famous jury theorem. Condorcet's theorem says that if voters are addressing a common question with only two possible answers, one of which is correct and one incorrect (such as the guilt or innocence of an accused criminal), and if the average probability of each voter choosing the correct answer is greater than .5, the probability that the answer chosen by a majority of them will be the correct one increases to certainty as the size of the group increases (Condorcet 1976, pp. 33–70) . The theorem is really a consequence of the law of large numbers and does not attribute any magical power to group decision making. The best way to see this point is to note that if the probability of an individual choosing the correct answer falls below .5, the probability of getting the correct answer for the group as its size increases goes to zero. Changes in group size can also have other consequences. For example, as the group increases in size, it may become more difficult for each one to identify with the group, as Grofman and Feld (1988, p. 572) put it, "in such a way as to prevent their decision making being distorted by bias and interest." Still, the theorem is inviting, and a welcome corrective to the negative view of group decision making based on the Arrow problem that groups are necessarily prone to instability. However, there is a third condition necessary for the theorem to hold: the individuals must decide independently. To the extent that they do not, that is, to the extent that they form a herd or a faction where each individual decision is based on the group, the process to reach the right decision is lost.

he will be able to arouse in himself his own antagonist, the general will, and thus he will become a true citizen of the body politic. (1963, pp. 78–79)

Hence the French Revolution, classically associated with the birth of human rights and democracy, is also the fountain of nationalism (as we explore in more detail in Chapter 7).

In modern times the quest for solidarity in politics has often led to extremist movements. One way to see this is to look briefly at the two most famous forms of extremism in the twentieth century, fascism and communism. Both were produced by the advent of mass politics in the nineteenth century. For large numbers to beat small numbers, solidarity was central. Marx thought this could be produced simply by poverty, although he also reasoned that work in the machine shop is collective work, and so the modern industrial enterprise could be a school for collectivism that could unite the working class (Meyer 1962, pp. 24–25). But the real source of solidarity, in his view, was common exploitation and misery. By the law of the workings of a capitalist system, known as the "increasing immiserization of the proletariat," the workers would become poorer and poorer, until finally they would recognize their common plight and act together to throw off their chains. But growing general prosperity in the late nineteenth century invalidated the law, and the extension of the franchise in many countries meant that the class consciousness of the worker did not appear in the way foreseen. Instead the international solidarity of the labor movement gave way to particular sentiments and loyalties. The effectiveness of class as a reference point for political organization was definitively dissipated with the catastrophe of 1914 (Gregor 1969, p. 89).

Lenin understood that, for revolutionary consciousness to be aroused, leadership was required. In *What Is to Be Done?* he famously argued that "*There could not have been* social democratic consciousness among the workers. It would have to be brought to them from without. The history of all countries shows that the working class, exclusively by its own effort, is able to develop only trade-union consciousness, that is, the conviction that it is necessary to combine in unions, fight the employers, and strive to compel the government to pass necessary labour legislation, etc." (Lenin 1969, p. 32).

So working-class solidarity required leadership and Leninism. In turn, in the early twentieth century, the specter of the communist movement gave birth to a form of extremism at the opposite pole in the form of fascism. The map of fascist movements in Europe follows closely if not exactly two other maps: that of defeat in World War I, and the map of attempts at a

Bolshevik revolution during the period when communism seemed likely to spread beyond its borders at home (Paxton 2004, pp. 80–81). Fascism was the major political invention of the twentieth century. It arose first in Italy, then spread to other countries, and developed its most spectacular and virulent form in Germany under the dictatorship of Hitler.

What was the essence of fascism? The question is still debated, but one thing is not under dispute: the centrality of the ideas of solidarity and group struggle. Thus according to Linz's authoritative formulation, the aim of fascism is "national social integration" (Linz 1976, p. 12). In Paxton's recent account, fascism is "true" insofar as it helps to fulfill the destiny of a chosen race or people or blood, "locked with other peoples in a Darwinian struggle" (Paxton 2004, p. 16). In turn participants in the movement are rewarded not least with "[t]he warmth of belonging to a race now fully aware of its identity . . . the gratification of submerging oneself in a wave of shared feelings, and of sacrificing one's petty concerns for the group's good" (Paxton 2004, pp. 16–17).

And again, there is the principle of the leader. In Italy, Mussolini liked to declare that he himself was the definition of fascism. The will and leadership of a Duce was what a modern people needed, not a doctrine (Paxton 2004, p. 17). Later, in Germany, the *Führerprinzip* was applied in even more dramatic fashion, with Hitler at one point declaring that Germany was not governed by laws, but only by his "will."[15]

But we are getting ahead of our story. Perhaps enough has been said to indicate that solidarity is central to the ideology and workings of extremist groups, a point to be elaborated further in Chapter 5. On the other hand, some forms of social interaction are typically held to be the foundation of democracy rather than dictatorship, whether of the fascist or communist or any other varieties. Foremost among these is social capital.

2.4 Social Capital

In *Making Democracy Work,* Putnam (1993) argued that social capital is what makes for good democratic government. Indeed, he says that "happiness is living in a society where horizontal trust [social capital] is high." Social capital there is measured by the density of horizontal associations. He provided evidence that those regions of Italy which are well governed have high social capital measured this way, whereas those which are badly governed have low social capital. He also conjectured that social capital is amazingly durable, as shown by the apparent facts that the geographical

---

[15] For details, see Wintrobe (1998a), chap. 15.

pattern of good and bad government in Italy in the late twentieth century appears to be the same as it was in the nineteenth century and even, though with less certainty, similar to that which existed in the fifteenth century.

Paldam and Svendsen (2002) presents some evidence that supports Putnam's thesis in general, while criticizing the idea that social capital is very long lasting. In fact, they suggest that it lasts a few decades, which seems much more reasonable. Even on their account, it would appear that social capital is more long lasting than solidarity. Perhaps the reason is that social capital is unlike solidarity in that it is embedded in the rules or norms of society, whereas solidarity is often nothing if not temporary. This is particularly true when it involves empathy with large numbers of individuals who are not part of any permanent group. Thus the solidarity that toppled the East German government or that which appeared in opposition to the Chinese dictatorship at Tienamen Square, or the solidarity that many people in the West felt with the victims of the 2004 tsunami tragedy all appear to have been temporary manifestations of solidarity.

In sum, solidarity would seem to be more fragile than social capital, but the fragility of both is a subject that is very unsettled. With respect to social capital, Putnam's next book, *Bowling Alone* (2000), deployed a battery of indicators to show that social capital has been steadily falling in the United States since the 1960s. The evidence is often compelling, but the analysis of why this has happened appears less so. The main reasons appear to be the growth of television consumption and "generational change" – a catchall phrase referring to the passing of the "great civic generation" comprising those born in the years 1925–1930 who became adults during the 1950s. Many of the correlations Putnam presented are fascinating, especially the ones between those who agree relatively strongly with the statement "TV is my primary form of entertainment" and various measures of civic engagement, such as the number of club meetings attended, whether the person worked on a community project, and even the mean number of times a driver "gave the finger" to another driver last year.

While there is little doubt that the book is a grand accomplishment, its underlying logic is not without its problems. For example:

1. If social capital could have fallen so dramatically in the United States in a few decades, how could it have persisted in Italy for hundreds of years, as asserted in his previous book, *Making Democracy Work* (1993)?
2. Perhaps most important, here as elsewhere, the question arises, just what is "social capital"? The same term appears to be used to mean different things. For example, whereas the 1993 book on Italy is concerned with horizontal trust, and indeed draws a significant contrast

between the properties of horizontal trust (which it is argued is good for democracy) and vertical trust (bad for democracy),[16] in the new book extensive reference is made to "social capital" and the distinction between horizontal and vertical trust seems to be lost.

The distinction between horizontal and vertical trust was first, to my knowledge, made in Breton and Wintrobe (1982) and then elaborated in Wintrobe and Breton (1986), among other places, in the context of organizations like government bureaucracies and business firms. We argued that horizontal networks (Th) lowered an organization's productivity – that is, no matter how beneficial they might be from the point of view of the personal well-being of subordinates, such networks tend to reduce the efficiency of the business firm or bureaucracy from the point of view of the organization's principals. The reasons are such things as the fact that horizontal networks make it easier for subordinates to distort information to their advantage, cover for each other, and so forth. On the other hand, vertical networks (Tv) raise productivity, for example, by improving communication between subordinates and superiors. Consequently it is not the level of trust that is important for an organization's efficiency but its distribution.

Although the trust concepts in Breton and Wintrobe and in Putnam are certainly similar, if not identical, it is interesting that their normative roles are reversed: in Breton and Wintrobe, vertical trust raised organizational productivity, whereas horizontal trust lowered it; in Putnam (1993), horizontal trust is good for democracy, whereas vertical trust is bad for it. Of course, one could reconcile the two positions by saying that one refers to politics, the other to bureaucracies or business firms, but this leaves a number of questions unanswered.

In the work of Knack and Keefer (1997), Fukuyama (1995), and Inglehart (e.g., 1999) among others, there has appeared yet another concept of trust: "generalized social capital." Unlike Coleman's concept of social capital, or Breton and Wintrobe's vertical or horizontal trust, this refers to the extent to which a person is willing to trust a stranger. One problem is that social capital in this sense and that in the sense of Breton and Wintrobe or Coleman are sometimes negatively related. That is, the more trust there is within a group, the more distrust there may be of outsiders. Hence the strange result in Fukuyama (1995), for example, that Italy and Japan are "low-trust"

---

[16] Indeed, it is emphasized that the problem of poor government in the Italian South is not due to the fact that the people in places like Sicily and Calabria have no or too few networks, but that they have the *wrong kind* of networks: vertical (patron-client, mafiosi, etc.), as opposed to horizontal networks, such as voluntary associations.

countries. One explanation for this result is that in those countries trust tends to be particularized within groups, and people are divided into "ingroup" and "outgroup." No matter how strong the level of ingroup trust, such societies will score low on the Fukuyama–Knack and Keefer definition of trust. But maybe the classic instance of this kind of theorizing is Banfield's concept of "amoral familism," invented to explain the strange patterns he discovered in a small town in southern Italy. Again (as in Putnam 1993), the concept is invented to understand how Italian life and society work. Perhaps the right conclusion is that this task is essentially hopeless for North Americans. But another big problem is China, where indexes of high levels of corruption seem to go hand in hand with high trust (see, e.g., Paldam and Svendsen 2002).

One point Putnam does not explore is the connection between trust and corruption. It would seem that corruption is the exact opposite of trust, that is, if corruption is observed, it means that that person could not be trusted, or it means a *breach* of trust. Della Porta (2000) argues and provides evidence from Italy that corruption destroys trust in government. She also shows in a cross-country analysis that the lowest satisfaction with democracy is reported for those countries that score high on the corruption index, like Italy, and the nations that are most satisfied with democracy are those where corruption is lowest (Della Porta 2000, p. 209).

In sum, social capital appears to come in many variations: positive social capital, negative social capital, corruption, generalized trust, horizontal trust, vertical trust, and solidarity, among others. It follows that, as Jean Cohen puts it, one basic issue is whether "'inherited social capital' is the right concept to use for six rather different things: interpersonal trust, social solidarity, general norms of reciprocity, belief in the legitimacy of institution-alized norms, confidence that these will motivate the action of institutional actors and ordinary citizens [social solidarity], and transmission of cultural traditions, patterns, and values" (Cohen 1999, p. 220).

Although we cannot solve all of these conceptual problems here, it may be useful to introduce some simple notation and definitions that I believe will clarify quite a few of them and show the precise relationships between solidarity, trust, social capital, and related concepts. I do this in the appendix to this chapter.

2.5 The Production of Trust and Social Capital

If trust or social capital is like other forms of capital, one should be able to describe the investment process by which it is produced, and the conditions under which it depreciates. In the work of Becker (1996), Putnam (1993, 2000), and many other social scientists on trust or social capital, the investment process is mysterious and typically the amount available is described as the amount inherited (see, e.g., Becker 1996, Putnam 2000, or Cohen 1999). Putnam appears to believe that trust is produced (or at least maintained) through participation in group activities. However, it seems unlikely that participation alone can create trust: for example, if there were serious disagreement among the participants, it is not obvious that social capital would be created rather than destroyed.

In a similar vein, Uslaner (1999, pp. 145–146) argues that social capital is produced by participation in sports but not by visiting arts museums. He also discusses experiments done in the 1960s by Muzafer Sherif et al. (Uslaner 1999, p. 145) where attempts were made to rebuild horizontal trust among two groups of campers after it was destroyed. The main finding appears to be that the only thing that worked was if the two groups were compelled to cooperate toward a common goal. For example, a field trip in a truck was organized for the groups in which it was arranged for the truck to break down. The two groups had to work together to fix the truck, and this seemed to rebuild social capital. Breton and Wintrobe (1982) described one analytical process for creating trust. In their analysis, a person invests in trust with another person by making an initial sacrifice or gesture on his or her behalf or by forgoing an opportunity to cheat that person. The amount that could have been earned by taking the lost opportunity to cheat or the size of the gesture measures the size of the investment. How much trust capital is produced for any given investment depends on a number of things, especially how well the "signal" given by forgoing the opportunity to cheat is received by its intended recipient(s), that is, on how easily the individuals communicate with each other, and so forth.

It is no accident that secret and especially criminal organizations like the mafia or youth gangs typically recruit members by presenting highly structured opportunities for newcomers to invest in. In this context, Uslaner's illustrations like the sports example or the field trip experiment could be seen as special cases of the Breton and Wintrobe framework in that they provide plenty of opportunities for each side to make appropriate investments in trustworthiness and for these signals to be observed by the other group. The same concept can be used to describe the creation of solidarity in the family, as described previously. The head of the family generates trust through his gifts, the other members through not taking opportunities to "cheat" (profit at the family's expense). Similarly, in the army, solidarity appears to be created through sacrifice (by the officers or the informal leaders of the group) and through constant, repetitive instances where people conduct disciplined activity (thus forgoing opportunities to cheat) together, that is, when they act as *one*.

Salmon (1988) described another process for creating trust involving conjectures and refutations. Coleman (1990) discusses the decision to extend trust in a number of social contexts.

2.6 Contagion

One proposition about social capital (or solidarity) has not yet been noted: social capital, like any other form of network externality, is *contagious* (Katz and Shapiro 1985; Becker 1996). One can generate this result in many ways: via interdependent preferences, network externalities (see, e.g., Katz and Shapiro 1985), asymmetric information (Mishkin 1996 explains the East Asian crisis this way), information cascades (Bikchandani, Hirshleifer, and Welch 1992), winner-take-all markets (Frank 1988), and self-fulfilling prophecies (Farmer 1999). Becker defines social capital in terms of interdependent preferences (Becker 1996; Becker and Murphy 2000). He uses the concept of social capital to refer to "the influence of past actions by peers and others in an individual's social network and control system" (Becker 1996, p. 4). So an individual's consumption (C_i) depends on that of other individuals (C_{jt-1}). He also introduces the concept of habit or "personal capital": an individual i's consumption in period t (C_{it}) depends on his consumption in a previous period (C_{ti-1}). Becker showed that these two variables, especially in combination, can generate very large elasticities of demand and instability.

One nice illustration is the consumption of addictive drugs. Suppose that the price of an addictive consumption good, C, rises. Then i's consumption C_i falls; so does C_j. In the next period, C_i falls further, both because C_{it-1} has fallen and because (C_{jt-1}) has fallen. These falls generate further diminutions and so on, until a "corner" solution (e.g., zero consumption) has been reached. At the other extreme, something that triggers an increase in the consumption of the good by one or more individuals can lead, by the reverse process, to the opposite corner, that is, addiction. Another model generates contagion from informational considerations (Banerjee 1992). In this model, a person observes the decisions made by other people and chooses whether to use her own information or to follow the decisions made by others. If a person decides to follow the herd rather than rely on her own information, she inflicts a negative externality on the rest of the population. If she had used her own information, her decision provides information to others, which in turn encourages them to use their own information as well. But when she simply conforms, her own information is lost. Banerjee refers to this as a "herd externality."

Another well-known source of contagion is network externalities (see, e.g., Katz and Shapiro 1985). The key reason for the appearance of network externalities is the complementarity between the components of a network. "Network effects" or network externalities" arise because the value of membership to one user is positively affected when another user joins and enlarges the network. For example, in a communications network, such as a network of electronic-mail users or a network of people who exchange files, each user desires to link directly to other users. So, as has long been recognized, the demand for a network good is a function of both its price and the expected size of the network.

Because of the strong positive-feedback elements, systems markets are especially prone to "tipping," which is the tendency of one system to pull away from its rivals in popularity once it has gained an initial edge. One implication is that in markets with network effects, there is a natural tendency toward de facto standardization, which means everyone is using the same system. Tipping has been observed in many situations, including typewriter keyboards, AM stereo radios, FM versus AM radio, color versus black-and-white television, and VHS versus Beta in videocassette recorders (Katz and Shapiro 1985).

The contagion property is particularly important in politics, where genuine information is weak and the incentive to collect it is not there because of the free-rider problem. Indeed, it is well known that ideas and political support are contagious: hence, the name bandwagon effects. Things like bandwagons and fads can be explained by the desire for social cohesion. People adopt an idea in order to be "in," that is, to be either in the vanguard of or at least a part of the group or movement that promotes the idea. It need have nothing to do with the logical case for the idea (if any) at all. Thus, there has never really been a case on aesthetic, medical, or logical grounds for hula hoops in the 1950s, tie-dyed tee shirts in the 1960s, disco culture in the 1970s, backward baseball caps in the 1980s, or wearing earrings in your tongue in the 1990s.

It is easy to think that where there is social capital, that is, lots of horizontal associations a la Putnam, this acts as a bulwark against instability. But that may be exactly wrong: there is evidence that the more social capital there is, the more *unstable* the polity. The classic example is the Weimar Republic. It was thought that Hitler rose because Germany was an "atomized" society with few individuals members of groups or voluntary associations – but, in fact, exactly the opposite was true: Weimar Germany was particularly rife with horizontal associations, with lots of social capital in precisely Putnam's (2000) sense.[17] Indeed, many groups joined the Hitler movement *as a group*, encouraged by their leaders.

It follows that, paradoxically, the more social capital there is, the greater the demand for constitutional protections in the form of checks and balances. One important application of these ideas is the reasoning of Madison and others in *The Federalist Papers* about the design of the American Constitution. There the case for a constitution is made on grounds of the instabilities due to passions. And one major source of instability was said to be bandwagon effects, especially under the influence of the wrong kind of political leaders. The Founding Fathers were especially worried about demagoguery: the notion that citizens could be "misled by the artful misrepresentations of interested men," or by the "wiles of parasites and sycophants, by the snares of the ambitious, the avaricious, the desperate."[18]

Another implication of contagion is that it shows one reason why the decline of social capital in the United States could have been so precipitous as it appears in Putnam's charts: because it is contagious, once it starts to decline, the process sets up expectations that are self-fulfilling. And there are also applications to other societies. Thus, in Russia, the fall of the communist system left lots of social capital, now unconnected to the Communist hierarchy, and these horizontal connections gave birth to the "anti-modern society" of contemporary Russia, to use Richard Rose's (1999) phrase.[19]

2.7 Conclusion

In this chapter I reviewed some of the literature on social interactions, trust, social capital, or solidarity. The literature on these topics is huge, and I have made no attempt to be comprehensive. One point made here is that the concepts are often used imprecisely, with the same word used to mean the different things at different times. In the appendix I give precise mathematical definitions of trust, social capital, and solidarity and show the close relationship between these concepts.

The most important point made is that introducing social interactions in any of these forms often changes the behavioral prediction made (the next chapter provides some illustrations of this phenomenon). I have also

---

[17] See Wintrobe (1998a) and references therein.

[18] Federalist Paper 71, p. 432, quoted in Page and Shapiro (1989), p. 57.

[19] This argument is also spelled out in Wintrobe (1998a).

described some processes by which social capital or solidarity is produced (or destroyed) and illustrated these with solidarity in the family, the army, and religious and extremist groups, and with social capital in politics. Finally, because social capital is contagious, it can rapidly rise or decline in certain circumstances.

APPENDIX: THE DEFINITIONS OF SOLIDARITY, NETWORKS, TRUST, AND SOCIAL CAPITAL

In this appendix, I introduce some notation and definitions to make the concepts of solidarity, trust, and social capital more precise, and to show the relationships among them. To begin with trust or networks, assume, following Breton and Wintrobe (1982) that $_aT_b^{1.00}$ represent the degree to which a person a trusts that another person, b, will not cheat him on a transaction where the potential gain to b from cheating is $1.00. I assume trust in this sense has the following properties:

$$0 < {}_aT_b^{1.00} < 1, \text{ that is, } {}_aT_b^{1.00} \qquad (A.1)$$

represents a probability that is between zero and one.

Note that this implies that trust between two persons is never either zero (nonexistent) or one (perfect trust). This assumption is not necessary (we show later when it might be reasonable to modify it), but it seems reasonable when describing person-to-person interactions. Note also that the degree of trust is specified for a given opportunity to cheat (represented by the sum $1.00). An individual may say in ordinary parlance that he trusts his grocer to always give him the correct change, but this does not mean he trusts him if the possible gain to the grocer is much larger than this (e.g., in a business deal worth millions). Presumably,

$$_aT_b^{1.00} < {}_aT_b^{2.00} \qquad (A.2)$$

and so on for larger and larger opportunities for b to cheat. More generally,

$$_aT_b^{y} < {}_aT_b^{x} \text{ if } y < x \text{ where } x, y = \$.01, 1.00, 2.00, \dots \dots \$\infty. \qquad (A.3)$$

For simplicity, in what follows, we assume that all the x's move up or down together, for example, if a believes that c is more likely to cheat her than b for a gain of $5.00 $({}_aT_b^{5.00} < {}_aT_c^{5.00})$, then she also thinks that c is more likely to cheat her when the gain is larger or smaller than this (e.g., $_aT_b^{\$100} < {}_aT_c^{\$100}$). Similarly, if something happens that raises a's trust in b when x is one value, say x = $5.00, it raises it for all values of x. It is possible to think of exceptions here, but if they were common it is hard to know how people could use the word "I trust her" or "I trust him more than I do her" in everyday parlance as a shorthand for expressions like "$_aT_b^y$" as I assume they do.

We can use the same notation for *generalized trust*, or *general social capital*, that is, the degree to which an individual trusts a stranger. This is the sense in which it is used by Fukuyama (1995) or Knack and Keefer (1997). This is just

$$_aT_j^x \ j = 1, \cdots\cdots N, j \neq b, x = \$.01, 1.00, 2.00, \cdots\cdots \$\infty \qquad (A.4)$$

where j represents any *stranger* rather than an individual b who is in a's network, or with whom a has a specific relationship. The community is represented by members $j = 1, \ldots N, j \neq b$, and again the degree of trust is specified for a given opportunity to cheat (\$x). Of course for people in a's network (the b's in expression equation A.2 or A.3), the level of trust will be higher than this. But presumably if equation A.4 and expressions like it for different members of the community were typically zero in a community, then it is hard to know how everyday activities like buying a dress or investing in a mutual fund could go on without a great deal of thought about how the contract will be enforced.

The level of trust will typically be higher in a network than it is for generalized, impersonal contacts and contracts with other people whom a does not know. Indeed, a's *networks* may be defined precisely as all those people b for whom

$$_aT_b^x > \ _aT_j^x \text{ for any } x = \$.01, 1.00, 2.00, \cdots\cdots.\$\infty. \qquad (A.5)$$

That is, a person may be said to be in another person (a's) *network* when a trusts him more than he does a stranger in the community.

Now let us turn to solidarity. Here we could again refer to a transaction – since presumably solidarity affects (lowers) transactions costs – but more commonly when speaking of solidarity people are referring not to a transaction but to a group or community that is involved in some common enterprise. An individual now has the choice not between honesty or cheating a particular individual but whether or not to cheat the whole community. He can cooperate, express his solidarity, do his duty, be "loyal" (by making his contribution), and so forth, or he can decide to cheat (by free-riding, cheating, or defecting). Solidarity with a community means identifying with it, and to the extent that someone feels that way they are likely to support it rather than free-ride and let others carry the burden.

Consider first solidarity in the family. Suppose the head h cares for another member of the family r, who is rotten, that is, he only cares for himself. Nevertheless, because he receives gifts from the head, he will not take an opportunity to profit himself by b if it would reduce family income by c, where b < c. Thus the head's gifts mean that he can trust the kid even if he is rotten. His gifts create a feeling of solidarity with the family on the part of the kid. The value of this trust or solidarity might be

$$_h T_r^x = .7. \qquad\qquad (A.6)$$

This just means that the head trusts (believes that there is a 70 percent probability) that the rotten kid will not cheat the family when the gain to the kid is x. But note three things that appear here that were not in Becker's formulation: (1) The trust is not perfect. It is possible that the kid would still cheat, particularly if he is not positive that the gifts will continue. For example, if the kid thinks the probability that the gifts will continue is 70 percent, that would explain the value ".7" in equation A.6. And the larger the value of "x" in equation A.6, the lower the trust, until for very large values it becomes very low, a point obscured in Becker's formulation where it is assumed either that negative transfers are possible or that gifts always continue. (2) The trust of the kid is a capital asset to the family, which any head would want to create, not just one who loves the kid. (3) The extent to which the head trusts the kid depends on the extent to which the kid trusts the head,

$$_h T_r^x = f\left(_r T_h^x\right), \ f' > 0. \qquad\qquad (A.7)$$

Thus, the higher is $_r T_h^x$, that is, the more the kid is convinced of the affection of the head and therefore the more he believes gifts from the head will continue, so he cooperates with the family, leading the head to trust him in return. So trust and solidarity tend to be reciprocal in close relationships like those in the family.

In larger groups, such as firms, political parties, communities, or nations, the degree of *solidarity* can be expressed as follows. Let $S_a^{1.00}$ represent the probability that a will cooperate or make a sacrifice for the group – pay his taxes, give to charity, clean up after his dog, vote, work on weekends for the party or community, and so on – rather than cheat, free-ride, or defect when the cost to him of doing so is $1.00. In general, S_a^x indicates the degree of solidarity a has with the community or group. Here, it seems reasonable to assume that

$$0 \le S_a^x \le 1. \qquad\qquad (A.8)$$

Note that in this case the strong inequalities (in equation A.1, for trust) have been replaced by weak inequalities. This is to include two interesting special and extreme polar cases: $S_a^{.01} = 0$ at one extreme and $S_a^{\infty} = 1$ at the other. The first of these could be taken to represent pathological individuals, for whom $S_a^{.01} = 0$ (where the sum .01 is taken to represent the smallest possible sum). Such individuals never give to charity, vote, go to community meetings, clean up after their dogs, pay their taxes, or participate in group affairs if they can avoid doing so. Some people think that professional economists belong in this category, but this is mostly a misunderstanding.

The second relationship described for trust also holds for solidarity, that is,

$$S_a^y < S_a^x \text{ if } y < x, \text{ for example, } S_a^{1.00} < S_a^{2.00}. \tag{A.9}$$

That is, people are more likely to cheat or defect, the larger the gain to them from doing so, which seems reasonable.

This gives rise to a second extreme possibility, which is the possibility that

$$S_a^{\infty} = 1, \tag{A.10}$$

that is, of perfect solidarity with the community. An individual will not defect no matter how large the potential gain to him from doing so. Perhaps suicide martyrs belong in this category, a possibility that we return to in Chapter 5.

These examples suggest that generalized trust is closely related to solidarity (or social cohesion). To see their relationship, let us make the following assumption, which seems reasonable: *An individual who will not cheat the community when the gain to her from doing so is x also will not cheat an individual within that community in order to gain the same amount.*

With this assumption, *generalized trust is the same thing as solidarity*, that is,

$$_a T_j^x = S_a^x. \tag{A.11}$$

The term on the left-hand side of equation A.11, generalized trust, just specifies the probability that a will not cheat an individual in the community when he can gain x by doing so. The term on the right, which represents solidarity, says that a will not cheat the community when he could gain the same amount by doing so. These two are the same by the assumption just made.

Why do people sometimes talk about generalized trust (even at the popular level, as in expressions like "No one trusts anybody else in this company") and at other times they use the word "solidarity"? The difference in usage comes about because trust refers to a relationship, whereas solidarity describes a feeling or an aspect of preferences. But the actions that result are the same.

However, one could define a different category of trust, namely the degree to which an individual trusts someone whom he neither knows nor who is a member of the community, that is, a "complete stranger," $_a T_k^x$ where $k \neq b$ or j. Neither solidarity nor generalized trust includes this category as they are defined here. If the concept "generalized trust" is meant to include this category, the proposition about the equivalence of generalized trust and solidarity does not hold. Still, ordinary persons sometimes do feel solidarity with complete strangers, as many people worldwide seemed to feel in the aftermath of the tsunami tragedy.

If we neglect the category of trust described in the previous paragraph, then solidarity is closely related to social capital. An individual a's stock of social capital is

$$\sum_b \left(_a T_b^x \right) + S_a^x \text{ where } j = 1, \cdots\cdots N, \, j \neq b, \tag{A.12}$$

that is, the sum of his personal networks (the first term in equation A.12) and his degree of solidarity with the community (the same thing as the trust he extends toward strangers within the community).

The community's stock of social capital is

$$\sum_a \sum_b \left(_a T_b^x \right) + \sum_a {_a T_j^x}, \tag{A.13}$$

that is, the sum of the networks of all of the individuals in the community plus the stocks of generalized trust within the community held by each individual. If, for simplicity, each person has the same level of generalized trust, then equation A.9 may be simplified to

$$\sum_a \sum_b \left(_a T_b^x \right) + n_a T_j^x. \tag{A.14}$$

It is immediately clear that the definition of social capital used by Coleman (1990) or Breton and Wintrobe (1982) neglects the second term, while the Fukuyama and Knack and Keefer type of definition excludes the first. And it is easy to imagine a society (Italy, Japan?) where individuals have strong personal networks (the first term in equation A.14 is high) but do not trust strangers (the second term is low). At the other extreme, one can imagine a society where individuals typically have a basic trust in strangers but personal networks are weak (the United States?). Indeed, if the formal institutions of a society (markets, courts, and governments) function efficiently, one might expect individuals to dispense to some extent with personal networks and rely on these institutions for many of their business activities. In that society, it would not be surprising if people exhibit a basic trust in strangers because the reputations of individuals are easily documented, redress can easily be had to well-functioning courts when one is cheated, governments support the possibility of individual formal transactions with infrastructure, and so forth. On the other hand, when these formal institutions do not work well, personal networks may be substituted for them. So it is not difficult to imagine that generalized trust or solidarity and personal networks are sometimes inversely related because they are substitutes.

Suppose for a moment that we drop the distinction between personal networks and generalized trust and just let $_aT_j^x$, $j = 1, \ldots N$ indicate the extent to which a person a trusts another person, where i refers to both strangers and persons in a's network, when the opportunity to cheat is again any sum \$x. Then we can define a's *social capital* simply as

$$\sum_i \left(_aT_i^x \right) \tag{A.15}$$

where i refers to any person in the community. An individual's social capital is then measured by the extent to which he trusts the other people in the community in which he lives.

In the same way, the *community's social capital* is just

$$\sum_a \sum_i \left(_aT_i^x \right) a, i = 1, \cdots\cdots\cdots\cdots\cdots N. \tag{A.16}$$

This provides a rationale for commonly used expressions that refer to the "social capital" of a community. What else is the social capital of a community but a group that is composed of individuals who will cooperate with and not cheat each other, or the community, and forgo an opportunity to profit at the expense of the whole community, or of some people within it? But note that survey questions, such as that used in the General Social Survey (as by Knack and Keefer 1997 or Alesina, Glaeser, and Sacerdote 2000) asking how much trust an individual puts in strangers, will not give an accurate picture of social capital in the sense of equation A.15 or A.16. Instead, these will measure *either* networks *or* solidarity, respectively.

Finally we can also define such things as *reputation* this way. If $\sum_i \left(_aT_i^x \right)$ refers to the extent to which a trusts others, then a's reputation is simply given by the extent to which individuals in the community trust *him* (a):

$$\sum_i \left(_iT_a^x \right). \tag{A.17}$$

Obviously a could also be an organization, such as a business firm or government. If all trust relationships were exactly reciprocal, equations A.17 and A.15 will be the same. Otherwise they will not.

To sum up, we now have precise definitions of trust, networks, generalized trust, social capital, reputation, and solidarity or social cohesion. Clearly, in these definitions, solidarity, social capital, reputation, and generalized trust are all closely related to each other. But, depending on how they are defined and measured, they are not always the same and sometimes they move in opposite directions. The important lesson of this section is that the concepts are all valid, *provided one keeps the group or individual with whom trust or solidarity is held clearly in mind.* Is it one's personal relationships, a particular community, or group, or society in general? Once the group is specified, terms like social capital, solidarity, or trust do have a clear and unambiguous meaning.

THREE

Some Illustrations and a General Framework

3.1 Introduction

All of the work described in the preceding chapter, despite its obvious importance, only gives us part of the picture. All the behavior described there is demand-driven. For example, contagion effects imply that people who are involved in social interactions end up at corner equilibria. This implication is used, for example, by Becker in his (1996) model of addiction. A person enjoys a cigarette or a drug with his friends today. Tomorrow he wants to have more, partly because he had some yesterday, partly because his friends did, and he likes to do what they do. This escalates until he is addicted. But in this case, as in others, there is usually some attempt at a solution, that is to say, some attempt to form a group or structure or other form of organization or in some other way to endeavor to internalize the externality. In the case of smoking, for example, people who wish to stop may see a doctor, get Nicorette gum or the patch, or join a group to help them in this purpose, rather than just continue to hang out with their addicted friends and let the situation escalate.

With network externalities, property rights may help solve compatibility problems and investment problems in networks. For example, when there is a single owner of the network, that firm may be willing to sponsor the network by making investments in its growth that competitive hardware suppliers would not.

At the same time, these solutions seldom work perfectly. There is usually a characteristic problem that blocks the solution from being realized, or the solution possesses some characteristic defect. The patch causes stomach problems. Standardization of computer platforms brings monopoly and monopoly abuses; this was the U.S. government's and the European Union's case against Microsoft.

In response to this incomplete or inappropriate private response, public policy can take one of two forms: a price solution that sometimes ignores the social interaction (e.g., in the case of the problem of crime, the "price" solution might take the form of raising penalties for criminal activity), and a solution based on the interaction (e.g., community-based policing). It seems reasonable to conjecture that the more important the social interaction, the more the interaction-based solution will in fact be more appropriate than the solution based on individualistic behavior and prices alone.

To pursue this idea, let us look at a few more illustrations. Then we will return to the all-important policy issue. The next two sections discuss crime and poverty alleviation. Section 3.4 turns to social interactions in international finance (herd behavior and corruption). Section 3.5 presents a table that summarizes and tries to generalize about these examples, and then further develops the policy implications of the analysis.

3.2 Illustration 1: Crime and Social Relations

Economists have typically analyzed criminal behavior following the framework set out by Becker (1968) in his path-breaking article. In that article, and in much (but not all) of the subsequent work, an individual decides whether to commit a crime depending on what he or she anticipates getting out of it in terms of monetary (or nonmonetary) return, and on the risks of the activity. Social interactions with others do not enter the picture. At the policy level, the Becker approach focused on the use of prices – deterrence variables such as punishments and levels of policing as a crime prevention strategy. The basic model (Becker 1968) looks at an individual's interactions with the justice system as represented by two policy variables: the probability of arrest and conviction, p, and the size of the punishment, f. An individual looks at the utility of his expected return from crime (monetary or psychic) and compares this with the disutility of the expected punishment and, on this basis, decides whether to commit a crime or not.

Thus, although Becker himself was instrumental in the development of the economics of social interactions, social interactions involved in criminal behavior were initially ignored in his approach to criminal behavior, perhaps in order to bring this subject into the standard economic approach.

It is worth repeating the list of social interactions involved in crime:

1. A great deal of crime in Canada and the United States is committed by young people who are part of gangs.
2. Punishment in the form of jail terms automatically exposes the criminal to opportunities to socialize and form networks with criminals.

3. Punishment carries stigma, and as a result of being punished, individuals may find it harder to get a job than before, thus again increasing the relative gains to illegal activity.
4. The most serious form of crime is often organized crime.
5. We would expect to see more crime wherever there is not much social capital.
6. Too high punishments often mean that the community will no longer support the police in catching offenders. As a result, excessive penalties may have the counterproductive effect that the probability of a criminal getting caught may actually fall.
7. As the punishment is increased, juries may become less willing to convict; thus, increasing the penalty lowers the probability of conviction.

Thus the interactions of the individual potential criminal that are ignored include those with the people with whom he is involved in committing the crime and others who may be involved in some way, for example, other gang members, the police, the community, the jury considering his case, and the prisoners with whom he may be incarcerated. They raise a question: is it a coincidence that all of these social interactions reduce the effectiveness of the legal remedy derived from atomistic behavior?

Obviously, the existence of all of these social interactions casts doubt on the standard, individualistic way of approaching the crime problem, and on the remedies that are derived from an approach that ignores them. Is there an alternative? A social relations approach to crime has been developed, which emphasizes "Fixing Broken Windows," to use the title of the of the article by Kelling and Wilson (1982) that introduced the approach and of the book by Kelling and Coles (1996), both of which emphasize the role of social relations in reducing crime. Many observers believe the adoption of this approach is responsible for the fact that, after many years of increasing, crime rates fell dramatically in New York after the program was introduced in the early 1990s. However, this claim is hotly contested, as we shall see.

The "broken-windows" approach emphasizes that behavior commonly classified as "disorderly," while not as serious as crime, nevertheless can create fear and criminogenic conditions. Like broken windows left unrepaired, such behavior tends to create an atmosphere that criminals might find congenial but ordinary citizens would not. By "disorderly" Kelling and Coles (1996, p. 20) refer to acts such as "aggressive panhandling, street prostitution, drunkenness and public drinking, menacing behaviour, harassment, obstruction of streets and public spaces, vandalism and graffiti, public urination and defecation, unlicensed vending and peddling, unsolicited window washing of cars ('squeegeeing') and other such acts." The result is that "disorderly behaviour unregulated and unchecked signals to citizens that the area is unsafe. . . . Responding prudently, and fearful, citizens . . . stay off the streets. As citizens withdraw physically, they also withdraw from roles of mutual support with fellow citizens on the streets, thereby relinquishing the social controls they formerly helped to maintain with the community."

In New York, disorder grew partly as a result of the "reform policing model" common in many American cities at that time, which concentrated on rapid response to distress calls. Thus "success" on that approach was measured by how quickly a car got to the scene of the crime. But taking police out of the neighborhoods and putting them in their cars reduced the interaction between police and the community and made it difficult for the police to establish trust relationships with the citizenry. The result was that neighborhoods deteriorated and citizens withdrew, in turn spawning further deterioration and withdrawal and social decay. So on this line of thought, disorder and crime are contagious. The mechanism may be represented as the *disintegration of social capital*, as follows:

Disorder → Fear → Citizens withdraw → Social capital falls → Crime increases.

The program to combat disorder began in the New York subway system, which by the 1980s had deteriorated considerably under the onslaught of widespread fare beating, aggressive panhandling, graffiti, and so forth. In some cases groups of youths would literally take over a subway station, disable all the token receptacles, hold open gates, and collect fares from persons entering the station (Kelling and Coles 1996, p. 119). William Bratton, later to head the New York City Transit Authority, describes one of these incidents that he witnessed himself:

I tried to put a coin into a turnstile and found it had been purposefully jammed. Unable to pay the fare to get into the system, we had to enter through a slam gate being held open by a scruffy-looking character with his hand out; having disabled the turnstiles, he was now demanding that riders give him their tokens. . . . Other citizens were going over, around, or through the stiles for free. It was like going into the transit version of Dante's *Inferno*.[1]

One innovation was the antigraffiti program, inspired in part by Nathan Glazer's 1979 article "On Subway Graffiti in New York," which argued that graffiti was part of the appearance of disorder that encouraged crime. In

---

[1] William Bratton, *Turnaround: How America's Top Cop Reversed the Crime Epidemic* (New York: Random House, 1998), p. 141.

response the 1984 Clean Car program adopted a simple idea: once a train was entered into the program and cleaned, it would never again be used while graffiti was on it. Once cleaned, any further graffiti would be removed from cars within two hours or the car would be taken out of the system. Thus, graffiti artists would never see their handiwork (Kelling and Coles 1996, p. 116). Another important innovation was the introduction of the post of "station manager" by the New York City Transit Authority. Prior to 1990, no single individual was in charge of any one station. The NYCTA operated functionally – at each station, cleaning issues would be dealt with by one department, safety by another, repairs by a third, and so on. The position of station manager introduced an element of quasi "ownership" to the management of the subway (Kelling and Coles 1996, p. 134).

The program was an enormous success in the subway and in other public spaces in New York where similar ideas were tried. Subway felonies declined by more than 75 percent and robberies by 64 percent in the early 1990s, with the onset of decline beginning almost immediately after the order-maintenance program was begun (Kelling and Coles 1996, p. 152). The subway experience then provided the blueprint for the changes in the police system, both as an intellectual model and because the person responsible for implementing many of the changes in the subway, William Bratton, would later become police commissioner. Programs embodying similar ideas were subsequently implemented by the New York City police. A program of "aggressive order maintenance" involving the heavy use of community policing ideas such as foot patrols and citizen involvement, but also involving the targeting of minor offenses, was implemented. Thus the program focused on minor rather than major problems and in some ways reversed the emphasis on "marginal deterrence" for bigger offenses that is characteristic of the individualistic approach. Whether the program was responsible or not, there seems little doubt about the drastic decline in serious crime: within five years, from 1992 to 1997, murders had fallen by 64.3 percent, and total crimes had been cut in half (Massing 1998, pp. 33–34).

However, whether it was the application of the "broken-windows" approach that caused the decline in crime or some other factor is hotly disputed. Lochner (2005) looks at individual perceptions of the probability of being arrested based on data from the National Longitudinal Survey of Youth and the National Youth Survey. He provides interesting evidence that individual perceptions of arrest rates appear to be unresponsive to information about the arrests of other random individuals and local neighborhood conditions (while positively correlated with local arrest rates). Levitt (2004) argues that the fall in crime in big cities was the result of two factors: the abolition of constraints against abortion culminating in *Roe v. Wade* in 1973, which on his evidence accounts for 50 percent of the drop in crime across the United States in the 1990s; and, in New York itself, the addition of 45,000 new police officers. Once these two factors are entered in, there is no role left for the broken-windows approach. However, his own self-reported confidence in this result is "low." And the extension of his econometric model of crime rates backward to the 1980s predicts exactly the opposite of what actually happened (Levitt 2004). That is, the model predicts a decrease in the crime rate (mainly as the result of increased incarceration), whereas the rate actually increased in the 1980s despite increased incarceration. In the twenty-first century crime rates have continued to fall in New York City and it would be interesting to see if this new result, which is clearly unrelated to the change in the abortion laws, and easily explained on the broken-windows idea that crime is contagious, can be accounted for with Levitt's simpler model.

Another study, by Corman and Mocan (2005), does find a significant result for the broken-windows approach. In that study, serious crimes are regressed on misdemeanor arrests as a measure of broken-windows policing. Arguably this understates the significance of the approach – for example, the effect of community policing in reducing misdemeanors and other crimes directly *without* arrests does not get included this way – but the study does show at least this aspect of the broken-windows approach to have validity in the case of robbery, motor-vehicle theft, and grand larceny. So the full story is not yet in on the usefulness of this approach in reducing crime.

Other theoretical arguments also support the general "broken-windows" story. After all, the most basic element of the story is that crime is contagious. Glaeser, Sacerdote, and Scheinkman (1996) provide systematic evidence that crime is contagious (without necessarily embracing the broken-windows idea, not the subject of their paper). Thus, it may be that the presence of "broken windows" acts as a signal to potential criminals that the area is not well maintained and that no one is watching, and therefore it is a safe place to commit crime. However, another possibility is that the Bratton strategy had the effect of arresting hardened criminals, but on lesser charges and more frequently. This version would minimize the role of social capital in the community in reducing crime. On the other hand, Kelling and Coles emphasized that the presence of an active and vigilant citizenry was necessary to keep the crime rate low, and this idea is supported by other communities with low crime rates, such as Japan.

While criminal behavior is typically understood in individualistic terms, much crime in the United States is committed by youth gangs. Gangs are not well understood. For example, gangs are not necessarily disliked by the citizens of the communities in which they operate. Jankowski's famous (1991) study showed that gangs appear to be viewed by their communities in surprisingly positive ways. This provides the basis for Akerlof and Yellen's (1994) model in which whether punishments for criminal activity are effective or not depends crucially on whether citizens side with the police or with the gang. In the model, citizens have a concept of a "fair" punishment, and if the punishment is raised too high, citizens may switch from siding with the police to siding with the gangs, even hiding gang members from the police. This is one way punishments can be counterproductive. The theory is similar to Andreoni's idea that juries may be unwilling to convict if the penalty for an offense is too high: thus the increase in the punishment (f) results in a reduction in the probability that it is actually applied, and the net consequence may be to increase rather than reduce the incentive to commit crime.

In a similar way, the application of the broken-windows theory is itself sometimes misplaced and can be counterproductive. Thus, Borooah (2000) points out that, in England, police tend to stop blacks with much higher frequency than whites.[2] The result may have been a poisoning of race relations, something that has also occurred to some extent in New York under Mayor Giuliani. In the long run, in turn, this could easily worsen the crime problem itself if the result is greater separation and more racial discrimination. Procedures that may involve police harassment of minority groups, sometimes called "racial profiling," represent a misreading of the broken-windows story, in which it is central that the citizenry be on the side of the police and citizen involvement is key to reducing crime. Indeed, *racial profiling is the antithesis of that approach.*

The idea that crime is contagious explains another puzzle: why so-called victimless crimes are usually outlawed. By these crimes I refer to such things as illicit drug use, prostitution, or gambling. In all these cases, there are no direct damages to the community, as in arson or theft or murder. Instead, in each case the "crime" is a transaction in which the "victim" voluntarily engages. Consequently, the only person actually harmed is the person who

---

[2] If crime commission differs among races, for example, if blacks commit crime more frequently than whites, one can derive an "optimal" or efficient level with which members of each race should be stopped based on racial characteristics (Borooah 2000). However, it is not obvious that such racial differentiation is genuinely efficient, especially if it perpetuates stereotypes and statistical discrimination, which in turn generate a greater propensity to commit crime. In other words the price policy (race-based arrest procedures) would not be efficient if the second (social interaction) effect dominates the first (price) effect.

does not want the activity outlawed because he or she is the one who wants to do it. It is true that there are so-called third-party effects – the neighborhood in which drug dealing, gambling, or prostitution takes place is apt to be rather unpleasant – but that is mostly the result of the activity being illegal. When these activities are legalized – witness the casino at Schipol (Amsterdam) airport, for example, or the legalized (and government-operated!) lotteries all over Canada, or the marijuana coffee shops in the Netherlands – these third-party effects tend to disappear. For these reasons, people who have written on crime from a rational choice point of view have great difficulty explaining why these activities tend to be criminalized in the first place.

One answer suggested by the present approach is to begin by recognizing that, even though an individual may want to engage in one of these acts, he or she might still view them as harmful in the longer run. It is no doubt a great pleasure to inject heroin at the time, but the consequent addiction is not fun to get rid of. Second, all of these activities are contagious, in two senses. The first is that they are habitual, as discussed previously: an ex-smoker who does not want to start again may still want a cigarette but recognizes that one is seldom enough. Thus, although he would like to have one, he does not light up because he is afraid that having one will only lead him to want another one. Similarly, observing other people lighting up may stimulate his own desire to smoke. For this reason he may prefer not to be around people who smoke. In the same way, the individual who lives in a society where drugs, prostitution, and gambling are legal and easily available may be tempted to engage in these activities himself. And he may fear that doing them once may simply result in his wanting to do them again and again. These beliefs – in the "contagion" within oneself, as well as that between people, that is, the temptation arising from the activities of others – are the foundation of Alcoholics Anonymous (Galanter 1989), a very successful program for treating alcoholics that emphasizes complete abstinence from drinking and the crucial role of support groups. In this case, the "poison" is within oneself to some extent, and it may be that many citizens, knowing or suspecting that they will be tempted, and not wanting to put themselves in that position, rationally agree to have the activities outlawed.

3.3 Illustration 2: Poverty and Microfinance

Although considerable work has been done on the *causes* of poverty in the developed world in terms of group behavior – for example, on the social isolation of racial groups, culminating in the concept of a black underclass and other work along those lines[3] – I focus here on group-oriented *solutions* to the poverty problem, which have become enormously important lately. In particular, one solution to the poverty problem that has received widespread attention recently both in theory and in practice is the idea of "microfinance" – making tiny loans available to the poor, as pioneered by the Grameen Bank in Bangladesh and other institutions in the developing world. One of the important distinguishing features of these programs is that, typically, liability for repayment falls not on individuals but on self-selected groups of individuals. For example, in the Grameen Bank, loans were originally made to self-formed groups of approximately five individuals. The basic idea is that the group can be creditworthy even though no individual within it is. So joint liability may perform "the apparent miracle of giving solvency to a community composed almost entirely of insolvent individuals" (Plunkett 1904, quoted in Ghatak and Guinnane 1999). They can get a loan at a lower rate, or where the individual wouldn't have been able to get a loan at all.

The programs appear to have had enormous success in the developing world. Currently, the Grameen Bank lends to about 2 million people, mostly rural, landless women, in Bangladesh. It operates in 36,000 villages, or about half of all the villages in the country (Ghatak and Guinnane 1999, p. 213). In all the major programs, repayment rates are very high, more than 95 percent. As of 1999, about 8 to 10 million households were served by microfinance programs, and some advocates are pushing to expand to 100 million by 2005 (Morduch 1999, pp. 1570–1571). The idea for the Grameen bank originated with an economist, Muhammad Yunus, who explains how it came about: "Bangladesh had a terrible famine in 1974. I was teaching economics in a Bangladesh university. You can guess how difficult it is to teach the elegant theories of economics when people are dying of hunger all around you. Those theories appeared like cruel jokes. I became a dropout from formal economics. I wanted to learn economics from the poor in the village next door to the university campus" (Yunus 1995, quoted in Morduch 1999, p. 1575).

Yunus began by lending the villagers money from his own pocket, and within ten years he set up the bank, drawing on his experience. Since then, many other programs have been started. The programs have been implemented in various ways, and the institutions involved in the programs differ

---

[3] On the concept, see Wilson (1987), and Sawhill (1994) on the measurement and growth of the underclass, which in 1980 she and her associates measured at about 2–3 million in the United States.

substantially from one another. Thus, other members may be made liable for the actions of each member, part of each loan may be financed by another co-op member, and the interest on the part of the loan financed by other members may be increased. In the Grameen Bank, members of the peer group are jointly liable for repayment of loans, and none of them can gain access to new credit from the bank until the debts of the group are repaid. This provides an incentive to members of the group to monitor each others' activities, including the riskiness of projects, possible misuse of loans, and any other matters that may result in default.

The success of group lending has many possible explanations. Perhaps the simplest is that the individuals in the group know more about each other than a bank does or could discover at low cost. Thus one simple possibility is that group members may face a lower cost of verifying each others' performance. For example, if the condition of the loan is that repayment is warranted when output is high but may be deferred if output is low, neighbors may be able to ascertain that better than a bank could. If the projects undertaken by different members of the group are simple and similar in terms of their characteristics, then the bank can avoid the cost of performing its own audit every time a borrower claims she has low output by inducing her partner(s) to undertake liability for her. In this way, group lending economizes on transactions costs.

Another reason group lending may be effective on informational grounds is because it allows the bank to *screen* borrowers by varying the degree of liability and thus overcome the adverse selection problem. Group lending may provide this screening function because members self-select into groups. The reason is that, while all borrowers may prefer to have safe partners, safe borrowers value safe partners more than risky borrowers because they repay more often and, as a result, are more likely to realize the gain of having a safe partner. So in equilibrium borrowers end up with partners of the same type, and the result is that banks can screen borrowers by varying the degree of joint liability. Risky borrowers will have risky partners and will prefer a contract with less joint liability than will a safe borrower.

Another possible explanation for the effectiveness of group lending is that it is not due to superior information but superior enforcement, either because of social ties, peer pressure, or peer sanctions. In this way, group lending can overcome the moral hazard problem. For example, a major source of market failure in credit markets is that a bank cannot apply financial sanctions against poor people who default on a loan, because by definition they are poor. Poor people's neighbors may be able to apply sanctions under conditions when a bank could not. More subtly, Besley and Coate (1995) show how joint liability affects the *willingness* to repay. Group lending has two opposite effects on repayment rates: on the one hand, the advantage of groups is that they allow a member whose project yields very high returns to pay off the loan of a partner whose project does badly. On the other hand, the disadvantage is that a moderately successful partner may default because of the burden of having to repay her partner's loan. Besley and Coate (1995) show that if social ties are sufficiently strong, the net effect is positive. The implication is that, under circumstances where social ties are weak, as may be the case in many parts of North America, group lending may not be effective (Ghatak and Guinnane 1999, p. 201).

Wydick tests a number of these hypotheses on Guatemalan data and finds evidence that "the success of group lending is derived from peer monitoring and the willingness to apply internal pressure on delinquent members rather than the institution's ability to harness *previously* existing social ties to improve loan repayment" (1999, p. 471). In fact, one of the central findings of his study is the surprisingly small degree to which social ties within borrowing groups affect group performance. Indeed, he finds that "Previously existing social ties may even create a conflict of interest for borrowing groups, making threats of expulsion from the group more difficult and less credible" (p. 474). If social ties are unimportant, then the reasons for the failure of the programs in North America are less obvious.

Group lending is not the only mechanism that differentiates microfinance contracts from the usual loan contracts. Many of the programs also use dynamic incentives, regular repayment schedules, and other devices to help maintain high repayment rates. For example, all lend in increasing amounts over time ("progressive lending"), and most require weekly or semiweekly repayments starting soon after the loan is given out. Most programs begin by lending just small amounts and then increasing loan size upon satisfactory repayment (Morduch 1999, pp. 1580–1585). One implication of a repayment process that begins almost immediately is that the household must have an additional income source on which to rely.

In addition, for group monitoring to be effective, the cooperative structure must create the proper incentives for its members to monitor one another. For example, Banerjee et al. (1994, p. 492) discuss three ways that the group "constitution" may provide the right incentives: the other members are made liable in whole or in part for any loan on which the co-op defaults; part of each loan may be financed by another co-op member; and the interest on the part of the loan financed by other members may be varied, enhancing or diminishing the stake of the co-op in ensuring that the loan is repaid.

In the end it is striking that the same variables – focusing on the group rather than the individual, leadership on the part of the financial institution, and structuring the loan repayment process so that small, incremental decisions are substituted for big, discrete ones – are essential for the program to be a success. These variables resemble those in our first example of crime prevention. Here, as in crime, the question addressed is not whether the cause of poverty is itself social, but whether a social solution can be found that is superior to that based on the individualistic approach.

3.4 Illustration 3: International Finance – The Asian Crisis

Another area where social interactions have been neglected is in financial markets. One important source of contagion there derives from asymmetric information. Thus, depositors typically do not know the quality of the loan portfolios of the banks in which they have deposited their money. If there is a deterioration in performance, individuals may wish to withdraw their deposits, thus generating a contraction in the banks' ability to make loans and causing a further contraction. In turn, by a familiar process, this may cause panic, further withdrawals, bank failures, and so forth. In the absence of a government safety net, contagion may spread from one bank to another, causing even healthy banks to fail.

Less well known, or at least less well emphasized, is that social relations lie at the heart of these phenomena. To see this point, note first that one important type of social relation is networks and the potential for corruption between banks and their loan clients. At the heart of the asymmetric information problem is that there is information that the financial intermediary possesses and the depositors do not, namely, "To whom is the bank lending its depositors' money?" (Mishkin 1996). Close social connections between the banks and their clients are therefore naturally cause for concern among their depositors. These issues came to dominate financial news in 1997–1998 with the collapse of the East Asian and Russian "emerging" markets. To look at what happened in East Asia, the starting point in much of the analysis of what happened there can be summed up in the phrase "crony capitalism." That is, connections are the main mechanism for allocating credit in Indonesia and other Southeast Asian countries.[4] Banks owned by politically well-connected individuals are used to finance the operations of affiliated companies. In Indonesia, for example, almost every major corporation had

---

[4] See Campos and Root (1996), Krugman (1998), Sachs and Radelet (1998), or Bhagwati (2000).

its own bank, and the line between the two entities was often blurred (Sachs 1998, p. 22).[5] Companies were usually tied up in hard-to-value webs of interlocking shareholdings and government connections. So the essence of crony capitalism in East Asia is that the process of loan allocation is, to westerners, "corrupted," and the corruption is not easy to discover.[6]

The flip side of this corruption is that it makes loans possible, whereas in its absence perhaps the market would have been much smaller. In Indonesia, for example, much of the private sector economy is dominated by Chinese trading networks. They survive on *guanxi* – personal relationships built on trust in an individual's ability to carry out his promises. Sanctions are personal or communal in these situations, partly because the system of formal legal contractual compliance is underdeveloped or itself corrupted. Consequently, the choice, to some extent, is between crony capitalism and no capitalism at all. Currently, there are widespread calls for more transparency in the finances of these markets, but such appeals miss the point that loans made on the basis of loyalty and in secret are part of the essence of the political economy of these countries, and part of what makes their economies a success as well. (See Campos and Root 1996 for a detailed exposition of this point of view.)

The second important social relation involved is the interaction among lenders – and the potential for herd behavior. Thus, even more spectacular than the rise of crony capitalism was its spectacular collapse in 1997–1998. One of the simplest and most compelling analyses of what happened is that, on the basis of early success, and partly under pressure from what Bhagwati christened the "Wall Street–Treasury complex," Southeast Asian countries liberalized their financial markets to allow foreign investors in on a grand scale. However, there was no understanding that capital markets, unlike goods markets, are subject to manias and panics and therefore need to be monitored and regulated carefully. Hasty financial liberalization meant a rapid inflow of short-term capital, but these enormous levels of short-term borrowing raised the vulnerability of these companies, and as it was discovered and then became widespread knowledge that it was not always

---

[5] Krugman (1999) points out that one reason the Mexican devaluation turned into a panic was the fact that some Mexican businessmen appeared to have been informed in advance of the devaluation; this made foreigners want to get out as they realized a distinction was being made in the treatment of insiders versus outsiders.

[6] More recently and with respect to other places the word has come to be used in a different way, for example, it is used by Bhagwati to refer to the Clinton administration and its Hollywood "cronies" (Bhagwati 2000) and by Krugman (2003), with reference to the Bush administration and its ties to energy companies.

obvious where the money went once it was invested, panic developed and investors followed other investors out of these markets even more rapidly than they went in. One important point, stressed by Paul Krugman (1998) among others, is that the unique aspect of Asia's comeuppance was not so much the awfulness of the system there from an economic point of view, but the severity of the punishment. As both Krugman and Sachs and Radelet argue, what turned a bad financial situation into a catastrophe was the way a loss of confidence turned into a self-reinforcing panic. In 1996 capital was flowing into emerging Asia at the rate of about $100 billion a year; by the second half of 1997 it was flowing out at about the same rate. Thus it is possible in principle that a loss of confidence in a country can produce an economic crisis that justifies that loss of confidence – that countries may be vulnerable to what are aptly called "self-fulfilling speculative attacks." Or, as U.S. Treasury Secretary Robert Rubin said at the time, a "herd mentality" developed among investors and contributed to the recent broad-based losses in emerging markets and other asset classes.

Further work showed that the two social interactions were linked. For example, Wei (2001) argued that domestic crony capitalism made a country more dependent on the more fickle type of international capital flows (e.g., international bank loans) rather than the less volatile type (e.g., foreign direct investment, or FDI). He presented statistical evidence that the degree of domestic crony capitalism was indeed associated with a higher ratio of external loan to FDI. This type of capital flow has been identified as being associated with a higher incidence of a currency crisis. So crony capitalism increased the likelihood of a currency crisis.

To summarize, the first important social interaction emphasized here with respect to international financial markets is the networks between firms, banks, and politicians in Southeast Asia that permitted loans and investments in the absence of well-defined contractual rights enforcement – a system that in its glory days was referred to as "alliance" capitalism and only later came to be known as "crony" capitalism. The second social interaction discussed is herd behavior on the part of international investors themselves – which occurs when investors make loans where and on the basis of whether others are making loans and not on the quality of the investments themselves. In an era of widespread ownership of mutual funds, indeed, such activity is probably the norm: creditors act on the basis of the actions of other creditors, not on the basis of the debtors' fundamentals as perceived by the individual investor.

On this way of thinking, these two social interactions combined with premature capital market liberalization to produce the panic in emerging markets that began in 1997 in Southeast Asia. Suppose this analysis is accepted. What policy implications follow? Once again, there are two possible types of policies to follow, one based on price and another on social interaction. The price policy consists in raising interest rates to high enough levels to induce investors to return: this was the IMF policy. But if social interactions are dominant, then interest rates are neither the primary determinant of investment within Southeast Asia (networks are) nor are they the determinant for outside investors (conformity or herd behavior is). So the policy followed by the IMF might have been ineffective and even counterproductive and many leading international economists, including Bhagwati, Krugman, and Sachs, have argued that it was. Moreover, as Wade and Veneroso (1998) emphasize, the ratio of debt to equity in many Southeast Asian countries is typically higher by an order of magnitude than it is, say, in the United States. Consequently, raising interest rates imposes a correspondingly larger burden on the firms and threatens many of them with bankruptcy.

3.5 Policy Implications

The examples discussed in this chapter and the preceding one are summarized in Table 3.1. All of the cases in the table appear to fit the same pattern. First, all show the importance of social interactions and contagion, as has been discussed throughout the chapter. Second, all display some kind of structure or hierarchy or organization formed for the purpose of internalizing the externality. Third, associated with the structure is some characteristic problem – what I refer to in the table as "poison." Fourth, in each case the interactions take a stepwise pattern. The "small steps" that are characteristic of all the different social interactions are not identical. In the microfinance case, the role of small, frequent repayments may be related to enforcement limitations: the cost of nonrepayment is social sanction, roughly speaking; this cost is also, roughly, invariant to the size of the missed installment. Small, frequent repayments, therefore, may be meant to ensure that the sanction for nonpayment is greater than the benefits of nonpayment. If large, discrete repayments were allowed, this might not be the case. In fighting crime, the focus on "small events" may signal that the authorities are emphasizing law-abiding behavior as a broad social norm. But, to me at least, it is striking and merits further investigation that, in each case, there is this stepwise pattern.

Finally, from the policy point of view, there is both an individualistic price policy (P) and a policy that takes into account the existence of social

Table 3.1. *Five Issues Where Social Interactions, Not Prices, Are Key to Understanding and Policy*

Issue	What Makes Them a Group?	Social Interaction (Contagion)	Structure/Hierarchy	Problem or Poison W: without hierarchy H: due to it	Stepwise Interaction	Policy P: price SI: nonprice
Family relations	The family	The rotten-kid theorem (solidarity is contagious)	The family needs a head	W: powerlessness of other members H: authoritarianism breeds disincentives, Samaritan's dilemma	Repeated interaction	P: price incentives create division SI: automaticity of gifts breeds solidarity
Military power	The army	Sacrifices by leaders breed solidarity (solidarity is contagious)	Formal discipline, informal leadership by example	W: panic, disintegration H: excess conformity breeds stupidity	Marching	P: discipline alone does not create a strong army SI: solidarity conquers fear
Poverty/ microfinance	Know each other well	They can get loans together but not separately	Structure of mutual monitoring, leadership by the bank	W: no loans or repayment H: moral hazard	Dynamic small repayment incentives	P: raise interest rate, adverse selection SI: group liability
Crime	Criminals: gangs Citizens: community	Neighborhood deterioration demonstrates to criminals that the neighborhood is "safe" for crime, to people that it is unsafe	Subway "station manager"; community involvement on the side of the police	Gangs: W: dead end H: boss takes the cream Community: W: vulnerable to gangs H: racial profiling	Smaller offenses lead to bigger ones	P: price: p↑ or f↑ SI: maintain order and police small offenses/community involvement
International finance (the Asian crisis)	2 groups: 1/ alliance capitalism (cronies); 2/ the electronic herd	1/ corruption 2/ buy or sell because others are buying/selling	1/ Asian hierarchies: Japanese firm, *chaebol, guanxi* 2/ Federal Reserve/ IMF	(IMF) W: vulnerability, panic H: moral hazard	Stepwise adjustment in interest rates is difficult in a panic	P: interest rates ↑→ bankruptcy SI: property rights, general trust

interactions (SI) and tries to increase the level of trust or solidarity within the group. As is normal in the analysis of these phenomena, I suggest that there is a "tipping point," where the social interaction effect becomes more important than the price effect. In other words, for each of these problems there are two regions, in one of which changing prices on individual behavior is a good policy solution and others where this is not the case. For example, for U.S.-style economies with a shareholder system and in which firms are widely held, a policy of raising interest rates can be useful to moderate economic activity; but in the case of South Korea the structure of the *chaebol* and the social interactions involved may have made this policy too costly. In the case of crime in a middle-class suburb where criminal gangs are few or nonexistent, or of white-collar crime, a policy of raising the "price" of crime may act as a successful deterrent. In other cases where the social interaction element is more important (e.g., where there are potential racial problems, or where there is a dominant gang and it is vital to have the community on the side of the police in order to combat it), the social interaction problems may overwhelm the price effects and a policy of raising punishments may be counterproductive.

3.6 Summary

The basic message of the chapter is that the mainstream individualistic, market approach does not lead to understanding, neglects social interactions, and leads to policies that might be counterproductive when these are especially important. To begin with crime: from our discussion it is easy to imagine that an increase in the punishment for crime could actually raise the level of crime. For example, suppose that a lot of crime is committed by gangs, and that the key to reducing crime is to have the community on the side of the police rather than on the side of the gang. In that case, raising the penalty might make the community feel the penalty is unfair and then be less likely to assist the police. Or, in the case of crimes where guilt or innocence is decided by juries, raising the penalty might make the jury less willing to convict. Again, this would lower p, the probability of apprehension and conviction, and possibly increase the crime rate.[7] The "broken-windows" approach recognizes the social interactions involved: that whether an

---

[7] Of course, the social interactions approach can also be counterproductive: for example, extensive policing of minor offenses, as suggested by the "broken-windows" approach, might aggravate race relations, in turn raising the fears of minority groups of unjust prosecution and giving them less legitimate opportunities, thus possibly resulting in more crime.

individual commits a crime or not depends on his perception of what others are doing; it tries to create safety in part by maintaining order and in part by creating a general norm of law-abidingness within the community.

In the family, dealing with family relationships by price incentives can sometimes cause division. Thus suppose, as in Becker's model, that there is a "head" of the family who tries to encourage another family member to pursue a course of action. Sometimes price incentives might work (e.g., giving a son or a daughter fifty dollars to mow the lawn, or punishing a child by withdrawing driving privileges for driving while intoxicated). At other times, it can cause division and even tragedy (the Montagues and the Capulets of Romeo and Juliet are perhaps the most famous example of the latter). The gift giving by the head that generates unselfish behavior even by selfish family members in Becker's model is not a reward or punishment that is contingent on the behavior of individual family members, but the consequence of the "automatic" inclusion of the income or welfare of other members into the utility function of the head. It is this "social interaction" (i.e., the fact that the income or welfare of other family members enters the utility function of the head) that makes the family *one* (a solidary unit). Even where love is insufficient, the head's problem can still be viewed as one of raising the level of trust that each family member has in each other, and "automatic" transfers that make selfish behavior unprofitable have this effect. Such policies could also be adopted by families with multiple heads or nonheads.

In the army, the accounts detailed in Keegan (1976) suggest that it is not merely the discipline of rewards and punishments that wins battles. Rather, the army that retains solidarity triumphs over the army that disintegrates into the selfish behavior of its individual members. Fear is the fundamental problem faced by everyone in battle, and solidarity in battle is generated, according to these accounts, by the example and sacrifices of leaders, whose behavior helps each individual to overcome his fear. The social interaction is that the more others are willing to sacrifice, thus showing that they are not afraid, the greater the likelihood that any individual will overcome his fear and stand his ground. By contrast, a policy of punishments for not fighting well could easily be counterproductive. It could *increase* the individual's fear.

In the case of poverty and lack of access to credit, again, use of the price variable to control individual behavior – in this case, the interest rate applied to individual loans – does not necessarily provide a good solution. Many poor people are simply not creditworthy in the standard sense. Raising the interest rate on individual loans to the level appropriate for the riskiness of the loan may simply result in adverse selection: the best risks leave first, and in the end the bank ends up with the bad risks or even no market for loans at all. The problem is that, on normal banking criteria, the individuals in these situations may not be particularly creditworthy. On the other hand, advantage may be taken of social interactions: the individuals in the group may be better able to monitor or pressure each other than any external agency, and so the group as a whole may be creditworthy even when each individual within it is not. So by taking a group rather than an individual approach, and by utilizing the appropriate repayment structure, group lending may make the market work.

Finally, in the Asian crisis, the IMF has tried to solve problems by implementing structural adjustment programs. But it tended to ignore the nature of the social relations or the networks involved in alliance or crony capitalism in East Asia: these relationships implied high corporate debt ratios, so when the IMF insisted on its standard recipe of raising interest rates to solve the problem, it may not have understood how much larger the burden of adjustment would be in Asia. The herd behavior of outside investors compounded the problem. The result may have been needlessly costly adjustment.

PART THREE

EXTREMISM

FOUR

The Calculus of Discontent

4.1 Introduction

Extremist leaders often end up either as heroes or villains. Sometimes they can be both at the same time, depending on what you are reading or whom you are talking to. Vladimir Ilyich Lenin is usually considered a villain in the West, but to many people for a long, long time he was a hero. Mahatma Gandhi was often considered an extremist villain by the British government, as Nelson Mandela was to the apartheid South African government. Slobodan Milosevic is largely considered a villain now, but not by everyone, and he was once a hero to many Serbs.

One reason extremist leaders are either villains or heroes is that they have big goals – like a Communist society, independence for India, a democratic South Africa, or Greater Serbia. Leaders with big goals or radical agendas obviously are going to come into conflict with other groups in society who don't share those goals. The conflicts between communism and capitalism, independence and British rule for India, black votes and white rule in South Africa, and Serbian aspirations and those of the Croatians, Albanians, and Slovenians are obvious.

Our point of view is that extremists are rational. Their goals may be bigger than those of most of us, but from an economist's point of view, rationality just means that, whatever the goal, a person chooses the best means to achieve it. The goals themselves are neither rational nor irrational; we just take them as given. The simplest way to think of an extremist leader is someone whose goals or views are outside the mainstream on some issue or dimension. In the twentieth century, extremists were typically persons on the extreme right or the extreme left, but the dimension could also be nationalism, religion, or security or any other politically important dimension.

However, there is another way to think of extremism in politics, in which extremism refers to the use of extreme *methods* of political competition, usually violent ones, such as assassinations or terrorism. Often (not always) those with extremist beliefs also use extremist methods.

What leads political leaders to take extremist positions on issues? Why do they sometimes demand that their followers use violence or other extremist methods in order to achieve their goals? These questions are obviously of great importance today. In this chapter I do not have much new to say on the first question, but I do summarize the literature on it and discuss some of the most interesting answers proposed by others. I then come to my main subject which is the second question: what explains the attraction of violence to people with extreme goals? I show why, when a group has extremist goals, extremist methods are indeed more likely to be attractive to its leaders than if its goals were moderate. Indeed, I show that the more extreme the goals of the group, the more likely it is to use extremist methods to further those goals.

Of course, some leaders who have been labeled extreme have succeeded without violence. Some of these are heroes to many today. Mahatma Gandhi and Martin Luther King are the most obvious examples. They are both mainstream today, and in my view justly heroic, but they were considered extreme by many in their heyday, Gandhi by the British, King by many in the U.S. South. But they both expressed a profound moral aversion to violence. That they were able to succeed without it is, of course, in part, a tribute to their genius. But it is also because they saw the possibility of attracting mass support to their cause without it. And it is also because their goals were universal:

I have a dream that one day this nation will rise up and live out the true meaning of its creeds. We hold these truths to be self-evident that all men are created equal. I have a dream that, one day, on the red hills of Georgia, the sons of farmers' slaves and the sons of farmers' slave owners will be able to sit down together at the table of brotherhood. I have a dream that, one day, even the State of Mississippi, a state sweltering with the heat of injustice, sweltering with the heat of oppression, will be transformed into an oasis of freedom and justice. I have a dream.[1]

It's still moving to read that speech today, and it is hard nowadays to think of Martin Luther King as an "extremist." But from the standpoint of

---

[1] Martin Luther King Jr. (delivered on the Steps at the Lincoln Memorial in Washington, D.C., on August 28, 1963). From the Martin Luther King Papers Project at Stanford University, http://www-leland. stanford.edu/group/King/.

many in the southern United States in the 1950s and the early 1960s, where segregation was the norm, that's what he was. Of course, among civil rights leaders he was a moderate, and he was supported by many federal leaders, including the Kennedys. Extremism is always relative to a particular context, time, or place. But King was not afraid of the label:

Was not Jesus an extremist for love – "Love your enemies, bless them that curse you, pray for them that despitefully use you." Was not Amos an extremist for justice – "Let justice roll down like waters and righteousness like a mighty stream." Was not Paul an extremist for the gospel of Jesus Christ – "I bear in my body the marks of the Lord Jesus." Was not Martin Luther an extremist – "Here I stand; I can do none other so help me God." Was not John Bunyan an extremist – "I will stay in jail to the end of my days before I make a butchery of my conscience." Was not Abraham Lincoln an extremist – "This nation cannot survive half slave and half free." Was not Thomas Jefferson an extremist – "We hold these truths to be self-evident, that all men are created equal." So the question is not whether we will be extremist but what kind of extremist will we be. Will we be extremists for hate or will we be extremists for love? Will we be extremists for the preservation of injustice – or will we be extremists for the cause of justice? In that dramatic scene on Calvary's hill, three men were crucified. We must not forget that all three were crucified for the same crime – *the crime of extremism.*[2]

Nelson Mandela is another of today's heroes, and, like King, he is certainly a hero of mine. But he faced entrenched opposition from the apartheid government of South Africa, and sometimes he despaired of achieving his goals without violence. In 1961 he formed an armed wing of the African National Congress, arguing that the violence of the government could possibly only be combated by violence. He still advocated this on his release from prison in 1990:

Today the majority of South Africans, black and white, recognise that apartheid has no future. It has to be ended by our own decisive mass action in order to build peace and security. The mass campaign of defiance and other actions of our organisation and people can only culminate in the establishment of democracy. The destruction caused by apartheid on our sub-continent is incalculable. The fabric of family life of millions of my people has been shattered. Millions are homeless and unemployed. Our economy lies in ruins and our people are embroiled in political strife. Our resort to the armed struggle in 1960 with the formation of the military wing of the ANC, Umkhonto we Sizwe, was a purely defensive action against the violence of apartheid. The factors which necessitated the armed struggle still exist today. We have no option but to continue. We express the hope that a climate conducive to a

---

[2] Letter from Birmingham Jail, April 1963. From Martin Luther King Day quotes at http://grove.ufl.edu/~leo/mlk.html (emphasis added).

negotiated settlement will be created soon so that there may no longer be the need for the armed struggle.[3]

Of course, in the end, Mandela and the African National Congress won their fight for democracy in South Africa, and if it was not entirely without violence, there was no bloody revolution, and Nelson Mandela became the first president of an integrated South Africa.

Moving toward the other end of the "violence-nonviolence" spectrum, there is the case of Slobodan Milosevic. He did not shrink from using violence: he launched four wars during his time as president of Serbia. Ultimately he went to war with NATO. He lost that war and was put on trial at the Hague for "crimes against humanity." Few think of him as a hero today. But he too had big goals and dreamed of a greater Serbia. Three million Serbs were scattered outside the borders of the largest republic, Serbia, as Yugoslavia unraveled. Many of these people longed to be part of a greater Serbia. It was a dream the Serbian president encouraged.[4]

The explosion of nationalism in Serbia prefigured the explosion of radical Islamic nationalism. Both were "organic" movements, fueled by what to many seemed the disappearance of the basis of solidarity in their societies – communism in the former Yugoslavia, the Islamic community in the Arab world.

Yet a different kind of violence has been practiced by Osama bin Laden. His goals are big, too. He dreams of a truly Islamic society, like that in the prophet Mohammad's time. Among the chief obstacles to that dream are the secular, U.S.-supported governments in places like Egypt, and the United States and other secular, Western societies themselves, which bin Laden thinks of as living in a state of *jahiliyya*, or barbarism.

To most people in the West, myself included, Osama's methods are repulsive. But, to my mind, the best way to understand what he is about is to assume he is rational. His goals are huge, but they are hardly universal. And he faces entrenched opposition to his goals, not only from within Arab countries, but from much of the rest of the world.

Is Osama rational? The place to start in understanding Osama is that he is weak. From the military point of view, he is a Holy Warrior without an army. Politically, he does not command an organized political party that could take power anywhere in the Muslim world. Even in Afghanistan, bin Laden was at best the "guest" of the Taliban government. His choice of

---

[3] Nelson Mandela's Address to Rally in Cape Town on his Release from Prison, February 11, 1990, http://www.anc.org.za/ancdocs/speeches/release.html.

[4] Milosevic, *CBC Sunday Morning*, July 5, 1992.

methods may be gruesome, but it is not irrational. He needs his enemies to get so angry that they use their strength against themselves, judo-style. As has been said, George Bush has been his best "recruiting sergeant." But, it must be remembered, he has a lot of support. And he, too, is a hero to many.

Martin Luther King, Mandela, Milosevic, and Osama bin Laden were (or are) all considered extremists. They wanted to effect radical change in society. King abhorred violence. Mandela was willing to use it only reluctantly. For Milosevic, it was a principal tool. For Osama bin Laden, it is virtually the only tool, and he appears to see the hand of God in it.

What explains the attraction of violence to people with extreme goals? This chapter is devoted to this question. The basic argument is that leaders whose views are outside the mainstream adopt extremist methods when there is an indivisibility that characterizes the relationship between the intermediate goal of the group and its ultimate goal. In the chapter I look at three examples: communism (control over the means of production is an intermediate goal to the achievement of a communist society), nationalism (control over territory is an intermediate goal to the achievement of nationhood), and Islamic fundamentalism (ridding the Muslim nations of foreign and secular influences is an intermediate goal to the achievement of an Islamic society).

The most important policy implication of the chapter is that one should look at the goals of extremist groups in order to understand their actions. The reason is that it is the indivisibility of the goal that explains the extremism of the actions, and if one can unbundle the goal or make the indivisible divisible, then there may be ways to provide these goals in a way that satisfies some of the members of the group and thus dries up support for the grander ambitions of the leaders of extremist groups.

The next section looks at some of the reasons why political leaders sometimes adopt extremist ideologies. Section 4.3 looks at the ways in which extremist leaders can obtain power using moderate or peaceful methods. Section 4.4 outlines our basic argument about the attractiveness of extreme methods. Section 4.5 develops this model of the choice of method in some detail and shows the calculus of discontent – the conditions under which groups decide to use extremist methods. Section 4.6 then turns to methods of combating extremism.

4.2 Why Do They Choose Extremist Positions?

Groups may adopt positions outside the mainstream of their societies (extreme positions) for many reasons. Here I mention a few of the most important ones. Perhaps the most common idea about why groups choose extremist positions is that this is a response to the failure of the policies of more centrist groups. For example, the rise of the Nazi party is often analyzed as a response to the failure of the parties of the center to act on or satisfy the demands of the German people with respect to issues like unemployment and law and order in the 1930s.[5] Similarly it has been argued that the rise of fundamentalist Islam is a response to the failure of Arab governments (e.g., the failed socialism of Nasser – see Giurato and Molinari 2002, Zakaria 2003); in turn, this failure may be related to the fact that Arab governments have tended to be dictatorships, and not of the developmental kind. Yet another example is the United States in the 1960s, where the Vietnam war gave birth to the Weathermen and other extreme groups.

Extremism can also arise as a response to the "opening up of space" on the extremes that sometimes occur when formerly right-wing or left-wing parties move toward the center. One example is the rise of the radical right in Israel, which was born as the result of the Camp David accords (Sprinzak 1989). In the same way, Kitschelt (1997) explains the rise of first the extreme left in Europe and then the extreme right as due to the fact that conventional leftist and rightist parties had moved toward the center. He also notes the increased importance of the libertarian-authoritarian dimension in Europe in the 1990s, which he traces to changing production systems and the consequent new appeal of free-market policies as the result of the twin factors of globalization and the failure of communist systems. These two factors, he suggests, generated the policies of the extreme right in Europe in the 1980s.[6]

Finally the rise of "extremism" as a response to the fact that one's homeland is occupied by a "foreign" power, or as a response to a dictatorial government, or in societies where civil rights are limited is easy to explain.

4.3 How Do They Get Power? Democratic or "Moderate" Avenues

The general result of political competition under various assumptions (either Downsian, or multiparty with probabilistic voting) is the median voter theorem. The basic idea is that, by moving to the center, each party can gain more votes from centrist voters and, as long as there are only two parties, not lose any at the extremes. This median solution is also welfare maximizing (Brennan 2002, p. 93; Mueller 2003).

---

[5] For one version of this argument, and detailed references to the literature on it, see Wintrobe (1998).

[6] But note that, in Kitschelt's (1997) analysis, the opening up of space is not sufficient: one still needs the supply of entrepreneurship to account for what happened.

One can then list all of the conditions under which nonconvergence would occur, for example, many parties, ideological preferences (especially the preferences of party activists), extra dimensions. But these outcomes are inherently unstable and do not represent an extremist equilibrium (Brennan 2002). Public choice also looks for socially rational outcomes (Brennan 2002), and extremism is usually held to represent an irrational outcome.

How then can an extremist equilibrium result from democratic processes? The simplest way for an extremist group to obtain power is via a coalition, implicit or explicit, with centrists (e.g., the National Rifle Association in the United States and the fundamentalist Jews in Israel have obtained power to have their preferred policies implemented via formal or informal deals with centrist parties).

Another, more complex way that extremists can take power is via a coalition of "monomaniac" extremists. These are people who care only about one issue and take an extreme position on that issue. The idea was put forward by Pierre Salmon (2002). Thus two or more groups, each of which is "monomanical" in a separate dimension, can form a coalition large enough to win power. As Salmon explains:

> For instance, you could have a [monomaniac] coalition if you have 20 per cent of a group who are violently anti-homosexual, for instance, 20 per cent who are Catholic fundamentalists, 20 per cent who are anti-immigrants, 20 per cent who are anti-Semitic and 20 per cent who are in favour of complete free markets, then you could have a coalition in which, if you look at the overall figures, you would find only 20 per cent of the people being anti-homosexual, and this would be below the number which is given in moderate parties, in which you have more than 20 per cent of persons being anti-homosexual.[7]

So, even though most people in the coalition, let's say, might not be particularly antihomosexual, nevertheless, the position of the coalition is antihomosexual. Most people in the coalition might not particularly care about free markets, but the coalition, as a whole, has a very extreme position on free markets. So, *even though most people in the coalition are not extreme on most issues, because the group takes the position of the monomaniac extremists in the coalition on each issue, the group as a whole is extreme on every dimension.*

Pierre Salmon's ideas can be used to interpret the 2004 American election. Of course, there are some people who always vote Democrat and some who always vote Republican. But they didn't decide the election. George Bush won that election on a platform with three main components. All of them

---

[7] Interview with Pierre Salmon, in Wintrobe (2004).

seem radical or extreme by the normal standards of American politics. The first is that the way to prevent terrorists from attacking America is to wage unprovoked wars on countries that have supported terrorism, like Iraq, even if there is no evidence that those countries had anything to do with the 9/11 attack. The second is tax cuts that disproportionately favor the rich. And the third is religious fundamentalism, including opposition to abortions, stem cell research, and gay civil unions, and the promotion of religious censorship on television media and of a religious point of view in American life.

There are two ways to interpret his victory. The first is the median voter model, in which case one has to conclude that a majority of Americans are extreme on all these issues. That means the median American is a religious fundamentalist who is in favor of preventive wars and tax cuts for the rich. But most Americans don't seem to be like that. Salmon's ideas suggest a different interpretation. This is that Bush won because he put together a coalition of three groups of voters. For each of these groups, *one* of these issues was paramount and determined its voting. So the group in favor of tax cuts for the rich was not necessarily against gay unions or for preventive wars, but it voted for Bush because of his position on tax cuts. Similarly the so-called security moms may have voted for Bush for his stand on keeping American safe. But they are not necessarily extremist on the other two issues: it's just that those issues were less important to them. And the religious evangelicals may not have cared for Bush's stands on war and tax cuts, but for them the religious issue was paramount. So, in the end, a coalition was forged that was extremist on *all* of these issues even though the average American is not. This is another way of explaining his victory.

Some support for this interpretation can be found in a description by a leading conservative activist, Grover Norquist, of the strategy used in forging the U.S. conservative coalition. Norquist is the head of the advocacy group Americans for Tax Reform and was described by former U.S. House of Representatives Speaker Newt Gingrich as "the single most effective conservative advocate in the country" in a *New Yorker* profile by John Cassidy.[8] In the profile, Norquist talks to Cassidy about how to build a coalition:

If you want the votes of people who are good on guns, good on taxes, and good on faith issues, that is a very small intersection of voters ... but if you say, "Give me the votes of anybody who agrees with you on any one of these issues, that's a

---

[8] Quoted in Cassidy (2005), p. 42.

much bigger section of the population." To illustrate what he meant, Norquist drew three intersecting circles on a piece of paper. In the first one, he wrote "guns," in the second he wrote "taxes," in the third he wrote "faith." There was a small area where the three circles intersected. "With that group, you can take over the country, if you start with the airports and the radio stations," he said. But with all of the three circles that's sixty per cent of the population, and you can win politically. (Cassidy 2005, p. 46)

A third way in which extremism can come to power through normal democratic politics has been described in Amy Chua's *World on Fire* (2004). Her analysis looks at the likely political reaction to the simultaneous introduction of marketization and democratization, today's recipe for many countries to develop and modernize. In her analysis the majority sometimes unites in hatred of a "market dominant minority." This is particularly likely when the minority in question constitutes a separate ethnic group.

Her starting point is that, particularly in many developing countries, the distribution of the fruits of economic growth resulting from marketization are uneven: there are large gains to a few but losses to many. The fact that the overall level of measured GNP goes up – that there is measured economic growth – may be cold comfort to those who are hurt by the policy. Now, the introduction of democratization at the same time as marketization means that those who are injured have a way of making their feelings felt. Various manifestations of extremist violence tend to result when two conditions hold: first, there is what Chua calls "a market-dominant minority" – a minority group that is particularly good at operating in markets, and which obtains what to many may appear to be a disproportionate share of the gains from marketization; second, the democracy is "illiberal":[9] the country is democratic in that there are more or less competitive elections but constitutional protections for human rights and other checks and balances are weak or absent, as seems to be true in many places in the contemporary world. This provides an opportunity for those who are hurt by the policy to take extremist political actions against these minorities. The most obvious examples of market-dominant minorities are the Tutsis in Rwanda, the Chinese in Thailand, or the Jews in Russia.

To sum up, I have described some of the ways in which extremism can come to power by perfectly moderate or normal methods of democratic political competition. I now turn to an alternative way for them to come to power, via extremist methods.

---

[9] Zakaria (2003) has also discussed what he calls the rise of "illiberal democracy."

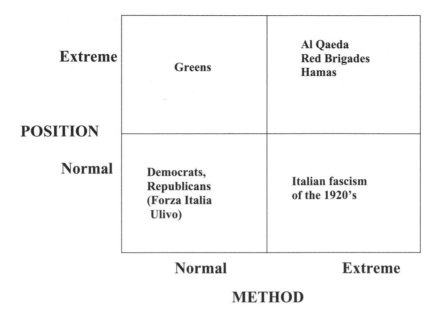

Figure 4.1. Two kinds of extremism (adapted from Galeotti 2002).

4.4 How Do They Get Power: Extremist Methods

At the beginning of this chapter I noted a common distinction between two kinds of extremism:

1. An extremist person or group can be defined as one whose equilibrium position is located at a "corner" rather than in the interior on some dimension (e.g., the left-right dimension in political space).
2. Alternatively, a political extremist could be defined as one who uses extremist methods, for example, bombings, inflammatory language, terrorist activity, and so forth, but whose platform is or may be centrist rather than extremist in political (left-right) space.

Some (e.g., Galeotti 2002) expand on this distinction to develop a typology of extremism. If we assume all types are possible, there are four combinations, as shown in Figure 4.1. The horizontal axis shows extremism in method, the vertical one extremism in ideological position. The Green Party, for example, adopts what to some is an extremist position with respect to the environment, but never uses terrorism or other violent methods of protest (although Greens have famously used civil disobedience). On the other hand, Italian fascism of the 1920s has been described as an "extremism of the middle" – that is, it was extremist in the use of violent methods of political competition, but its policies were centrist.[10] Modern Italian parties like the Ulivo and Forza Italia are centrist (center-left and center-right) in both method and policies, as Democrats and Republicans usually are in the United States. And groups like Al Qaeda, Hamas, and the Red Brigades are extremist in both their proposed policies and their methods.

However, there is something missing here that is central to many kinds of extremism, especially its historically most important kinds. This is the fact that in many cases the goals of extremist groups are indivisible. The most obvious examples are groups that feel dispossessed from their "homeland" and take extremist actions for this cause. A homeland can be larger or smaller but still there is this element: a group either has one or it doesn't. And there are minimum requirements. Is the area under the group's control sufficiently large that the government can provide the basic functions of the modern state? Does the group have sufficient control over citizenship, taxation, property rights, security, and the means of coercion and violence to function effectively? Similarly, for years many in the Communist Party fought for the goal of a communist society, and a central tenet of that movement is that the achievement of communism necessitated a revolution and the overthrow of the bourgeois order. One reason is that it is obviously difficult to implement central planning unless the government controls most of the economy. Nor can an economy that is half communist and half capitalist give birth to a communist society in the classic sense in which there would be a "new man" and so forth.

A third example is control over the means of violence. In successful states this is a monopoly of the state. It can be eroded through gangs or terrorism, but in the end the state is either basically "in control" of the means of violence or it is not, and when the state loses control over it, that state has essentially failed.

Yet another example is Osama bin Laden's goal of a restoration of Islamic rule in Arabic countries (see B. Lewis 2003; Zakaria 2003). Either a country is secular, based on Roman law or the Napoleonic code or some other secular source, or it is religious, based on a religious doctrine such as Catholicism or *sharia* law. Finally the same point applies to the aspirations for independence of a group that is under occupation. Let's look at some historical examples: either the British were going to leave India or Israel, or the French leave Algeria, or they were not; either the blacks were going to get the vote in

---

[10] Paxton (2004) suggests that the reason for this was the necessity to compromise with other groups in the fascist coalitions. At the beginning and at the end of the fascist era, this compromise was less necessary and the movement showed its true colors.

South Africa (in which case they would control the government, being an overwhelming majority) or they were not. All of these goals, which were, of course, achieved in the end, are indivisible.

In all of these cases, my basic argument is that there is a natural complementarity between the goal of the extremist group, which is indivisible, and the methods, which are extremist.[11] That is, there is a natural complementarity between extremist goals and extremist methods. Thus it is difficult to separate the two, as we have in Figure 4.1.

Other extremist groups have goals that are clearly divisible: examples include the Greens's goal of a cleaner environment, and the National Rifle Association's goal of fewer restrictions on gun ownership. Implicitly, I argue, these groups never reach the heights of fanaticism characteristic of groups that have indivisible goals.

4.5 Why Do They Choose Extremist Methods?

4.5.1 Extremist Methods Are Risky

Suppose to begin with that extremist methods are simply a form of political competition or rent seeking. If so, then the central difference between extremist methods compared with normal democratic methods of political competition or rent seeking is that extremist methods are *risky*. Because they are illegal, or can get out of hand easily, or can provoke a negative reaction either from the state or from other political groups, they are therefore more likely to involve greater losses than conventional politics. On the other hand, when they succeed they sometimes do so in a spectacular fashion. Consequently the choice between extremist methods and moderation can be analyzed in the same way as the choice between a criminal career and a legitimate one, as in models of the decision to commit crimes pioneered by

---

[11] Of course, other distinctions could be made. One of these is the distinction between ordinary extremism and what might be called "totalitarian" extremism. Members of totalitarian extremist groups, as exemplified by classical Nazism and communism, and possibly some variants of Islamic fundamentalism, tend to be extreme in their "world view," and this viewpoint dictates extremist positions on a whole host of issues, not just a single dimension. The classic analysis of American extremism by Lipset and Rabb (1970, 1978) implicitly referred to this type of extremism when they defined the essence of extremism as "monism" or "anti-pluralism." Thus their book was titled *The Politics of Unreason* and they described such people as unable to compromise. Their analysis points to another distinction – the *comprehensiveness* of the extremist outlook or the number of dimensions covered by the extremist world view.

Becker (1968). This point is explored in the model that follows.[12] I show that under certain circumstances the use of extremist means (e.g., terrorism, violence) follows from the extremist goals of the group. Thus it is no accident that the most serious forms of extremism also use terrorist methods. The main conclusion is that one has to understand the goals of the groups in order to understand their actions and to formulate policy toward them.

4.5.2 A Basic Model of the Calculus of Discontent

I assume a political organization with some ideological goal Z, which might be a state for the group that lacks a homeland, or a communist society, or a law banning abortions, or throwing all people of a certain race out of the country, or an Islamic society governed by *sharia* law. I do not inquire into the rationality of the belief in this goal but take it as given, as is normal in economic theory. The group tries to further this goal by exerting political pressure. So the product of either moderate pressure or terrorism is an increase in Z. Of particular importance, as emphasized previously, is that this goal is often indivisible, or displays increasing returns. This property is illustrated in Figures 4.2a, 4.2b, and 4.2c, where the horizontal axis indicates the level of an intermediate goal – land to the Palestinians or Jews, control over the means of production, the extent to which foreign forces are thrown out of the homeland – and the vertical axis the relationship between this intermediate goal and the final goal of the group (respectively, a Palestinian or Jewish state, a communist society, or an Islamic society). This is the relationship that displays an indivisibility or increasing returns.[13] In each case there is a critical point, where enough of the intermediate goal has been obtained that the final goal is possible.

Thus Figure 4.2a illustrates the case of Palestine-Israel, Figure 4.2b shows how communism displays this property, and Figure 4.2c depicts potentially Islamic societies like Saudi Arabia or Egypt and what appear to some to be their foreign-secular domination. In each case there is an indivisibility or area of increasing returns between the intermediate goal and the ultimate goal of the group.

---

[12] Landes (1978) and Sandler and Lapan (1988) have also exploited this analogy, though in different ways from that followed here.

[13] In turn, the indivisibility or zone of increasing returns arises because the intermediate goal can be likened to a missing "factor or production" in the production function of the ultimate goals.

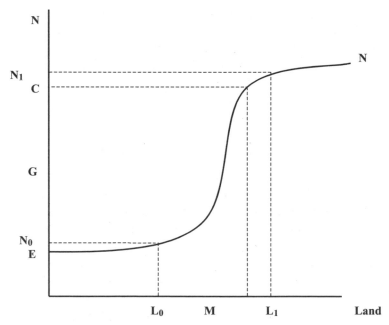

Figure 4.2a. Increasing returns in Palestine-Israel. N = nationhood. E = even with no land, the Palestinians are "conscious" of nationhood. C = critical point (where increasing-returns region ends), as (some) Palestinians feel that this is the minimum they need to form a nation. (Some) Israelis feel that if they give them that much, *they* won't have enough land to constitute a state because their borders will be insecure. So C is the critical point for these two groups. G = area where more land is still insufficient to provide enough space to enable the group to fully become a nation.

To fix ideas, it might be useful to think of an example where there is no indivisibility. The objective of reducing *income inequality,* for example, is *divisible.* The level of income inequality in a society is a continuous variable that can take on any level from complete inequality to complete equality. The most common way to represent this is via a Gini coefficient. A graph of this (not shown) would display no indivisibility or increasing returns. Hence income inequality as a function of, say, tax rates is not indivisible and does not provide a motive for extremist methods in the same way that nationalist or religious society aspirations do. Consequently, if the argument of this chapter is correct, the latter provide a more important source of extremism than the former.

However, income inequality could be an intermediate goal for some group, and the relationship between it and some ultimate objective indivisible. Marx, who relied on the income inequality of capitalist societies to

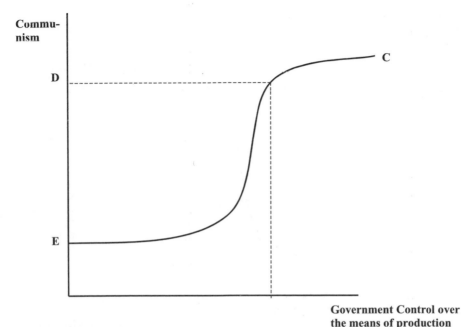

Figure 4.2b. Communism and control over the means of production. C = communism. At D, the state has sufficient control over the means of production so that C is possible, so D = critical point. E = some communism is possible even with no government control over industry.

provide the basic argument for revolution, substituted "class" for income. He argued that the normal workings of a capitalist economy would result in the proletariat becoming progressively poorer, and this progressive poverty would result, at some point, in the attainment of class consciousness. Here is an indivisibility (class consciousness as a function of inequality). But, instead, the poor got richer, and it turned out to be entirely feasible in many societies for many people to move from one class to another. The basic reason for the failure of Marxist predictions to hold is that the poor got rich in most Western societies, and many of them moved from working class to middle class, thus destroying the purported immobility between classes.

Perhaps this argument could be generalized, to the effect that indivisible variables are always the source of revolution.

How does the existence of an indivisibility explain why a group would choose methods like terror to pursue its objectives? According to the argument at the beginning of this section, the basic difference between terror

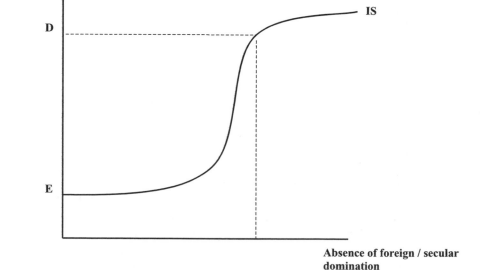

Figure 4.2c. Islamic society and foreign or secular domination. At D, enough foreign or secular domination has been removed to make an Islamic society possible. E = Even with total domination, one can still have a little bit of an *ummah*.

and moderate pressure from the point of view of the group is that terror is risky. I try to capture this feature in the choice among methods of pressure, for example, that between moderate and extremist methods.

Assume the organization has a production function that can either produce moderate (M) pressure or extremist incidents (I) in any combination from fixed levels of labor (L), capital (K), and organizational capacity (O). Of course, in reality there is a continuum of methods, beginning with voting, peaceful and lawful demonstrations, then continuing with civil disobedience, violence toward property, assassination of political enemies, and ending with violence toward innocent civilians. For the purpose of modeling I assume only two methods, one moderate (peaceful and lawful, and therefore riskless) and the other violent and risky. Then the level of moderate and extremist pressures are:

$$M = M(L_M, K_M, O_M), I = I(L_I, K_I, O_I) \qquad (4.1)$$

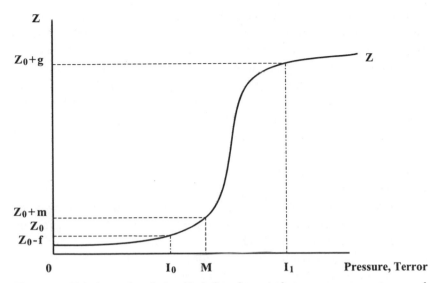

Figure 4.3. This shows the relationship believed to exist between pressure or terror and the level of the ultimate objective (Z) that is achieved.

in which

I = the number of violent Incidents and
M = the level of Moderate pressure.

The organization's total stock of L, K, and O are fixed:

$$L = L_M + L_I, \tag{4.2}$$

$$K = K_M + K_I,$$

$$O = O_I + O_M.$$

The organization can use any combination of moderate or extreme methods. The more it chooses extreme or violent methods, the greater the level of risk undertaken. Let us first illustrate the general argument with a simple example. Then we will develop it in more detail.

Figure 4.3 shows the goal of the group Z on the vertical axis. Z therefore represents variables such as nationhood N, communism C, or an Islamic Society IS in Figures 4.2a, 4.2b, or 4.2c. The horizontal axis shows the product of applying various methods of pressure. Suppose that from the risky method there are three possible "states of the world" – success (and the achievement of a high level of pressure I_1, in which case the level of the goal achieved is $Z_0 + g$, or failure (with level of pressure I_0). Failure results in one of two possible outcomes. In the first of these, the attempt to impose pressure fails and the outcome is simply the status quo Z_0. In the second, the attempt also fails, and, in addition, the leadership is caught, convicted, and sanctioned, retarding the goals of the group. If the value of the sanction *as measured by its cost to the goal of the group* is $-f$, then the outcome in that case is $Z_0 - f$. On the other hand, the outcome of applying a moderate level of pressure is always the level of pressure M, with gains for the group equal to $Z_0 + m$.

Thus $g =$ the gains to the group as estimated by its leader from using its organization and other factors of production to produce successful terrorist incidents I, and $m =$ the (certain) gain to the group from using only moderate methods of pressure. Then one dimension of the level of increasing returns may be summarized by the ratio g/m. This is the ratio of the gains from successful terrorist pressure to moderate pressure. The higher this is, the more the function displays increasing returns.

> $q =$ the probability that extremist methods succeed and the state accedes to the demands of the group
> $1 - q =$ the probability that the methods fail
> $p =$ the probability that, in addition to failure, the leadership of the extremist group is caught, convicted, and sanctioned
> $f =$ the cost of the sanction to the goals of the group
> $Z_0 =$ status quo income
> $U =$ the utility function of the leadership

Then extremist methods will be chosen if:

$$qU(Z_0 + g) + (1 - q)pU(Z_0 - f) + (1 - q)(1 - p)U(Z_0) > U(Z_0 + m). \tag{4.3}$$

This equation shows how terror can be a rational choice. A moderate level of pressure may leave the group stuck in the region of increasing returns, with the goal hardly advanced. With terrorist or risky methods, on the other hand, it is *possible* that the group can achieve its goal. Of course, it is also possible that the group will fail, but note that the costs of failure may not be that large if there are increasing returns ($Z_0 - f$ is not that far from Z_0). Thus, given that the goal displays increasing returns, terrorism may be a rational choice.

Whether terrorism is rational also depends on other elements in the structure of opportunities. The greater the indivisibility, the larger the ratio g/m, and the more likely extremist methods will be chosen, as shown in equation 4.3. An increase in the likelihood that the methods succeed (q) will also raise the likelihood that these methods are chosen. Similarly, an increase in the capacity to manufacture terrorist incidents I would on the other hand raise the level of terror by raising the ratio g/m.

The other main determinants are the deterrence variables p and f. Equation 4.3 appears to imply that increases in these variables are effective in deterring extremism, if they can be raised high enough. But note that increasing returns may limit the effectiveness of these variables. If these are very large, as depicted in Figure 4.3, the enormous *potential* gains from terror explain the indifference of many extremist groups to loss of life, either that of their victims or the losses to members of the group who sacrifice themselves for the cause. Thus it shows that sanctions and other punitive measures against the group may not be effective. Second, raising p sufficiently high to act as an effective deterrent may involve a conflict with civil liberties, as is often remarked.

Finally, the figure shows the importance of paying attention to the goals of the group, as their indivisibility is central to the reason for the choice of terror as a mode of political competition. And one way to combat terror is to try to make the indivisible goals divisible.

4.5.3 The Argument in More Detail

Figure 4.4 shows the relationship between the instruments chosen (and therefore the level of risk) and the level of pressure exerted. At the origin on the horizontal axis, all of the factors of production are employed in moderate pressure, so the level of risk is zero. As we move along the horizontal axis, more and more of the factors are employed in the risky method, terror. The vertical axis shows the expected level of pressure that results. Each point depicts the maximum level of pressure that it is possible to produce corresponding to that level of risk. It seems reasonable to suppose that taking at least some risk increases the expected level of pressure, so the curve depicted is initially upward sloping. At some point, too much risk can be taken from the point of view of expending pressure and the slope of the curve turns negative. The maximum level of expected pressure is the point Q, but the actual level decided upon by the leader of the organization will depend also on his or her attitude toward risk.

The next question is the relationship between pressure and power. This depends on the structure of political institutions or the rules of the political game in the society where terrorist activity is undertaken. To take the most obvious case first, suppose that the country is a democracy and that the

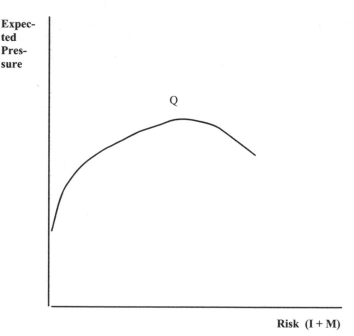

Figure 4.4. The choice among methods of pressure is essentially a decision about risk.

assumptions underlying the median voter model are satisfied. Then pressure succeeds only when the median voter is "persuaded," and it fails otherwise. Once it succeeds, further pressure does not produce any more power. In that case, pressure produces zero power until the median voter is persuaded; it produces "absolute" power at that point, and beyond that point further pressure produces no further increase in power. Of course, this depiction is extreme. One way to relax the assumptions but stick to the median voter model is to allow for some uncertainty as to the location of the median voter. Then the curve displaying the relationship between pressure and *expected* power will again display increasing returns until the expected position of the median is reached, and diminishing returns thereafter. Again there will be a critical point, depicted as A in Figure 4.5, and this will be at the location of the median voter if the estimate of this position is unbiased.

Other possible models of democracy do not necessarily display such stark levels of increasing returns – for example, if political parties maximize expected votes, as in probabilistic voting models.[14] Similarly, pressure group models do not display this property.[15]

---

[14] See Mueller (2003) for a survey.
[15] See Austen Smith (1997) for a survey.

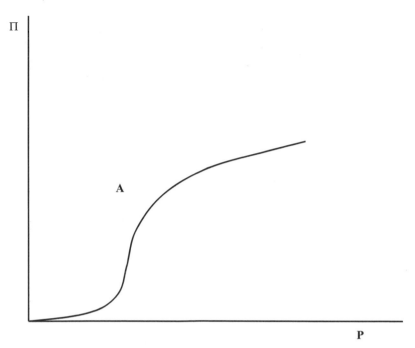

Figure 4.5. How pressure translates into power. The possibilities are: median voter, interest group equilibrium, or pressure versus dictatorship (e.g., tinpot or totalitarian). Under most possibilities there is again a critical point (A). But this is not the case with a pressure group equilibrium, or with models where parties maximize votes, as in probabilistic voting models.

Another possibility is that the regime is a dictatorship. Here, once again we would expect that the curve would display increasing returns. The point of "extremist" protest against a dictatorship is presumably to launch a revolution, and the point at which the state is weakened sufficiently for a revolution to take place is obviously a critical point. The increasing returns do not imply that any individual's action can get the bandwagon rolling, however. Short of having sufficient support to effect this revolution, most attempts at protest will simply bring problems for those who attack the regime. Indeed, in recent years, the literature on revolution is replete with such things as the possibility of bandwagon effects or the achievement of "critical mass" as depicted in Figure 4.5 (see Rasler 1996 or Opp and Ruehl 1990).

If Figure 4.5 does have the shape depicted, this only reinforces the degree of increasing returns to extremism and the basic argument made here. However, it is not necessary to our argument. Only if Figure 4.5 displayed diminishing returns throughout would the picture we are developing be possibly undermined.

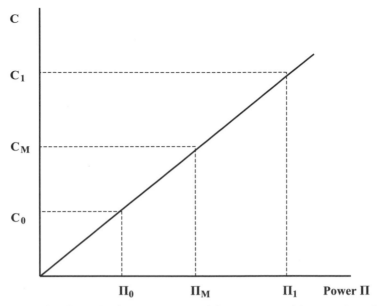

Figure 4.6. The relationship between power and the attainment of the immediate objective. Π_M = the level of power produced by "moderate" methods such as civil disobedience. $\Pi = \Pi_0$ or Π_1 = the level of power produced by extremist methods. The figure assumes a linear relation between power and the *immediate* objective C, either Control over land, Control over the means of production, or ridding the Country of non-Islamic authorities.

Figure 4.6 then displays the relationship between power and the immediate objective, represented by the variable C, as in Control of land for the Palestinians or Jews, Control over the means of production, or ridding the Country of non-Islamic authorities, domestic or foreign. There seems no compelling reason to believe that this relationship is nonlinear; hence it is depicted as a straight line.

One way to illustrate our basic point can be seen in Figure 4.7. Because we assume that the group leader can choose any combination of extremist methods and moderate methods, the level of risk that can be undertaken is completely variable. The horizontal axis displays this level of risk and the vertical axis the expected total returns to it, that is, the value to the group of the achievement of its final goals at different levels of risk.[16] The curve EZ in Figure 4.7 displays the risk – total return relationship for a group that is contemplating various methods of pressure from fixed resources. U is the

---

[16] Note that the vertical axis depicts the *total* proceeds or return from a given "portfolio" of moderate and terrorist actions, not the average expected return on the portfolio.

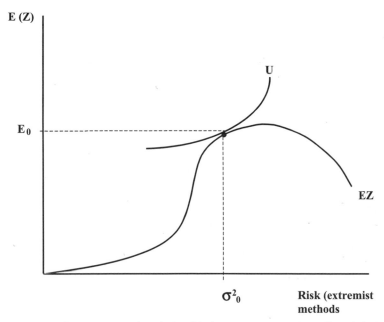

Figure 4.7. Another way to see the relationship between pressure (or risk) and the level of the ultimate objective achieved. The figure shows an equilibrium (E_0) where the indivisibility is present.

utility function of the group leader. Equilibrium is at the point E_0, σ_0^2, if the group decision maker is risk averse. The indivisibility implies that, from the point of view of the group's decision makers, very little is to be expected from moderate methods of pressure, and even switching some resources into extremist methods does not advance the goals of the organization very much. As pressure is ratcheted up, the gains from it increase at an increasing rate over a substantial range. Ultimately the rate of increase of these gains tapers off, and they continue to increase but at a decreasing rate. So only at high levels of pressure do the gains become sufficiently large that the objective can be said to be reached. Finally a point is reached when so much risk is taken that it actually becomes counterproductive, that is, after that point returns are negatively correlated with risk. But the essential point is that the larger the range of increasing returns or the greater the indivisibility, the more likely the group is to choose extremist or terrorist methods compared with moderate measures of pressure.

To see this point in a more dramatic way, look at Figure 4.8. Suppose that the leadership of the group becomes more extreme. This possibility is

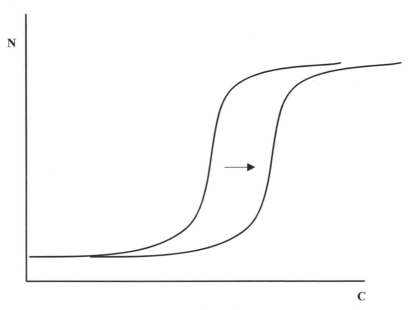

Figure 4.8a. A movement to the right implies a more extremist position.

displayed in Figure 4.8a. There, the leadership becomes more extreme in the sense that it believes that *more* of the group's intermediate objective is required before the group can achieve its goal. Thus, to illustrate with the Israel-Palestine question, a group may be said to become *more extreme* when it believes that only when it is in possession of *more* of the total land in Israel-Palestine can a Palestinian or Jewish state be achieved. Thus the curve and its inflection point move to the right in Figure 4.8a. If we assume for simplicity that the data underlying Figures 4.3–4.6 are unchanged, the result in risk-return space is as depicted in Figure 4.8b. The new equilibrium is at E_1 in Figure 4.8b. Note that the return to risk has fallen (for any level of risk, the return $E(Z)$ is lower). Nevertheless, the leadership will decide to take more risk, as shown by the point E_1 compared with the original equilibrium at E_0. A sufficient (though possibly not necessary) condition for this result is that the utility function is homothetic. In that case, our basic result follows: *the more extreme the goals of the group, the more it will tend to use extremist methods.*

Of course, mistakes are possible. Extremist methods might have been chosen by mistake. For example, the curve may be misestimated so that moderate methods of pressure such as civil disobedience would actually have been sufficient. In this case, the production function actually has its

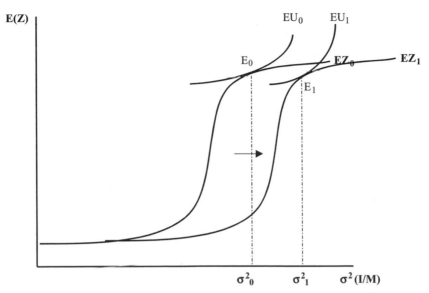

Figure 4.8b. A turn to a more extremist ideology (shown by the arrow) implies greater use of violence (extremist methods), shown by the shift from E_0 to E_1.

critical point at a fairly low level of Z. But equilibrium (because of the misestimation) is at a high level of risk or extremism.

The capacity for mistakes implies that terrorists sometimes end up on the downward sloping portion of the curve (this portion of the curve is displayed in Figure 4.7). They go too far. Perhaps the most outstanding recent example was the killing by the Red Brigades of Aldo Moro in Italy in the 1970s, which seemed to everyone, ex post, a mistake and after which support for the terrorists dried up and the era of terror ended (Drake 1995; Ginsborg 2003). However, recall that their basic objective was achieved in that the Communist Party never did join the government.

4.5.4 Mathematical Summary

The model depicted in Figures 4.4–4.8 can be summarized as follows:

$$Z = Z(C) \qquad (4.4)$$

where Z = some ultimate goal like a communist society, nationhood, or a new *ummah* (religious community), and C = the intermediate input – Control of land (N), Control of the means of production (C), or the Capacity to

remove foreigners and secular influences (IS). And $\partial Z / \partial C > 0$, $\partial Z^2 / \partial C^2 >$
0 until the "tipping point," after which $\partial Z^2 / \partial C^2 < 0$.

$$C = f(\pi) \tag{4.5}$$

where π = power, as described in Figure 4.6.

$$\pi = g(P, ST) \tag{4.6}$$

where P = pressure, from Figure 4.5, and ST = aspects of the STructure of
the political system.

$$E(P) = P(K, L, O, \sigma^2), \text{ from Figure 4.4} \tag{4.7}$$

where $E(P)$ = expected pressure, "O" = organizational capacity, and $\sigma^2 =$
the level of risk, $\sigma_P^2 = h(I/M)$, and K, L are the fixed quantities of capital
and labor.

Equations 4.4–4.7 can be solved by simple substitution to yield the equation for the constraint in E, σ^2 space:

$$E(Z) = g(K, L, O, \sigma^2 z) \tag{4.8}$$

$$\text{where } \sigma^2 z = h(I/M). \tag{4.9}$$

Finally, the group leader's preferences can be represented in the usual way
for mean-variance type models:

$$E(U) = k(Z, \sigma^2 z). \tag{4.10}$$

Equations 4.8–4.10 constitute the complete model of the extremist leader's
behavior. The group leader maximizes equation 4.10 subject to the constraints equations 4.8 and 4.9, as in Figure 4.8. Given the fixed stocks of
K, L, and O, he chooses to allocate these assets between the moderate and
extreme methods of pressure I and M. In mathematical terms the model is the
same as the choice between a riskless asset M and a risky asset I in portfolio
choice models. The main differences are that the extremist leader maximizes
the expected utility of the final goal Z rather than the utility of wealth, as is
usual in mean variance models of portfolio choice, and of course, the shape
of the constraint equation 4.9, which here displays the indivisibility.

4.5.5 Why Can't Terror Be Eliminated?

The central question from the policy point of view might appear to be as
follows: Look first at the simple version of the model in equations 4.1–4.3.
Is it not possible that if one could raise p and f sufficiently, terror could
be eliminated? Why cannot the state raise p and f sufficiently high so that

"terrorism doesn't pay" in the same way that Becker suggested might be done for ordinary crimes? Again, the most important reason why this deterrence approach might not work is the indivisibility. This implies that the gains to the group, if successful, are so large that it may be impossible to deter it by the kinds of penalties that would be considered by civilized societies. Moreover, if the group is very far from its goal, as in Figure 4.3, the losses to the group from the penalty do not leave it all that much further away, again a consequence of the indivisibility. So we return to our basic point. *What limits the possibility of eliminating terrorism by deterrence is the indivisibility.*

Other reasons can be elaborated if we recall that further work on crime, especially by Akerlof and Yellen (1994) and by Andreoni (1995), suggests that there are other limits to punishment besides the cost of the resources used in pursuing criminals and punishing them discussed by Becker (1968). The first is that too high punishments could lose the support of the community and that often this support is critical to catching offenders. Thus an increase in f can reduce p. The second reason is that that juries might be less willing to convict in the case of capital punishment, because they would be more afraid of making an error. So on both counts, the limit to f is that $p = p(f)$, $p' < 0$. Now, if we apply this reasoning to the case of terrorism, the first of these limits is even more pronounced, essentially because the implementation of punishments that are "excessively" high, thus causing the community to react against the government and on the side of the terrorists, is often exactly what the terrorists are hoping for.

The possibility that a critical mass or bandwagon effect takes place again differentiates the world of terror from the world of crime, namely that the key in terrorism is to increase support for the cause, whereas no such goal – and no such dependence on an external audience of potential supporters – exists in the world of crime. Support for the cause may increase if the state imposes penalties that are "too high." So this provides another reason why ordinary, non-risk-preferring leaders of pressure groups would choose terror over moderation.

To understand this point, let us modify the simple model in equation 4.3 to include bandwagon effects. Thus let $r =$ the probability of an outcry or bandwagon effect that gains $+ h$ to the group as the result of the overreaction of the state. Then the choice between methods becomes

$$qU(Z_0 + g) + (1 - q)prU(Z_0 - f + h) + (1 - q)p(1 - r)U(Z_0 - f)$$
$$+ (1 - q)(1 - p)U(Z_0) > U(Z_0 + m). \qquad (4.11)$$

Clearly, the payoff to terrorist methods is larger, the larger the level of r.

The other important social interaction that could be introduced is the probability of a violent response, not from the state, but from another political group, located at the other extreme. This might result in losses to the group $-l$. Alternatively it might produce gains $+l$ if the reaction of the other group helps it in its cause. For example, the extreme right and the extreme left in Italy in the 1970s often reacted violently to extremist acts by the other side. At the same time, they both had a common interest: the destruction of more centrist political parties.

To model this, introduce s = the probability of a violent response from the group at the other extreme; and that this results in losses to the group $-l$ (or gains $+l$). If we suppose it results in gains $(+l)$ to the group, for simplicity equation 4.11 is modified to give:

$$s[qU(Z_0 + g) + (1 - q)prU(Z_0 - f + h) + (1 - q)p(1 - r)U(Z_0 - f)$$
$$+ (1 - q)(1 - p)U(Z_0 + l)] + (1 - s)[qU(Z_0 + g)$$
$$+ (1 - q)prU(Z_0 - f + h) + (1 - q)p(1 - r)U(Z_0 - f)$$
$$+ (1 - q)(1 - p)U(Z_0)] > U(Z_0 + m). \tag{4.12}$$

Again, the effect is to make extremism more attractive if l is positive (as in equation 4.12). The reverse would be true if l were negative.

These difficulties with eliminating terror through policing and sanctions leads to the consideration of other methods, which fall into three main classes: to reduce the gains to the group by providing alternative sources of social cohesion; to emphasize human rights, in the hope of reducing the control of extremist groups over the individual; and to make the indivisibility divisible. The first two of these policy options are elaborated in Chapter 5. The third is discussed shortly. But first let us turn to the comparative statics of the model.

4.5.6 Comparative Statics

The simple version of the model in equations 4.1–4.3, combined with the informal reasoning of section 4.3 of this chapter leads to the following predictions. The level of extremist methods chosen will be higher $(+)$, or lower $(-)$, in the following cases:

1. The probability that extremist methods will succeed increases (implying a rise in q) $(+)$.
2. The state's capacity for repression increases (decreasing q) $(-)$.
3. Perhaps most interestingly, suppose that the utility of the status quo to the group decreases – that is, $U(Z_0)$ falls. Here it seems that the model

makes no prediction, contrary to the popular belief that this should positively affect extremism. So long as both moderate and extreme methods are available, a change in $U(Z_0)$ affects both sides of equation 4.3–4.5 symmetrically. Only if extremist methods were the only ones available would a fall in $U(Z)$ affect the calculus of discontent.

4. The probability that state repression will lead to an outcry increases (+).
5. The probability that the violence of the group provokes a violent response from those at the other extreme increases. This gives rise to two contradictory ripple effects: a multiplier effect that weakens the state (+); and the possibility that the other side will win increases, making the group worse off than under the status quo (−).
6. The probability that nonextremist methods or moderate methods will produce the goal that is desired increases (−) Thus the existence of barriers to entry into normal politics, promotes extremism (+).
7. The possibility of forming coalitions with those in the immediate center increases (−). For example, one could ask how quickly losses to the group increase as the group changes its position and moves toward the immediate center. The sharper the rate of increase of these losses, the more "rigid" the position of the group, and the more likely it is to use extreme methods. (−)
8. The larger a group is, the greater the likelihood that nonextremist methods will be successful in a democracy (−).
9. Social variables: for example, if it is not possible to communicate with others outside the group, this alienation might increase the likelihood of the use of extremist methods (+); or if norms exist that would be violated through the use of extremist methods, this would decrease it (−).

4.6 Making the Indivisible Divisible

In section 4.5.5 I suggested some limitations on sanctions as a solution to the problem of terrorism. Other policies that might be used to combat it include policies that break the hold of the group over the individual, a subject discussed in more detail in the next chapter. For example, state provision of public goods and of transfer payments such as welfare, unemployment insurance, or family allowances may enhance the workings of families, firms, and social organizations within the society and in this and other ways reduce the dependence of the individual on extremist groups. Another possibility is that the state can produce public goods. The more successfully it does so, the more favorably individuals may view the state, and the less they may be willing to join or take actions sponsored by organizations that are fundamentally hostile to the state and engaged in trying to weaken it.[17]

An emphasis on human rights might also reduce the power of the group over the individual. I treat this matter in considerably more detail in the next chapter on the supply of suicide martyrs.

The present chapter focuses on the demand for (rather than the supply of) suicide martyrs and for other forms of terrorist activity. The basic policy implication from this point of view would appear to be that to understand and to combat extremism, it is necessary to take the objective of the group seriously and to find ways to provide that objective to some extent and thus to satisfy the demands of moderates and potential participants of extremist movements without going all the way to satisfying the extremists' demands. The way to do this is to "unbundle" the theoretically indivisible objective and to show that it may be met without the radical overhaul of society demanded by extremist leaders. Here are a few examples.

The advent of Keynesian economics in the 1930s showed that the state could solve the problem of unemployment without giving up on capitalism. In this sense Keynes "saved" capitalism, as is often remarked. There is a certain sense in which communism is divisible, and its indivisibility is a feature of its ideology and not of the goals to which that ideology is supposed to point, such as greater freedom, security, more equality, or greater economic security. Thus, although no society has ever "given to each according to his needs and taken from each according to his ability," some societies do this more than others. And the instruments of the welfare state, such as welfare programs, unemployment insurance, transfers to the poor, training programs, and universal medicare, all have the effect of providing some of the objectives of communism without comprehensive state control over the means of production.

In the same way, problems of ethnic conflict have been solved in Canada and in many other states through institutions that give different minority ethnic groups a formal share in power. Thus features like federalism, the division of powers, checks and balances, and proportional representation all give ethnic groups some power without satisfying what they thought was an indivisible objective (their "own" state). In the same way, explicit power sharing has long been a familiar feature of so-called divided societies. Even

---

[17] A similar point is made by Berman (2003).

in post–Saddam Hussein Iraq, the basic idea implemented with respect to the Shiites, Sunnis, and Kurds is to give each group a share in power.

In many societies where there are problems of conflict between ethnic or other groups, the solution sometimes advocated is to provide a division of powers among different levels of government. Some advocate a form of *group rights* (Kymlicka 1995), though this idea remains extremely controversial. Canada is among the countries that has proceeded farthest along the lines of decentralization. Canada has gone very far in the direction of federalism, and there is an elaborate division of powers between the different levels of government. In the case of Quebec, a linguistic (federal) minority controls a powerful provincial government. It is possible to use Jewish law in Canada to solve disputes (when both parties agree), and there is currently a movement to allow the use of *sharia* law for the same purpose. Thus the specific demands of religious and ethnic groups may often be accommodated within an otherwise secular and democratic society. Of course, such an approach is not without its defects: one danger with this strategy is that, to the extent that it enables such groups to prosper, the (possibly coercive) hold of those groups on the individuals within it may increase. Presumably this is the logic behind the recent French legislation banning the display of prominent religious affiliations at public schools. This strategy is the opposite of the Canadian approach.

4.7 Conclusion

The basic point of this chapter is straightforward. Under certain circumstances, groups that take extremist positions on issues tend also to use extremist methods such as terrorism, violence, and assassination, to pursue those goals. To understand why, we started with the idea that the basic difference between extremist methods of political competition and moderate or accepted methods is that extremist methods are usually risky. In that sense the chapter takes the same starting point in understanding extremism as Becker took in understanding crime. Indeed, extremist methods such as terrorism are simply politically motivated crime. Like ordinary crimes, extremist methods can either succeed or fail, and if they fail, they invite possible criminal prosecution and punishment. Unlike ordinary criminal offenders, extremists usually have political goals, and failure also means retarding these goals as well. Apart from that, terrorism often represents the ultimate in crime, because particularly in its modern form it often results in the deaths of innocent civilians, and in any of its forms it represents a direct challenge to the state. Thus the state often reacts to it with the most severe punishments available to it.

Extremists in position adopt extremist methods when there is an indivisibility that characterizes the relationship between the intermediate goal of the group and its ultimate goal. In this chapter I look at three examples that represent the three most common kinds of extremism in the twentieth and twenty-first centuries: communism (control over the means of production is an intermediate goal to the achievement of a communist society), nationalism (control over territory is an intermediate goal to the achievement of nationhood), and Islamic fundamentalism (ridding the Muslim nations of foreign and secular influences is an intermediate goal to the achievement of an Islamic society based on *sharia* law). Metaphorically, in each case, the leaders of these groups are in the position of someone contemplating a long journey, starting at the beginning of a long desert at the end of which there is a mountain, and only when the top of the mountain has been reached can the group be said to achieve its goal. The longer the desert, and the taller the mountain, the greater the temptation to use extremist methods. Moreover, the larger the indivisibility, the more the group leaders will tend to be indifferent to sacrifices of human life by both victims and members, because the potential gains to the group from reaching its goals will be large compared with any conceivable losses. In turn, conflict between each of these and opposing groups (respectively, capitalism, other nations with the same territorial ambition, and secularism), is inevitable as it results from the conflict between their ultimate goals.

On the other hand, extremists with divisible objectives – less income inequality, a cleaner environment, fewer abortions, fewer controls on guns – do not typically use extremist methods. And those who do, I submit, are those who tend to perceive an indivisibility, as in the case of antiabortionists who see the fetus as a complete human being at an early stage of development, or those environmentalists who perceive a potential "catastrophe" and not a continuity in the level of destruction of the environment. Thus, once again, the use of extremist methods follows from a perceived indivisibility in the extremist's position and is not a separate feature of preferences.

If correct, the chapter would appear to raise a troubling challenge to liberal theory. Freedom of thought is central to liberal theory, provided that democratic methods are used to pursue that goal. If there tends to be a correlation between extremist positions and extremist (nondemocratic) methods, then it may be difficult for the state to combat the latter without imposing controls on the former. Such laws are in fact in force in some countries as exemplified by laws against "hate" speech. But how far can one go along these lines and still remain democratic?

The most important policy implication of the chapter is that one should look at the goals of extremist groups in order to understand its actions. The reason is that it is the purported indivisibility of the goal that explains the extremism of the actions, and if one can unbundle the goal or make the indivisible divisible, then there may be ways to provide these goals in a way that satisfies some of the members of the group and thus dries up support for the grander ambitions of their leaders. In turn, this policy implication shows the difficulties with the implication of the previous paragraph: the more one sanctions and prevents freedom of speech, the less likely is it that moderate forces will be able to understand the case for and against the goals of the extremists, and the more difficult it will be to satisfy the demands of moderates, driving them into the arms of extremists.

FIVE

Can Suicide Bombers Be Rational?

5.1 Introduction

The preceding chapter addressed the demand for extremist acts. But what about the supply? What leads people to demonstrate and to participate in acts of civil disobedience, terrorist acts, assassinations, and other forms of extremist activity? In this chapter we discuss supply with special focus on one example: suicide martyrdom. We focus on the supply of suicide martyrs because it is an extreme case, one that is particularly difficult to understand. But the analysis applies to any form of extremist participation, as the reader will see.

In suicide martyrdom, the perpetrators are willing not merely to risk their lives but to commit themselves to die for their cause. This apparent readiness to make the ultimate sacrifice is what makes the threat of suicide terrorism so large and so incomprehensible. Perhaps more than anything else, it marks off "them" from "us," as most of us cannot imagine ourselves committing such an act. In this chapter, I argue that it is possible to explain suicide martyrdom in rational choice terms and, although such acts are indeed extreme, they are nevertheless an example of a general class of behavior in which all of us engage.

One reason people join or participate at any level (e.g., participating in activities such as demonstrations or protests, bombings or assassination, as well as suicide martyrdom) in extremist groups is to obtain "solidarity" (or social cohesion or "belongingness"). As suggested in Chapter 2, solidarity is typically acquired through group-directed activity, especially in gangs, cults, unions, political parties or movements, and religious sects. In this chapter, I analyze the production of solidarity as a trade involving *beliefs* or values – the individual adopts the beliefs sanctioned by the group and receives the benefit of social cohesion in exchange. I construct a simple formal model to illustrate this process and then develop the conditions under which rational suicide for a cause is possible.

Members of extreme groups tend to exhibit an unusually high level of conformity. They tend to share beliefs that to outsiders may seem strange and even bizarre. I explain this with the "solidarity multiplier," perhaps the central result of the chapter. The idea here can be grasped if we consider what happens when, for some reason, an individual wants more group solidarity than before and intensifies his participation in group activities in order to get it. Because solidarity implies conformity to the beliefs of the group, when a person wants more solidarity she has to give up more of her own values in order to conform to the beliefs of the group. She is more and more giving up her identity for that of the group, perhaps as personified by its leader, and losing the capacity to make decisions based on values other than those of the leader. Then the normal tendency for the marginal value of solidarity to diminish as a result of choosing more of it will be reversed to some extent, as she incorporates more of the group's values into her own utility function. Consequently, she ends up choosing *more* solidarity than she would have on the basis of the "original" or "autonomous" utility function. This is the "solidarity multiplier." Under certain conditions, this self-reinforcing process of choosing more solidarity will approach a corner solution where solidarity is maximal and the individual's utility function is entirely that of the leader. Near to or at a corner, rational suicide for the group is possible.

The outline of the chapter is as follows. The next section outlines the process in which beliefs are traded for solidarity. Section 5.3 describes the solidarity multiplier. Section 5.4 indicates why a solution at or near the corner indicates a willingness to sacrifice oneself for the group and compares this explanation to other explanations of suicide martyrdom that have been offered. Section 5.5 looks at various alternative organizational "technologies" for producing solidarity and considers the structure of Al Qaeda in particular. Section 5.6 combines this model of followers' behavior with the model of the leader developed in the preceding chapter; then it shows how the two models are linked by examining a comparative static implication: the effects of a change in organizational technology on the leader's choice of extremism. From this, some important policy implications are developed. Section 5.7 concludes the chapter.

5.2 The Demand for Solidarity

Though the claim is not common in popular accounts, many social scientists who have studied the problem of terrorism have maintained that the actions of the participants are rational. Thus, Crenshaw (1990) lists the "costs and benefits" of terrorist activity. The costs to the organization include the likelihood of a punitive government reaction and the possible loss of popular support. The advantages include the benefits of agenda setting, demoralizing the administrative cadres of the government, disruption of the rule of law, and the inspiration to others to resist. Bruce Hoffman (1998, p. 7) prefaces his well-known book on terrorism with the observation that most terrorists appear to be normal and that, for many members of terrorist groups, "terrorism is (or was) . . . an entirely rational choice."

Suicide attacks are a small proportion of the total number of terrorist attacks. For example, in Pape's (2002) dataset, which covers the modern period since the contemporary practice was born during the Lebanese civil war in the 1980s through 2001, there are a total of only 315 incidents. On the other hand, the total number of international terrorist attacks over that period was 9,928 (U.S. State Department, *Patterns of Global Terrorism,* 2004). So suicide terror constitutes a small subset of the total number of terrorist incidents. But it represents the most difficult challenge to explain. Pape (2003, p. 4) develops a "strategic logic" of suicide terrorism in particular and shows that, "[v]iewed from the perspective of the terrorist organization, suicide attacks are designed to achieve specific political purposes: to coerce a target government to change policy, to mobilize additional recruits and financial support, or both." With reference to the universe of suicide attacks of 1980–2001, he shows that most suicide attacks occurred in organized, coherent campaigns, were aimed at democracies (which are more vulnerable to this kind of pressure), and were specifically directed at nationalist goals.

Other evidence is provided by Krueger and Maleckova (2003), who perform a statistical analysis of the determinants of participation in Hezbollah militant activities in Lebanon. They find that having a living standard above the poverty line or a secondary school or higher education is positively associated with participation in Hezbollah. They also look at data on Jewish settlers who attacked Palestinians in the West Bank in the early 1980s, indicating they were largely from high-paying occupations. These data agree with the general conclusion of sociologists studying protest activities, who find that such people, rather than marginal, isolated, poor, and uneducated, are typically better educated and better off economically than average (Sears et al. 2003; Knoke 1990).

Other work also takes a rational approach: Azzam (forthcoming) models the decision of suicide martyrs as a rational choice, based on the altruism of the martyr to supply public goods to the next generation. Suicide bombing is, in his framework, an extreme act of "saving" in which current consumption is lowered to zero. Note, however, that this kind of altruism is of a different nature than that used in the economics of the family. It is altruism toward the next generation, or, at best, "nephews and nieces," as Azzam puts it. This "generalized altruism" would seem to be of a different nature than that of a mother toward her children. On the other hand, to the extent that various organizations sometimes offer cash payments to the families of martyrs, a different kind of altruism on the part of suicide martyrs would be relevant, that toward their parents rather than the next generation.

Berman and Laitin (forthcoming) use a "club good" approach. Following Iannacconne (1992), they argue that religious groups are particularly good at designing signals of commitment that will distinguish the members who have the right degree of commitment from those who might pull out or defect. Religious sects (and possibly other groups, such as ethnic groups) are particularly capable of solving this problem because they possess mechanisms that tend to exclude free riders, such as sacrifice: for example, the requirement that years of study in a madras or yeshiva are necessary for entry and continuation in the community. Prohibitions (such as peculiar dress codes or dietary or Sabbath restrictions) that act as a "tax" on secular consumption also dispose members to increase their association with group members and contributions to the club good.

So the group's social cohesion is explained on the ground that less-committed individuals will be screened out. Berman (2003) extends this analysis to terrorism. His key point is that the level of commitment or loyalty that is characteristic of religious sects makes them particularly adept at activities like terrorism. The reason is that such activities are particularly dependent on loyalty: indeed, in the case of terrorism, defection or disloyalty by one person can destroy the project of the whole group. Consequently the religious group, with its high level of cohesion, is particularly suited to the performance of tasks associated with terrorism.

To explain suicide terrorism in particular, Berman and Laitin (forthcoming) extend this model by augmenting the utility function to include terms reflecting either altruism or "the utility of the hereafter" and to omit the terms representing the payoff for loyalty in the present world. Thus, in the case of suicide martyrs, the social cohesion of the group is not sufficient. One still needs to assume that the individual either believes in the hereafter and that his or her suicide martyrdom will be rewarded there, or is altruistic toward future generations and believes that his or her suicide bombing will enhance their lives.

One problem with this analysis is that the sacrifice and prohibitions that religions use to screen out the less committed implies that high-wage individuals tend to be screened out as less reliable, because their options outside the group are better. Yet the evidence from Krueger and Maleckova (2003) does not indicate that suicide martyrs are typically lower-wage individuals.[1] The authors amply recognize this point and argue that higher-wage individuals would have to make a "credible claim to loyalty," for example, that agents of the state murdered the claimant's brother. But, in that case, this implies that the martyr is not performing the action out of either altruism toward the next generation or a belief in the afterlife but out of solidarity with his brother, an entirely different class of explanation, which we expand on later.

The Berman-Laitin paper also suggests another possibility that has been much speculated on, namely that suicide martyrdom occurs because the individual believes that God will reward him for his actions with the promise of an afterlife. The majority of suicide attacks are not done for religious reasons, according to Ricolfi's (2005) dataset. However, this still leaves a large number where this motivation cannot be dismissed outright. This possibility is so important that I devote the next chapter to discussion of it.

This kind of work is extremely valuable in explaining the demand for suicide martyrs and explains why suicide campaigns are such effective weapons for certain kinds of organizations when pursuing political goals. However, there still remains the question of what motivates the suppliers of suicide. Unlike terrorist leaders, the goal of the organization cannot be the motivation for suicide martyrs themselves. From the point of view of the individual suicide martyr, the achievement of the goal of the organization represents a pure public good. Whatever the goal of the organization – a national homeland for Palestinians or Kurds, the removal of "foreign" domination by the Indians in Kashmir or the Russians in Chechnya, or the removal of U.S. troops from Saudi Arabia, the IDF from Lebanon, or the Tamils from Sri Lanka[2] – the individual's own contribution to this goal cannot be significant no matter how large his personal sacrifice. Therefore, he will tend to

---

[1] Nor are they always men, as is sometimes asserted. According to Bloom (2005), a third of the Sri Lanka bombers and a significant number of those in Chechnya and among the Kurds in Turkey have been female.

[2] These goals of terrorist organizations are listed in Pape (2003), p. 23. In his article and book (2005) Pape advances the thesis that suicide bombing is always a strategy of liberation from national occupation. Laquer (2005) takes issue with this, suggesting that in Algeria, Central Asia, and the Philippines this was not the case and that many of the bombings in Iraq are directed at fellow Muslims. Laquer suggests instead that suicide terror has simply become the preferred tactic in all kinds of civil wars.

"free-ride" rather than sacrifice himself, no matter how much he cares about the welfare of the next generation. Consequently, a rational choice explanation of individual participation must look elsewhere to understand the motives of individual suppliers of suicide martyrdom.

To be sure, there are individualized rewards – a place of glory, the possibility of monetary rewards to the bomber's family, and the possibility of volunteering for the act, but hoping never to be actually asked to do it, thus obtaining the benefits of martyrdom fame without enduring the costs (as described in Ferrero 2003). And there is the odd case where an individual's value of the pure public good is so large that he contributes to its supply. Somehow these do not appear to add up to a sufficient motivation to call forth a reliable supply.

In sum, one cannot explain the actions of suicide martyrs in terms of altruism or furthering the goals of the group. Yet there appears to be no shortage of would-be martyrs ready to sacrifice themselves for the goals of certain groups. Why? What motivates them?

One clue to supply is implicit in what has been already said, namely that nearly all of the research that has been done, including B. Hoffman (1998), Pape (2003), Crenshaw (1990), Post (1990), or Ricolfi (2005), indicates that suicide martyrs do not commonly act alone but are usually members of groups who "demand" their services. Ricolfi (2005) finds that suicide missions are hardly ever isolated actions by single individuals. "Behind a SM [Suicide Martyrdom operation] there is usually an organization or one of its local cells, which, as we shall see, finely dose and regulate SM" (Ricolfi 2005 p. 83).

Research into the internal workings of extremist groups has suggested two other things. First, these groups are characterized by a high level of social cohesion or solidarity. Thus, as Post (1990, p. 31) suggests, "For many, belonging to the terrorist group may be the first time they truly belonged." Second, members of such groups usually hold, in common, a set of extreme beliefs. Islam as used by Al Qaeda is not a purely religious doctrine but one that has been intensely distorted to serve the ends of the group (Black 2001; Gunaratna 2002; Ruthven 2000). Some other extremist groups have bizarre beliefs: for example, the Christian Identity movement in the United States apparently believe that the lost tribes of Israel are composed not of Jews but of "blue-eyed" Aryans' and that Jesus Christ himself was an Aryan (B. Hoffman 1998, p. 112).

The next section addresses these two features of extremist groups – their depth of solidarity and the extremity of their beliefs – and tries to explain them both.

5.3 Trade in Beliefs

In Marc Galanter's (1989) fascinating book on cults, which sums up fifteen years of his research on the psychology of charismatic groups, the power of group solidarity is described in the following manner by a heroin user who joined the Divine Light Mission: "Once I got to know them, I realized they loved me.... When I wanted to take heroin, or even to smoke [marijuana], I knew they were with me to help me stay away from it, even if I was alone. And their strength was there for me.... I could rely on their *invisible hand*, moved by Maharaj Ji's wisdom, to help me gain control" (1989, p. 27; emphasis added).

Another, fictional, account of intense solidarity is provided by Arthur Koestler. In his famous novel *Darkness at Noon* (1941), the hero ends by sacrificing the truth and ultimately his life for the good of the party.

The other remarkable feature about many situations where solidarity is particularly intense is the beliefs that people sometimes hold. How is it, for example, that a number of Americans, mostly members of paramilitary groups, would come to believe the view expounded in Mark Koernke's 1993 video, *America in Peril*, that "elements within the U.S. government are working with foreign leaders to turn the United States into a dictatorship under the leadership of the United Nations" (Karl 1995, p. 69)?[3]

To summarize, in many extremist groups, two remarkable features are the extremity of the beliefs and the depth of solidarity. I contend that neither of these two phenomena is necessarily irrational, and indeed that the key to understanding both of them is that they are related to each other. More precisely, they are the outcome of a process whereby beliefs are traded in exchange for solidarity or social cohesion. Thus, Galanter notes that many subjects experienced a decline in symptoms of psychological distress upon joining the group, and that, in his statistical analysis of the reasons for this, 37 percent of this overall decline could be attributed to an increase in social cohesion (1989, p. 32). While Galanter, a psychologist, does not model this process, the basic elements involved seem straightforward. The person who gives up his or her beliefs loses something, which could be called one's true "identity" or "independence of thought" or "autonomy." On the other hand, he or she gains the experience of greater solidarity or social cohesion or "belongingness."

In this chapter I assume, then, that the production of solidarity involves conformity or the acceptance of beliefs of the organization. To sketch a model

---

[3] This example was suggested in the introduction to a recent book on extremism (Breton, Galeotti, Salmon, and Wintrobe 2002).

of how this process operates, assume that an individual is endowed with a certain set of beliefs and, corresponding to this, a certain identity. If a person agrees to join a group, the price of admission is, in part, adoption of certain beliefs that are sanctioned by the group. Additional requirements might be to participate in group activities or in some other way to demonstrate that he shares in the beliefs and goals of the group.

The organization, in turn, supplies the individual with the sense of belonging to a community, by organizing events or activities that individuals can attend and participate in, sometimes by providing a place where members can meet and get to know others in the organization, and most especially by providing a framework of beliefs that the individual can adopt and identify with. The set of beliefs is common to all members to a greater or lesser degree. From the organization's point of view, the more united the membership is in its beliefs, the greater the willingness of the members to sacrifice their time and energy and other resources in support of the goals of the organization, and the greater the organization's capacity for action or power.[4] The organization often exercises some control over the information available to the members of the group: hence Hardin (2002) refers to the "crippled epistemology" of extremist organizations, and Geertz their "totalitarian" thought structure (2003): however, note that this aspect of extremist organizations, to the extent that it makes their members more united, increases the organization's power.

Why do people join extremist organizations or participate in extremist acts? The most obvious reason that might be suggested is that they believe in the goals of the organization, and they participate in its activities in order to bring them about. However, once again, it must be emphasized that there is a "free-rider" problem with participation in political activity: because one's own contribution toward the achievement of the goals of the organization is likely to be small, why not "free-ride" and hope that others will make the necessary effort? In the case of extremist organizations, which, as, we saw in the preceding chapter, usually have goals that are grand and distant, this problem is particularly acute.

However, the free-rider problem does not apply to the receipt of solidarity: that is a private good. Moreover, if solidarity is desired, this can also explain why a person joins organizations with beliefs and goals that are similar to his, and why people who have the same beliefs as extremist organizations tend to join or participate more than those who do not. The basic reason

---

[4] See Wintrobe (1998a), chap. 11, who provides a formal model of the proposition that a government's capacity for action is related to the similarity of beliefs of the groups within it. Here we are simply extending this idea to any organization.

for participation is the desire for solidarity with others who share the same beliefs. The more the beliefs of the individual are in agreement with those of the organization to begin with, the smaller the sacrifice required in terms of the individual's own autonomy necessary to receive a given level of solidarity. Consequently *an individual joins an organization whose beliefs are close to his not because he thinks that his own efforts will make any palpable difference to the achievement of the goals of the organization, but because that way he obtains the desired solidarity at the lowest "price."*

There are three further aspects of the process that seem important: participation, enforceability, and leadership.

Presumably, in order to be accepted for membership, a certain minimum sacrifice of beliefs and a certain minimum level of participation will be required.

How are the trades enforced? One cannot make a binding contract stating that person A will receive x amount of social cohesion in exchange for his agreement to subscribe to beliefs y and z. The reason is not only the issue of enforceability, that is, determining whether the social cohesion supplied was deficient, or whether A really changed his mind in the ways agreed to. The very making of the contract would imply that neither party was sincere, and deprive A of his social cohesion and the group of knowing that A subscribed to the requisite beliefs. However, this does not imply that the trade cannot take place, only that the mechanism of enforcement is more subtle: some proof is required on both sides of sincerity.

The organization's history provides some indication as to whether it typically lives up to its side of the bargain. For the entrant, some demonstration that the person has given up some of his autonomy and accepted the beliefs of the organization may be required. Churches have rituals of "conversion" and complex and sometimes arduous demonstrations of faith. Admission to a youth gang (see Jankowski 1991) may require "jumping in" – for a male, that he participate in the commission of a crime; for a female, that she sleep with one or more members of the gang. Admittance to the Mafia is governed by complex rituals that have a similar purpose (Gambetta 1993; Hess 1973). Gunaratna (2002, pp. 98ff.) describes recruitment and qualifications for entry into Al Qaeda. The Italian terrorist Giorgio, writing anonymously (1981, 2003), describes some of the complex and mysterious procedures for entry and advancement into the Red Brigade terrorist group, active in Italy during the 1970s.

Finally there is the vital element of leadership. Who is it that determines the beliefs of the group? Who is that decides when these beliefs have to be changed? How is the minimum level of participation decided? Who decides whether cohesion is given out or withheld? The point is vital, because it suggests that in many solidary groups there is a strong element of hierarchy, just as we saw earlier in Chapter 2 for the family, the army, and the classical extremist movements of communism and fascism.

In so-called charismatic groups, such as the Branch Davidians, the Scientologists, Divine Light Mission, and the Aum Shinrikyu, the psychiatrist Mark Galanter found that social cohesiveness was tied to a charismatic leader whose flock "revered" him (1989, p. 12). In the Branch Davidian cult, for example, compliance with the leader's expectations (David Koresh) was promoted by a series of reinforcements. According to Galanter, these produced a relief in depression and anxiety to the degree that a believer accepted the group's creed and its rules of behavior. By virtue of this relief effect, a member's mood became dependent on the degree of his or her commitment in the group. Indeed, Galanter shows that cults often act like emotional pincers, promoting distress while providing relief. The consequence was that, as Galanter notes, "This emotional dependence on the group and its beliefs left the sect members fully responsive to Koresh's demands, which escalated to include beating young boys and engaging young girls in sexual activity" (Galanter 1989, p. 170).

The main implication of this way of thinking is that a person who holds a belief that appears on the surface to be irrational may not be: *the rationality may consist not in the content of the belief but in the reason for holding it.* On this reading, the person who believes there is a UN plot to take over the U.S. government is no more irrational (in principle, if not in degree) than the professor who states to the officials in the administration of his university that his department, more than any other in the faculty, deserves more resources: in both cases, the reason for the belief may be solidarity or social cohesion, not the coherence of the belief itself.

It is simple to formalize the basic proposition of the model, that is, that social cohesion (solidarity) and conformity (unity of belief) are positively related. To do so, assume that individuals have utility functions in which both autonomy and solidarity are positive arguments:

$$U = U(A, S) \tag{5.1}$$

where the functions have the usual properties

$$U_a > 0, U_s > 0, U_{aa} < 0, U_{ss} < 0, \text{ and } U_{as} > 0.$$

Individuals are willing to trade autonomy for solidarity, and the way they do this is by adopting the beliefs demanded by one or more suppliers of solidarity. These suppliers may include religious organizations (organized religions and cults), gangs, political parties and movements, unions and

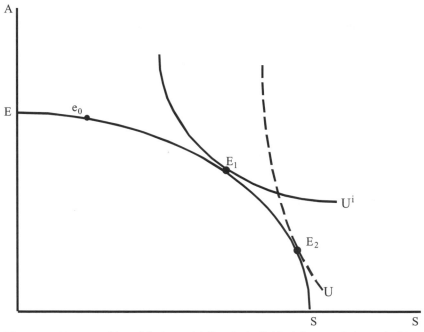

Figure 5.1. Because of the solidarity multiplier, the individual chooses E_2 instead of E_1.

business firms, and other organizations. The "industrial organization" of solidarity is complex because solidarity tends to be produced in the process of working toward some goal or participating in some activity and thus is usually supplied together with that activity.

An initial depiction of the trade-off between solidarity and autonomy for an individual is provided in Figure 5.1. The indifference curves correspond to equation 5.1, $U = U(A, S)$.[5] The individual maximizes utility subject to a constraint in the form of a production function

$$f(A, S) = 0 \qquad (5.2)$$

---

[5] In an early formulation of a related problem, Margolis (1982) develops a form of a utility function in which both the group interest and the individual's self-interest enter as arguments. However, in his model the individual's group interest is altruistic. Thus he tries to reconcile this with evolutionary selection and develops some interesting arguments along these lines. Work on group selection has continued in economics (for a survey, see Bergstrom 2002). In the model here, the issue of the survival of "group preferences" does not arise, because I assume people are selfish (they like being part of a group but that desire is purely selfish and gives rise to the private benefit of a feeling of solidarity). I do not rule out altruistic behavior, but I prefer to see how far we can get on the simple assumption that people desire solidarity.

depicted as the production possibility curve between solidarity and autonomy ES in Figure 5.1. The production possibility curve is depicted as having the usual shape, implying diminishing returns to the conversion of autonomy into solidarity and vice versa.[6]

A typical individual will have an endowment point like e_0 and will trade autonomy for solidarity by giving up his own beliefs in the manner discussed, ending up at an equilibrium like E_1. The rate at which he can trade off autonomy for solidarity depends on the technology available for doing this, as summarized in the production function. Thus, churches have a "technology" for conversion involving rituals, dogmas, and ceremonies by which individuals are assisted in becoming believers. Other organizations may have twelve-step programs, identification rituals such as "jumping in" to a gang, and so on.

One possible objection to the preceding analysis might be that, so far, there has been no discussion of empathy and its relationship to solidarity. Empathetic beliefs and sympathies for the plight of the poor are highlights of Catholic doctrine, which constitutes one of the loci classici of the concept of solidarity; equally, these beliefs are central to socialist doctrine, perhaps its other major source.

One way to incorporate this idea might be to modify the utility function to explicitly include empathy as distinct from solidarity. Thus one could write individual i's utility function as $U^i = U_i(A, S, C_j)$, where C_j indicates the consumption level of any of the j others in the group. Then empathetic feelings could be represented by $\partial U / \partial C_j > 0$, indicating that individual i feels better when the j others in the group have more to consume. It seems reasonable to assume that an increase in empathy would raise the utility of solidarity in the utility function, that is, that $U_s / U_{Cj} > 0$. Moreover, one might assume that the more empathy an individual feels, the smaller the trade-off between autonomy and solidarity, that is, the flatter the slope dA/dS of the ES production possibility frontier in Figure 5.1. That is, the more-genuine caring an individual feels for the others in the group, the greater the possibility of a disagreement with them while maintaining solidarity with them. However, some trade-off will still remain.

---

[6] The technology for converting A into S, where the level of S = solidarity, general social capital, or other types of social capital within the group is one way of specifying one aspect of organizational technology O mentioned in the previous chapter. Thus the analysis in this chapter can be combined with the leader's choice of methods of pressure discussed in Chapter 4. Later, in this chapter, we show one way of using this combined model to generate implications about changes in organizational technology for the development of extremism.

One example of solidarity in this sense might be the ideal of Christian teaching as practiced by Jesus. He preached concern for others, especially the less fortunate (see, e.g., Bokenkotter 1977). However, as soon as a doctrine such as Christianity is institutionalized into a bureaucratic organization, the possibility arises of deviance, and practices are instituted to repress dissent. Otherwise the original doctrine may be lost. Because of these repressive practices, over time conformity increasingly replaces autonomous thinking, and so over time the church increasingly fails to adapt. It might even be suggested that "false" solidarity (conformity) tends increasingly to replace "true" solidarity (genuine caring).[7] Hence the historical evolution of organizations like the Catholic Church, with its characteristic internal tension between the ideals of the church and its institutional practice, leading to periodic eruptions and protests by dissidents, constant reinterpretations of what the founders meant, and revolts on the part of those who think that the church has lost its way and who wish to go back to its true doctrine.[8]

One implication is that social cohesion will tend to be positively related to the extremity of beliefs. The reason is that if the views of the group are really extreme, people who wish to join will typically have to give up much of their original (more mainstream) identity to adopt them. Hence they will demand more social cohesion in return for adopting them.

The process also explains how religiously based organizations that deal with social problems like juvenile delinquency (e.g., Teen Challenge, Straight Ahead Ministries, and Nation of Islam) can sometimes be successful where government agencies fail: these organizations supply troubled people with social cohesion in addition to direct training or rehabilitation.

---

[7] The distinction between true and false solidarity may not be so simple. Thus, consider another case, where individuals give to the group, not because they care about it or the individuals within it, but because they expect to get something in return for their gifts (e.g., in the case of the church, some might make gifts hoping for the afterlife in return). The utility function remains as before ($U = U(A, S)$), but the individual can also obtain solidarity through making gifts. This suggests that solidarity can be produced through conformity to the beliefs of the group (giving up autonomy), or through gifts (giving up one's own consumption C_i), as in the production function $S = S(A, C_i)$. Which is the true solidarity? How do you distinguish those who give because they care for the group from those who give because they hope for something in exchange? Indeed, more typically an individual will be at an interior solution, making a combination of gifts and "giving up" beliefs in the production of solidarity. This might appear to show that the relatively rich would give more cash, and the poor "give up" beliefs more, implying that in a sense only the poor would really "believe" in the church's ideals. However, the poor tend to make a surprisingly high percentage of their income in gifts, mostly to the church (see Becker 1974).

[8] See, for example, Bokenkotter (1977) or Duffy (1997).

However, this analysis leaves out something important: once an individual i has made the choice of giving up some of his autonomy A in exchange for solidarity S, he has given up some of his autonomy and therefore his capacity to choose. For small changes this might not matter, but for large ones it obviously does – to some extent he has given up the control of the choices he might make to the leader of the group L. We will see in the next section that this gives rise to a very different picture.

5.4 The Solidarity Multiplier

In the preceding section we showed that an individual obtains solidarity in part by trading away his beliefs for those of the group, as personified by its leader L. If so, we can substitute the leader's utility function for i's utility function to the extent that i chooses solidarity S over autonomy A. Perhaps the simplest assumption to make about the utility function of the leader is that she cares only about the aggregate level of solidarity of the members:[9]

$$U^L = U^L(S) \text{ where } S = \sum s^i. \tag{5.3}$$

Presumably the only dimension of the leader L's utility function that is relevant to member i's decision making is the level of i's solidarity s^i. So far as each member i is concerned, he can contribute to group solidarity only by choosing more S. It follows that we can substitute the relevant portion of the leader's utility function

$$U^L = U^L(s^i) \tag{5.4}$$

---

[9] In general it seems reasonable to assume simply that the group has some objective Z and that the group leader receives utility from the extent to which the goal is realized, as in the preceding chapter. The preferences of the leader and the subordinate are integrated into a single model in section 5.7. Here, we note that as far as the leader's preferences about subordinate behavior is concerned, they can be depicted as follows:

$$U^L = U^L(Z)$$
$$Z = Z\left(\sum a_i, \sum s_i, K, L\right) = Z(A, S, K, L).$$

In this formulation, A and S of the members are productive "inputs" to the goal of the organization along with capital (K) and labor (L). A and S are a way of specifying organizational technology O. If we assume K and L are fixed for simplicity then the only dimension of choice is the proportions of A or S to use in the production of Z. Thus S might be expected to raise productivity relatively more where the coordination of activities is important. On the other hand, A might be most important when the output of the team implies creative thinking. Thus it seems reasonable to suppose that for a university $\partial Z/\partial A$ would be relatively high and $\partial Z/\partial S$ low, and vice versa for a mass organization. For cults, we assumed simply that $Z = Z(S)$.

for that of the member U^i (a^i, s^i) to the extent that i chooses S. This gives a new utility function U for i where his choices are now only partly his own (to the extent that he chooses autonomy A). The other part of his choices is governed by the leader. Thus:

$$U = (s/a + s)U^L(s) + (a/a + s)U^i(a, s) \qquad (5.5)$$

where the superscript i on s and a has been dropped for simplicity, and s/a+s is the fraction of his choices (utility function) that are solidary, and therefore identical to the leader's choices. Similarly, a/a+s represents the weight on the "autonomous" portion of his utility function U^i. Both autonomy and solidarity can be thought of as capital, so the denominator in equation 5.5 can be taken to represent the sum of the individual's "autonomy capital" and "social capital."[10] Note that in this formulation some individuals have more of both than others, which seems reasonable.

This utility function may be assumed to have the usual properties: diminishing marginal rates of substitution and so forth. However, the leader is interested in the level of solidarity of the *group* and in that of individual members only to the extent that it contributes to group solidarity. Consequently, an increase in the level of solidarity of only one member will not have much effect on the aggregate, and therefore $\partial U^L/\partial s^i$ does not decline as rapidly with an increase in s^i as $\partial U^i/\partial s^i$. Indeed, if the group is not too small, it is not unreasonable to assume that the leader's indifference curves in this space are vertical lines, as shown in Figure 5.2.[11]

Moreover, as i chooses more solidarity, that is, a^i falls and s^i rises, the increase in s^i increases the weight of the leader's utility function in i's utility function. Consequently the decline in the marginal rate of substitution of s for a is less, and the slope of the indifference curve does not fall as much as it would if i were totally "in control" of his own decision making.

To see the effects on i's decision making, assume that i maximizes utility as described in equation 5.5 subject to the production function of the organization in equation 5.2. The first-order conditions are:

$$\partial U_s/\partial U_a = f_s/f_a, \qquad (5.6)$$

---

[10] A related formulation can be found in Becker (1996) who refers to an individual's "personal capital" and "social capital."

[11] It could also be assumed that the leader dislikes individual values that may conflict with those he wishes the group to follow, that is, $\partial U^L/\partial a^i < 0$. In that case the leader's indifference curves in a^i, s^i space are positively sloping upward lines, reflecting the idea that for him s^i is a "good" and a^i a "bad." In this case, as s^i continues to increase and the weight of the leader's utility function becomes sufficiently large, i's preference for S over A does not decline but actually increases as S increases, leading to an increase rather than a decrease in the slope $dA/dS = -MU^s/MU^a$. Ultimately, i's indifference curves would become positively sloped as they get close to the S-axis.

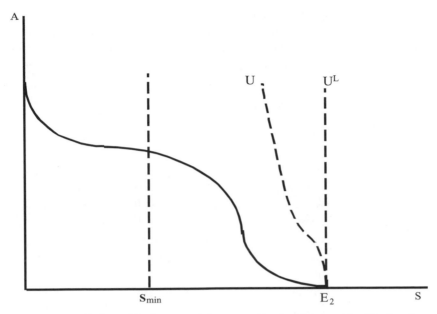

Figure 5.2. At (and possibly also near to) the corner E_2, the follower with utility function U will be willing to sacrifice himself or herself for the group. U^L is the leader's utility function, which depends only on the follower's level of solidarity.

that is, that

$$\frac{aU_s^i + s(U^Ls) + (a/(a+s))(U^L - U^i)}{aU_a^i + (s/(a+s))(U^i - U^L)} = \frac{f_s}{f_a}. \tag{5.6'}$$

The first term on the top of the left-hand side is the marginal utility of solidarity to i, weighted by the autonomous portion of his utility function. The first term on the bottom of the left-hand side is the marginal utility of autonomy to i, similarly weighted.

Equation 5.6′ shows how group preferences enter the individual's utility function. Thus, the second term on the top of equation 5.6′ is the marginal utility of i's solidarity to the leader, weighted by the portion of i's utility function that is identical to the leader's. The third term on the top shows the marginal gain and loss from the fact that as s rises, U^L replaces U^i in i's composite utility function U. Similarly, the second term on the bottom of the left-hand side represents the increased weight of the utility function of the leader (U^L) in i's composite utility function U as a falls. The larger is s, the greater the importance of these terms that represent the values of the group in the individual's preferences.

The term on the right-hand side is the slope of the production possibility curve, which shows the technology available to the individual for incorporating increased group preferences into the utility function. The greater the group's capacity to enable the individual to do this, the larger is the right-hand side f_s / f_a. At an interior solution, of course, the left- and right-hand sides of equation 5.6′ will be equal.

An indifference curve corresponding to the utility function described in equation 5.5 or 5.6, and equation 5.6′ is shown as the dotted line in Figure 5.1. As can be seen there, the normal tendency for an indifference curve to "flatten out" as S increases due to a diminishing rate of substitution of S for A is compensated for by its tendency to "steepen" as i increasingly adopts his leader's values. Consequently the indifference curves will be steeper than they would be if i could somehow choose more solidarity without substituting his leader's values for his own as he does so. The result is that i chooses a higher level of solidarity (E_2 rather than E_1 in Figure 5.1). The difference between E_2 and E_1 is the result of this solidarity "multiplier."

The intuition behind this result is straightforward: as the individual chooses more solidarity, in order to get it he adopts beliefs and values that are more akin to those of the leader. But, with these new values and beliefs, he finds that he prefers *more* solidarity than he did originally. In order to acquire still more solidarity, again his beliefs and values must change in order to conform to those of the other members of the organization. In turn, with this new utility function, he wants more solidarity than previously, leading him to change his values again, which again results in yet a further demand for solidarity, and so on. An interior equilibrium will result if these effects occur at a sufficiently diminishing rate, as shown in Figure 5.1.

One need not join an extremist group to observe the solidarity multiplier in action. I first noticed it (but did not understand it) years ago in the behavior of academic friends (not all economists) when they assumed important administrative positions such as department chair or dean of the faculty. Within a short time their values seemed to undergo a transformation: previously highly individualistic in many cases, their conversation was now laced with phrases like "the good of the department," the importance of promoting "institutional values," and so on. Their behavior seemed to change as well, as they now began to promote collaborative research projects and "loyalty" to the department.

One can also see the solidarity multiplier at work in the behavior of economists, who, with their powerful and mysterious paradigm of rational behavior, often misunderstood by outsiders, are often thought of as a cultlike group. The workings of the solidarity multiplier can sometimes be observed in graduate students, when they first grasp the essence of the economic way of thinking and begin to apply it to all sorts of situations, including those where it is inappropriate. Everyone has their favorite stories here but perhaps one example will suffice: that of an economist in a club or restaurant where it is possible to smoke, and who does so, and when another person complains, asks how much that person would be willing to pay to have him put his cigarette out, explaining that if it is less than the value to him of smoking the cigarette, it is "efficient" for him to do so.

Of greater importance is the possibility of temporary, rapid increases in solidarity, such as those noted by Ricolfi (2005) in his empirical work on Palestinian suicide martyrs. Ricolfi found that the desire for suicide martyrdom was often motivated by revenge or the desire to avenge tragic events such as the death of a relative at the hands of Israeli forces. "Revenge" is the classic motive in many studies of solidarity (e.g., Gold 2000). At the mass level, in Palestine, as in other resistance movements, the funeral of some important or tragic figure often becomes the occasion for stimulating revenge. The solidarity may be temporary, but that is enough to provide a mechanism for stimulating action.

The analysis in Figure 5.1 is incomplete. It is easy to imagine that the self-reinforcing process just analyzed leads to a corner rather than an interior equilibrium. The properties of the corner equilibrium are examined in the next section.

5.5 The Attraction of the Corner

At very high levels of S, i's utility function more and more becomes the same as the leader's, and his values his leader's values. A "corner" solution will be reached if the slope of the indifference curve is everywhere steeper than that of the production possibility curve:

$$\partial U_s / \partial U_a > f_s / f_a, \tag{5.7}$$

that is, that

$$\frac{s(U^L s) + aU^i_s + (a/(a+s))(U^L - U^i)}{aU^i_a + (s/(a+s))(U^i - U^L)} > \frac{f_s}{f_a}. \tag{5.7'}$$

Of course, at the corner $a = 0$, and so $s/a + s$ approaches 1, that is, i's utility function becomes identical with that of his leader. The easiest way to see this is to look back at equation 5.5. Substituting a = 0 there gives

$$U = U^L(s). \tag{5.8}$$

This corner solution is depicted in Figure 5.2.[12]

If the condition in equation 5.7, 5.7′, or 5.8 holds, individual i rationally chooses an equilibrium with all S, zero A. As equation 5.8 shows, his utility function at the point a = 0 is simply the utility function of the leader $U^L(s_i)$. The individual has no independent thought but is completely under the leader's control.[13] His values are completely those of his leader, and he will do whatever maximizes his leader's utility. If the leader wishes him to commit suicide for the goals of the group, he will do so. Note that he might do so even if he is not at a corner, but close to it, where the views of his leader or the values of the group contain great weight in his utility function. What is peculiar about the corner is not that only there is rational suicide possible, but that at a corner the individual will be particularly resistant to change. In particular he will be resistant to pressure from outside sources, such as threats or increases in the likelihood of prosecution or the size of the punishment for being a member of such a group.[14] And he will also be resistant to outside information that is critical of the group, unless that information comes from the leader. But although small changes will not cause any change in his behavior, very large changes will cause a substantial movement, as is usual for corner solutions.[15] This provides a key to policy.

---

[12] For the moment, ignore the new shape of the production function (it is discussed next) and note that a corner solution would still obtain in Figure 5.2 even with the same production function as in Figure 5.1.

[13] Note that the *leader* does *not* have an equilibrium at the corner E_0. Indifference curves like U^L do describe his preferences, but the constraint in Figures 5.1 and 5.2 describes the choices available to a subordinate or member and is *not* the constraint facing the leader. Hence the equilibrium autonomy and solidarity in Figures 5.1 and 5.2 is that of a member, not the leader. The leader's equilibrium cannot be described with this apparatus. The goals of the leaders of extremist organizations are discussed in note 9 and, of course, in the previous chapter. B. Hoffman (1998) and Pape (2003) in particular are also relevant to understanding the strategic choices of leaders of terrorist organizations.

[14] Sandler and Lapan (1988) and Enders and Sandler (2002) also consider the case of "fanatical" terrorists, defined as those who do not fear death, and suggest that deterrence is ineffective for such individuals. However, note that the point here is somewhat different: "fanatical" terrorists here are those who appear fanatically *loyal* or *obedient* to the organization's wishes. It is worth noting that sufficiently large penalties *can* be effective, as noted earlier. Finally, in this model solidarity, even when extreme, is always contingent. To illustrate this point, it is useful to recall that it is often suggested that no group ever demonstrated more loyalty to its leader than the SS to Hitler. Yet, toward the end of the war, when it was obvious that the Nazi regime was collapsing, these people deserted the regime in large numbers (see the analysis in Wintrobe 1998a, chap. 13).

[15] External changes that raise the "price" of solidarity would make the production possibility curve steeper in Figures 5.1–5.3 (not shown).

Onc way to see this point is to note that although a = 0 at the corner, the slope of i's indifference curve at the corner is not infinity, that is, it is not a vertical line like the indifference curve of the leader depicted in Figure 5.2. Substituting a = 0 into equation 5.7' gives the condition at the corner:

$$\frac{s(U^L s)}{(U^i - U^L)} > \frac{f_s}{f_a}. \tag{5.9}$$

The top shows the marginal utility of s to i, which is the same as that to his leader, because, at a = 0, i's utility function is the same as his leader's. The bottom shows that as i "tastes" a small amount of autonomy, the gain is his original utility function U^i minus the loss of the leader's utility function U^L. So even at the corner, where he has no autonomy, he is capable of getting his autonomy back.[16]

Further, it is vital to note that, while an individual who is at the corner may be extreme, *he is not irrational.* He possesses a well-behaved ordinal utility function and is perfectly capable of making choices that maximize his utility in the usual sense. Indeed, his behavior is merely an extreme version of a form of behavior that is extremely common, namely that, in part, he "internalizes" his values from the values of others, especially from those in a position of power over him. To obtain solidarity with the group of which he is a member, he adopts the group's values and beliefs. This is precisely what members of religious groups do when they agree to or "internalize" the values and beliefs of their religion, or what members of ethnic groups do when they subscribe to the belief that they "belong" together in some sense because they have as ancestors people who held similar beliefs, or what economists do when they write papers based on a certain set of assumptions that they share about human nature (e.g., that people are always rational!). The only difference in the behavior of the individual who is in equilibrium at a corner is the *extent* to which he behaves in this fashion. The behavior itself is perfectly "normal" and rational. And all of us are familiar with the internal struggle between doing what is right for the group and doing what is best for one's "self" felt by individuals who are not at a corner but near to it.

---

[16] A similar point holds at the opposite corner, where s = 0. The condition for that case is

$$\frac{a U_s^i + U^L - U^i}{a U_a^i} < \frac{f_s}{f_a}.$$

Even though s = 0, the partial derivative $U_s^i \neq 0$. The numerator shows what would happen if i moved away from the corner. He would gain U_s^i as usual, but in addition his utility function would change: to some extent, he would give up his "own" utility function and substitute that of the leader, as shown by the term $U^L - U^i$. Conformity is the price of solidarity.

Still, the analysis represents a considerable departure from standard economic theory. Can a more conventional approach explain as much? After all, economic theory does not usually invoke group preferences in this way. It is more common to modify the individual utility function to include altruism, as is commonly done in the economics of the family (e.g., Becker 1974). Both Azzam (forthcoming) and Berman and Laitin (forthcoming) take this route in explaining suicide martyrdom. But the main problem is the free-rider problem. Any "contribution" made to the welfare of the next generation by a suicide attack by, say, helping to rid the country of foreign occupation, is almost bound to be small, no matter how dramatic and effective and destructive that attack is. Thus the rational approach is to "free-ride," because the welfare of the next generation is a pure public good to an individual contemplating suicide martyrdom. Consequently, altruism does not solve the problem of reconciling suicide martyrdom with rationality.

In my analysis there is no free-rider problem because the individual has "internalized" the goals of the organization. Solidarity is not altruism, however. The individuals in this framework are entirely selfish. But they are responsive to social interactions and group pressures. Consequently, I believe that the most promising approach is one that incorporates group pressures into the individual's decision. This conjecture is bolstered by what by now is a fair bit of evidence that group pressures are important in suicide martyrdom (see especially Ricolfi 2005 or Gunaratna 2002). Suicide martyrdom operations are typically ordered, in campaigns that are started and stopped (Pape 2003; Ricolfi 2005). The individuals involved are often motivated by revenge (Ricolfi 2005) or by a felt external threat; they are members of organizations that have considerable control over the information they receive; and they are screened, trained, and prepared. Thus rather than focusing on how their actions result from their beliefs, it might be more plausible to speculate that their beliefs are the consequence of group pressures to perform the action. Finally, while this line of reasoning represents a departure from standard practice in economics, the whole point of this book is that there are many problems and circumstances where this departure is most welcome.

5.6 Comparative Statics

That an individual could completely or even to a large extent "internalize" someone else's utility function and become so deeply under her control is still bizarre. How can this take place? So far, we have described only one reason for this result – a strong desire for solidarity. Some other reasons can be described with the help of Figure 5.2. As illustrated in the figure, in high-solidarity groups there is usually some technological discontinuity or concavity in the production function. Thus for example, most organizations where solidarity is important have some ritual that requires the individual to commit to it, such as religious "conversions" or "jumping in" in the case of gangs or mafiosi. This makes the loss of A at the initial level of S discontinuous, as depicted in Figure 5.2. At the other extreme, where A is initially zero, the curve also displays increasing returns. The behavior of children provides an illustration. Thus, one can imagine that children brought up by their parents and initially lacking an identity of their own have to make a dramatic (discontinuous rather than marginal) change in order to get one. Thus they cannot move from A $= 0$ in small steps but need to "revolt" against their parents in order for this to happen. This point implies that from the point A $= 0$, the production possibility curve has an increasing rather than the usual decreasing slope, that is, initially $\partial^2 a/\partial s^2 > 0$, as also depicted in Figure 5.2. In turn, this also increases the likelihood that an individual who demands high solidarity will end up at a "corner." This struggle for identity is a well-known feature of adolescence. In a similar way, individuals who come under the spell of a charismatic leader may need to be "deprogrammed" in some way in order to return to "normal" society.

The analysis so far identifies people who might rationally get their identity almost entirely from membership in the group, including the possibility of committing suicide for the cause as a rational choice. The basic fact that might lead someone in that direction is a desire for a very high level of social cohesion or solidarity. So the first question one might want to ask is, Who is particularly likely to want very high levels of solidarity? Perhaps the most important category of such people comprises those who do not have much S from other sources, that is, people who are lonely and isolated and who therefore turn to the group for friendship and belongingness. One implication of this is that young people who are looking for solidarity from a gang would possibly be willing to join and participate in gang activities, even though monetary returns are low. This might possibly explain the extremely low values of life estimated for gang members by Levitt and Venkatesh (2000). Another implication is that in societies where social cohesion is difficult to get because social services are not well provided and there are few well-functioning organizations that provide it, for example, in so-called failed states, the demand for solidarity from those organizations is particularly likely to be high.

The analysis also points to a second characteristic: those for whom, at the margin, autonomy has low value. Presumably this would include people whose autonomy hasn't worked for them, that is, people who see themselves as "losers" or failures.[17] Another, related characteristic is a lack of a solid identity: those who lack one have relatively less to sacrifice in giving up their beliefs for those of the group. Thus young people without an established identity would be expected to be particularly vulnerable.

Are the poor particularly likely to be among those who especially seek high S, that is, is there some reason to think that solidarity is income-inelastic? From the economic point of view, perhaps the most straightforward way of looking at this matter is that the value of a life is positively related to potential lifetime earnings, and the larger these are, ceteris paribus, the more reluctant an individual would be to sacrifice his or her life.[18] This would provide the connection between poverty and the propensity to become a suicide martyr so often asserted in the popular media. However, note that matters are not so simple: if the demand for solidarity were sufficiently income-elastic, this could reverse this prediction. Indeed, studies of the relation between income and the propensity for suicide martyrdom essentially find no relationship to income or education (Krueger and Maleckova 2003).

While both the desire for solidarity, the relative absence of fixed beliefs, and the lack of a secure identity point to a negative proclivity between age and the potential to become a suicide bomber, the old have less to lose by taking this route (the remaining value of life gets smaller with age), and so the effect of age remains ambiguous. However, there seems to be no doubt that in fact terrorists are predominantly young people. This suggests that either the vulnerability of beliefs or the insecurity of identity dominates the economic factor of the value of remaining life.

With respect to price elasticity, if the equilibrium is at a corner, small changes in the cost of solidarity (in terms of autonomy) would not change behavior. But note that a sufficiently large change in price will have a truly dramatic change in the level of solidarity demanded, producing an interior equilibrium and reducing the demand for solidarity considerably. This would happen if the curvature of the production function were to remain as shown in Figure 5.2, and the change in price (not shown) tilted it up far enough to the right from the point E_2.

The dilemma for public policy toward groups that threaten public welfare is posed starkly if we consider those members of the group for whom the corner solution in equation 5.7 holds. Such individuals are resistant to change, and no policy is likely to be very effective. Thus, threatening, attacking,

---

[17] Some causes of low self-esteem are discussed in R. Baumeister, "The Self," in Gilbert, Fiske, and Lindzey (1998), chap. 15.

[18] I am indebted to Isaac Ehrlich for this point.

assassinating, bombing, and other policies that can be interpreted as changing the "price" of the group activity will often produce no change in the position of the individual within it at all. However, if the change in price were sufficiently large, it might produce the desired movement. Alternatively, attacks from "outsiders" may engender *more* solidarity within the group by the "security dilemma" mechanism: thus they may be counterproductive. But this problem does not arise for group members at the corner, whose solidarity is already maximal.

For those who are not at the corner, an external threat provides a unifying force that can cause the individual to choose more solidarity with the group. Indeed, as Posen (1993) showed for ethnic groups, an increase in cohesion among one possibly threatening ethnic group can make the threatened group more afraid, and this fear stimulates cohesion among the members of the threatened group in turn.[19] Moreover, a spiral can be set in motion with the "security dilemma" arising with cohesion or solidarity instead of armaments as the operative variable: increased cohesion within group j stimulates cohesion within group i, which stimulates further cohesion within j in turn, and so on. When this threat is or can be made present, therefore, initial moves in the direction of larger solidarity could be amplified in a process of positive feedback. An example of this dynamic is the rapid spread of nationalism in Serbia under Milosevic, which responded to and in turn stimulated the same behavior in Croatia under Tujman (see Chapter 8 for more detail). A similar dynamic characterizes the interaction between terrorist groups and their targets. Both acts of terrorism and the response to them typically provide casualties, and these provide plenty of opportunities for the emotionally binding experiences leading to the desire for vengeance, which substitute for the emotional binding within the group that characterizes cults.

5.7 The Structure of Supply: Alternative Organizational Forms

The types of groups discussed so far include cults and other organizations where individuals often participate together in group activities. However, these are not the only types of groups that can generate solidarity. For example, solidarity may be intense within a group even for a group that does not meet very often if the preferences of the members on important issues are relatively homogeneous to begin with, and if they have other means of communication and a leader with whom they identify.

---

[19] Some evidence that external threats promote group identification is reviewed in Huddy (2003).

In general, the better the technology or "production process" with which a group enables an individual to convert A into S, the more its members will choose high solidarity. As there is often little capital required in terrorist activity (except communication devices like computers, relatively primitive weaponry, and possibly physical space to meet in), the main determinant of technology is organizational structure. In what follows we first summarize some organizational characteristics of cults that have been only implicit in the preceding discussion and then consider some other organizational forms.

5.7.1 Cults

The cult form is characterized by small size;[20] a relatively fixed number of adherents, who in turn are in constant contact with each other, while relatively cut off from other sources of information; and often a charismatic leader (see Dawson 1996; Galanter 1989; or Appleby 1997). This implies some special features of the technology for converting A into S. First, inside the organization the individual is typically grouped with other, like-minded individuals, who are also involved in the transformation and subject to the same group pressures. Less committed individuals may also be screened out[21] through the sacrifices that are often demanded of the group, as discussed by Iannacconne (1992). In cults, even bizarre beliefs or practices may appear "normal."

Another important feature of the production process that affects the level of solidarity chosen is that it often takes place slowly or in small steps, as in Stanley Milgram's famous "obedience" experiments, and as Galanter observes for many cult groups. Thus, initially, recruits are usually exposed to relatively innocuous ideas and only as their involvement deepens are they treated to the full panoply of ideas, paranoid conceptions, and philosophical notions that characterize the group's ideology.[22]

---

[20] In turn this helps to explain why public goods are often supplied by small groups even though their benefits may be nonexcludable. It is more difficult for an individual in a relatively small group to free-ride because it is easier for the small group to give or deny solidarity according to an individual's contribution. So the small group, unlike the large one, has a way of enforcing contributions through the provision of the excludable private service of solidarity.

[21] Thus S_{min} in Figure 5.2 could be the minimum level of sacrifice demanded of a group member.

[22] Akerlof (1991) models Milgram's experiments with a "near-rational" model of obedience. The subjects in Milgram's experiments were indeed often horrified, ex post, at what they did (Milgram 1974). Galanter provides evidence that cults and other groups where solidarity

5.7.2 Netwar and Al Qaeda

Many of the new generation of terrorist groups are alleged to have more fluid organizational forms, with forms of organization, doctrine, and strategies attuned to the information age. This idea is often loosely expressed in the popular press. A precise formulation can be found in Arquilla, Ronfeldt, and Zanini (in Lesser et al. 1999), who suggest that "Islamic fundamentalist organizations like Hamas and the bin Laden network consist of groups organized in loosely interconnected, semi-independent cells that have no commanding hierarchy" (1999, pp. 56–57). Indeed in the archetypal case, they form an "all-channel" network. The all-channel network pictorially resembles a geodesic dome, in which each node is connected to each other node. There is no central leadership, no precise "heart" or "head" that can be targeted (1999, p. 51).

In turn, the capacity of the design for effective performance depends on the presence of shared principles, interests, and goals – at best, an overarching doctrine or ideology that spans all nodes and to which the members wholeheartedly subscribe. "Such a set of principles, shaped through mutual consultation and consensus building, can enable them to be 'all of one mind,' even though they are dispersed and devoted to different tasks; the members do not have to resort to hierarchy – they know what they have to do" (1999, p. 51).

How can the model of trade in beliefs apply to these forms of organization, which is, after all, the classic form of revolutionary (cellular) organization with network information exchange added? There appear to be three issues: do the members already share beliefs; how can they trade beliefs for solidarity if the members of the organization are dispersed and are not available to provide solidarity by hugging one another; and, if there is no hierarchy, who makes the organization's decisions and how are they communicated?

is high typically "brainwash" individuals in a series of steps, by initially coupling social cohesion with relatively innocuous ideas and only slowly introducing more radical ones. All of this suggests that individuals with accurate ex ante knowledge or expectations that in joining a group they will end up giving their life for it might decide not to join. On the other hand, the equilibrium in Figures 5.2 or 5.3 does not rely on any form of biased expectations or irrationality. Suicide martyrdom is widely reported today, and for people joining certain groups it must be obvious that there is a good chance that that is how they are going to end up. So it seems unwise to deny the possibility of completely rational suicide, fully expected prior to joining the group, while acknowledging that "near rationality" of the type suggested by Akerlof might make suicide martyrdom more likely for a larger class of people.

To address these issues, note first that, with respect to Al Qaeda, a more accurate characterization based on the evidence of its structure that we have as presented by Gunaratna is that it is "cellular" rather than "all channel":

> Al Qaeda's global terrorist network strictly adheres to the cellular (also known as the cluster) model composed of many cells whose members do not know one another, so that if a cell member is caught the other cells would not be affected and work would proceed normally. . . . Cell members never meet in one place together; nor do they in fact know each other; nor are they familiar with the means of communication used between the cell leader and each of its members. (2002, pp. 57, 76)

Some evidence that reinforces Gunaratna's view surfaced with the recent capture of the top Al Qaeda operative Khalid Shaikh Mohammed, of whom it was reported that "Hundreds of captured Al Qaeda operatives said during questioning that they had had a recent conversation with (Mohammed). . . . Often, according to intelligence and law enforcement officials, the captured suspects had no knowledge of each other but they had all been in contact with Mohammed" (*International Herald Tribune*, March 4, 2003, p. 6).

It is worth pausing for a moment to understand the implications of the cellular structure for how the organization functions and how it could be targeted by antiterrorist policy. Each cell operates under the command of a leader, who communicates information upward to his handler in turn. At the end, for operations where there are survivors, a report is sent upward and the operation is evaluated by the senior leadership. "Horizontal" communication between cells is strictly forbidden, and in any case the individuals in one cell do not know the individuals in other cells. Now, one reason often advanced for this structure is to preserve secrecy and to lessen the chances that, if one branch of the organization is discovered, the whole organization is destroyed. But there is another implication: *could there be a structure more conducive to authoritarian (hierarchical) control?*[23] In effect, with this structure it is only possible to communicate "vertically" (with superiors). Horizontal communication is minimized, and with it the possibility of any challenge to the leadership, or of organizing actions that feather the nest of subordinates but which are not in the interests of the leadership.[24]

---

[23] Breton and Wintrobe (1982, 1986) evaluated the efficiency of organizations in terms of the size and intensity of vertical as opposed to horizontal networks. On this approach, the cellular structure has much to recommend it in terms of the efficiency with which subordinates carry out the wishes of superiors. This and other economic approaches to bureaucracy are surveyed in Wintrobe (1997).

[24] Roy (2004, p. 322) denies that Al Qaeda is organized on the cellular principle and suggests that many of Al Qaeda's cadres, for example, the Hamburg cell that did the 9/11 operation,

In addition, what is minimized in this loose structure is *formal* hierarchical structure. But that does not mean that the organization is not authoritarian – quite the opposite. To illustrate, the Nazi party and the Nazi government, while it inherited a formal hierarchical structure from the Weimar regime, tended to bypass it in favor of the more informal bureaucratic structure of the Nazi party. At one point, Hitler declared that only the "will" of the Führer, not the laws of the regime, formally signified the intentions of the regime and the wishes of the government.[25] Descriptions of Al Qaeda "as a fluid and dynamic, goal-oriented rather than rule-oriented organization" (Gurantana 2002, p. 58) could equally well be made of the Nazi party structure (see, e.g., Arendt 1951, 1973). But does that imply that the Nazi party was not authoritarian?

Some evidence of direct hierarchical control over operations is also provided by Gunaratna. For example, he notes that "Osama directly coordinated important operations such as the September 11 attacks, and while Banshiri and his deputy Muhammad Atef worked on the ground in Somalia, Osama provided the strategic leadership for the East African embassy and USS *Cole* attacks, and reviewed the plans at every stage, pinpointing on photographs of the targets where the explosives-laden truck and boat respectively should be positioned" (2002, p. 77).

Traditional hierarchical relations are prominent in the modus operandi of Al Qaeda, as illustrated by the following account: "After the execution of an operation at the place and time specified, a full report identifying the strengths and weaknesses of the attack is prepared and sent to the head of Al Qaeda so that its impact can be gauged and the effectiveness of future operations improved. For instance, against his assigned role, the performance of each individual Al Qaeda cadre is evaluated for the purpose of rewarding or reprimanding him for his conduct: 'Those deemed weak or lazy were dismissed'" (Gunaratna 2002, p. 75).

Just as in cults, Al Qaeda also practices screening and sorting, training and indoctrination (Gunaratna 2002, pp. 81, 98). With respect to ideology, Islam,

are in fact good friends who know each other very well and socialize together in defiance of classical revolutionary cell structure. There is also no doubt that Al Qaeda was originally based on the personal links between veterans of the Afghan *jihad*. But he presents no evidence of contact between cells (apart from that among the senior leadership) that would contradict the picture presented in Gunaratna. Other sources support Gunaratna's account on this point (see especially Kean and Hamilton 2004). In any case, to the extent that it does operate the way Roy suggests, then my account of its informal authoritarian capacity here is still correct, only there is no problem of a distinctive "information age" structure to be addressed.

[25] See Breton and Wintrobe (1986) or Wintrobe (1998a), chap. 13.

and the promotion of it via the destruction of the anti-Islamic order, provides a common doctrine or set of beliefs that binds the members together, just as ethnicity or religion or communism have done for other solidary movements. Gunaratna emphazises the stringent emphasis on training and retraining (p. 70). But he also notes that "religious instruction . . . is considered far more important than battlefield or terrorist combat training" (p. 73). The organization also attaches great importance to propaganda, in particular the need for Muslim youths to reflect on the state of their societies (p. 88). Finally, Gunaratna suggests that "Although other terrorist groups driven by Islamic ideology, such as Hamas, prepare its fighters to die for the cause, no other group has invested so much time and effort as Al Qaeda in programming its fighters for death" (p. 91).

However, Islam as used by Al Qaeda is not a purely religious doctrine but one that has been distorted to serve the ends of the group (Black 2001; Gunaratna 2002). In particular, the religious doctrine is used to help motivate action: "The role of the *fatwa* and Islamic study committees is to justify Al Qaeda's actions. When a recruit is inducted, he agrees to pursue Al Qaeda's agenda and execute any order provided a *fatwa* justifying the action is cited, and Al Qaeda's religious scholars on the *fatwa* committee issue these Islamic rulings. They also preach and propagate Al Qaeda's model of Islam and ensure periodic indoctrination of the rank and file" (Gunaratna 2002, p. 84)

The next chapter examines the role of religion in promoting suicide terror, a subject that is often misunderstood, in more detail. To first sum up the argument in this section on the structure of Al Qaeda, it appears to be that of a cellular (and hierarchical) cult based on a distorted version of Islamic ideology that is used to further its goals. The evidence on the importance of training and propaganda and on the fact that the Al Qaeda version of Islamic doctrine is highly peculiar and specific to the organization suggests that if its members are indeed "all of one mind," this is an effect, not a cause, of the organization's operation. The structure is informal but that does not mean it is not hierarchical. At the same time, the structure is obviously fragile. With horizontal communication among the cells cut off to the point where those in one cell do not even know who the people in the other cells are, and with all communication directed upward through a single channel, the organization would appear extraordinarily vulnerable to the loss of a few key senior people. Since the invasion of Afghanistan, Al Qaeda may have become more of a "franchise" operation (Roy 2004, p. 323), engaging "subcontractors" to do its work, but whether the authoritarian aspect of its structure has basically changed is less clear.

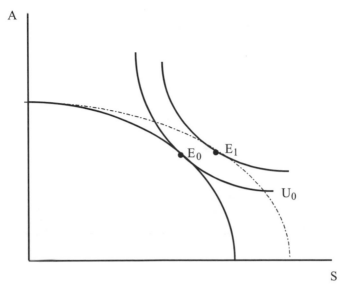

Figure 5.3. An improvement in the technology for producing solidarity leads members of the group to choose more solidarity.

5.8 Effects of Changes in Organizational Technology on the Leaders' Choice of Extremism, and Some Policy Implications

Now we look at how changes in organizational technology affect the leader's choice of extremism. At the same time we integrate the model of the leader's preferences in Chapter 4 with the model of follower's or subordinate's behavior in this chapter.

Equilibrium in the complete model implies that each individual within the organization is maximizing utility given the organizational technology for converting autonomy into solidarity, as discussed in this chapter; and the leader of the organization, given the preferences of his or her membership, the capacity of the organization to build solidarity, and his preferences for risk and the relationship between risk and return, is also in equilibrium, as discussed in Chapter 4.

To see how changes in technology affect extremism in this complete model, begin by looking at Figure 5.3. The figure displays the indifference curves (choice between autonomy and solidarity) of an individual member of an extremist group, and the constraint (indicating the group technology for developing solidarity among its members). Suppose now that there is an upward shift in the technology for producing solidarity (shown by the

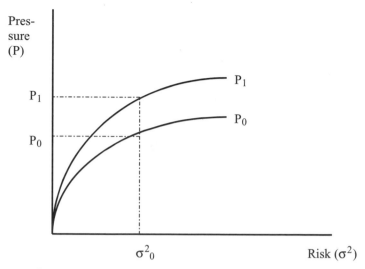

Figure 5.4. The group can now produce more pressure for any given level of resources K, L, and O and level of risk, because the members of the organization have chosen more solidarity than before as a result of the change in technology. Figure is adapted from Figure 4.4.

dotted line in Figure 5.3). This leads the typical individual to take more solidarity than before. Consequently, individuals are more willing to join extremist groups in order to get solidarity, and those individuals who are already members of such groups are more willing to be solidary with them. So the typical individual chooses E_1 rather than E_0, implying greater solidarity with the group.

Figure 5.4 shows the effect of this choice on the group's capacity to produce pressure. Because there is greater solidarity within the group, the organization can now produce more pressure for any given level of resources K and L. So, at any given level of risk (e.g., $\sigma^2 0$ in Figure 5.4), the amount of expected pressure increases (e.g., from P_0 to P_1). Because solidarity is more important for extremist methods of pressure than for moderate methods, the capacity of the group to produce pressure increases more the higher the level of risk taken, also as shown in Figure 5.4.

Figure 5.5 shows the effect of this change on the group leader's choice between moderate and extreme methods of pressure. As discussed in Chapter 4, this can be represented as the choice between a riskless asset (moderate methods of pressure) and a risky one (extreme methods). The level of extremism here is represented by the proportion of the "portfolio" in risky assets (I/M, where I is the number of extremist incidents produced and M is

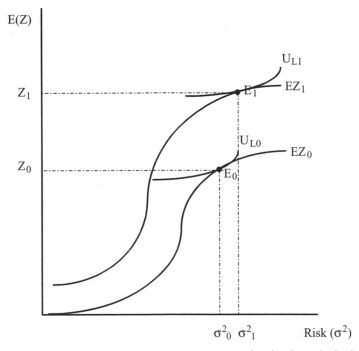

Figure 5.5. Because of the improvement in organizational technology, the leader now faces a better trade-off between risk and return. Provided either the substitution effect dominates the income effect, or relative risk aversion is either constant or decreasing as wealth (organizational capacity) increases, the leader chooses more extreme methods as a result. Figure is adapted from Figure 4.8b.

the level of moderate pressure, as in Chapter 4). Because expected pressure increases for any given level of risk, so does the capacity to achieve the goal of the organization (Z). In the figure, the relationship between risk and return (EZ) therefore shifts up (from EZ_0 to EZ_1). The increase in return for any given level of risk implies a substitution effect that favors risk taking, and an income or "wealth effect" due to the increase in the organization's capacity to produce pressure. The wealth effect favors risk taking (larger I/M) if the group leader's coefficient of relative risk aversion is decreasing as wealth increases. It is neutral if this coefficient is constant and negative (lower I/M) if this coefficient increases with wealth. Thus, *whether the degree of extremism increases or not depends crucially on the extremist leader's attitude to risk.* If the substitution effect dominates the wealth effect, or if the wealth effect is positive or neutral, he or she chooses more extremism as a result of this change.

This kind of analysis provides a clue for policy, especially with respect to the "carrot versus stick" debate that characterizes much of the policy debate over how to deal with terrorism.[26] Those who take the "carrot" position argue that we should look at the root causes of terror and offer potential terrorists an alternative path. To oversimplify, for the purpose of making my point, Pape (2003) suggests that the root cause of suicide terror is always occupation and proposes a simple solution – end the occupation. Frey (2004) argues strongly that deterrence does not work with respect to terror and proposes the carrot policy. On the other hand, the U.S. government since 9/11 has more or less exclusively followed a "stick" policy. Now it might be suggested that from the price-theoretic point of view it actually makes no difference, because the substitution effect tends to be in the same direction with either policy. To take a domestic policy that obviously applies to contemporary Britain, the government there could either suppress militant mosques and madrasses or subsidize moderate ones, with the same effect. But this conclusion neglects the income or wealth effect. While the substitution effect is in the right direction with either policy, the wealth effect may not be. And the wealth effect implicit in some antiterrorist policies is obviously very large.

From this point of view, the problem in deciding which policy is correct is that there is obviously no way to discover just what the attitudes toward risk of terrorist leaders might be, although the very fact that they are engaged in terror marks them as not terribly risk averse. Still the critical variable for assessing the direction of the wealth effect is the behavior of the coefficient of relative risk aversion as wealth changes, not an easily discoverable number about anyone, let alone about terrorist leaders. Consequently, the only policy that is guaranteed to be in the right direction (though not, of course, necessarily effective) is a policy of "carrot *and* stick." Technically, this neutralizes the wealth effect.[27] One place where the combination of carrot *and* stick has been tried is the British government's policies with respect to Northern Ireland in recent years, and it has indeed been argued that it is the combination of policies there that has promoted progress (McGarry and O'Leary 2003).

---

[26] Frey (2004) provides a comprehensive statement of the issues and argues for the "carrot" point of view.

[27] Note that the provision of the carrot along with the stick also tends to solve the difficulties with deterrence discussed in section 5.2. Thus strong penalties for terrorist activity are less likely to have the counterproductive effect of increasing support for the terrorist cause if positive opportunities are also provided at the same time for those who wish to renounce violence.

Still, other considerations may limit the effectiveness of carrots and sticks in any combination. Earlier I suggested an important reason why deterrence policies may be ineffective: the indivisibility of the goals of extremist leaders. It is not that the leaders are irrational, but because their goals are so large and the distance from them so great, the cost of the punishment pales in comparison. The same difficulty would appear to apply to the carrot solution or to the combination of carrot and stick. It is not obvious what kind of carrots can be offered to the truly millenarian. What kind of reward could compare in its appeal to Islamic radicals with, say, the reestablishment of a truly Islamic society along the lines of the caliphate? So the indivisibility of the goals of terrorist leaders create a problem for policies of either type. *The more millenarian the group, the less effective are counterterrorist policies of either the carrot or the stick.* This is the common sense behind the idea that it is impossible to appease someone like Osama bin Laden, whose goals appear to be the restoration of the caliphate and theocratic rule.

As to followers, millenarian groups and other very extreme groups are particularly likely to have members who are characterized by the "all-solidarity" corner solution described in this chapter. Such individuals are unlikely to be very responsive to either penalties or rewards offered by people coming from group outsiders.

Still, this does not mean the policies are necessarily ineffective. The point of carrot or stick policies is not to appeal to the committed leaders or devoted followers, or to deter those people, but to appeal to or deter those who are *on the margin* – people who might be tempted to join or participate in extremist groups and activities. The greater the elasticity of supply of these people, the more effective carrot and stick policies are likely to be.

Another possibility is social-interaction-based policies. For example, Frey (2004) lists the following carrot-type policies: reintegrating terrorists, that is, breaking up their isolation (pointing out that segregation reinforces extremism and vice versa). He suggests that terrorists can be involved in a discussion process that takes their goals and grievances seriously and, if compromises are feasible, tries to see how they should be granted access to normal political processes. The same principle can be applied to nations supporting or harboring terrorists, as Frey notes. Such policies include welcoming repentants, offering valued opportunities to them, and so on.

However, stick policies can also be social-interaction-based. The reason is that with violent extremism, the point about the policy is to *reduce* the capacity for solidarity within extremist groups and to increase that with elements of the wider society. For example, seeking help from Islamic moderates in identifying potentially violent individuals, and putting limits on free speech when it is used to advocate violence are stick policies that take into account the social interactions that breed violent extremism.

One way to interpret acts of terror like 9/11 or 7/7 is that they are a form of theatrical protest that is designed to demonstrate how deeply the group rejects the normal workings of the community (the same community that other members of society may find precious). And, it is worth recalling that suicide terrorism is most commonly associated with groups whose objective is the restoration of what they regard as their "homeland." So acts of terror are in fact deliberately antisocial – they imply a rejection of the existing community and argue for a new one, and in a way their appeal can only be countered with the promise of a different community, one to which they feel they can belong.

5.9 Conclusion

In this chapter I developed a simple model to explain the supply of extremist activity and focused especially on the question of how it is possible for a person to rationally commit suicide to further the goals of a group. In the model, an individual gives up autonomy for solidarity, that is, he trades his beliefs for a feeling of belongingness to a group. Small trades of this type do not result in unusual behavior, and most of us engage in such behavior all of our lives. At large levels, however, such trades imply that a person is increasingly giving up his identity for that of the group, perhaps as personified by its leader, and losing the capacity to make decisions based on values other than those of the leader. Consequently, the choice of larger levels of solidarity may drive a person close to or at a corner solution where her values are entirely those of the leader. Such a person is capable of rational suicide for the goals of the group. Some implications of this view are that small price effects will not change the behavior of the individual in question, and even very fairly large ones might not cause the person to revert to her old identity because she has given it up in exchange for solidarity. However, very large changes will cause a very substantial change, as is typical in the analysis of corner solutions.

Although such slavish devotion to the group is typically associated with cults, modern terrorist groups seem capable of producing such individuals, even though they are relatively large and dispersed. The structure of Al Qaeda is not only hierarchical but cellular, and this facilitates vertical control under these circumstances. This technological improvement in organization allows Al Qaeda to undertake more risky operations than if it were organized more conventionally, and it biases its choice of methods toward extreme methods.

The next chapter continues the analysis of suicide terror, with particular reference to the role of religion as a possible motivation for these actions.

SIX

Religion and Suicide Terror

6.1 Introduction

One interpretation of the behavior of the terrorists of 9/11 that has been commonly made is that they were motivated by religious belief. This interpretation was given credence by the evidence presented by Kanin Makiya and Hassan Mneimneh (2002), who described a manual apparently used by the hijackers, parts of which were found in the wreckage of one of the planes involved, and as well in a piece of Muhammad Atta's luggage, which, by accident, was not loaded on the plane at Logan airport. The manual consisted of instructions to the would-be martyrs that framed the act they were to undertake entirely as if it were to be done "to please God" (Makiya and Mneimneh 2002, p. 20), and there was no mention of any other motive or issue such as Palestine, Iraq, or U.S. global domination. Of course one could argue that the manuals were deliberately planted. But if the motives of the hijackers were more secular, what would be the point of planting such a manual?

In what follows I am going to assume that people such as those who carried out the 9/11 bombings are rational in the standard economic sense of that term, and ask if we can explain first why it is that rational people would adopt religious beliefs, and why and under what circumstances they might even be willing to sacrifice their lives for these beliefs. Thus this chapter explores aspects of the supply of this kind of terrorist activity.

The next section discusses the rationality of religious belief and, in particular, the idea of religious belief as a form of contract with God. Section 6.3 turns to another and in the end, I believe, more satisfactory foundation for religious belief – the desire for solidarity – and presents a simple model of how this is produced. Section 6.4 turns briefly to the "demand" for suicide terrorism and asks what makes leaders demand suicidal actions of their followers.

6.2 Religion as Contractual Exchange

Recently there has been a fair amount of work on the economics of religion, much of it inspired by the path-breaking work of Iannacconne (1988, 1992). However, one question that is not addressed in that work is *why* people need religion: for the most part, Iannacconne simply assumes that people derive utility from the consumption of "religious commodities" and does not inquire into the reasons for religious belief. An answer to this question is suggested by contractual theories, a line of thought initiated by Miller (1993). In these models, events described in the Bible are interpreted using the theory of contractual exchange. The most outlandish piece is possibly that of Raskovich (1996) who interprets the Jewish Covenant, which committed the ancient Jewish people to belief in the one God, as an example of "exclusive dealing" – that is, the Jews agreed to believe in only one God in exchange for being the chosen people.

No one can deny the centrality of the Covenant to Jewish history. As Finer (1997, p. 238) put it in his magisterial *The History of Government from the Earliest Times*,

The entire community had covenanted itself to God at Mount Sinai. This is the central event in Jewish history. Everything else was elaboration and commentary. At Sinai God gave out his law; it was written down and the people covenanted to obey it. So, each individual, and the community as a whole, was in direct communion with God.

Finer goes on to note some significant political corollaries, the most important of which is that the Covenant not only binds the people but also binds their secular ruler: "[T]he monarch is bound by an explicit and written law code imposed on him, coequally with his subjects, *from the outside*" (1997, p. 238). Thus what particularly distinguished the ancient Kingdom of Israel is that it was the first constitutional monarchy. The people were bound by the law, but so was the king.

Other monotheistic religions can be understood the same way, that is, in terms of a contract, although the contractual aspect of religion is less stressed in their founding myths. The early Christians modified the contract to one of belief. To put it simply, in the early Christian religion, if one believed, one was saved in return. The decisive turning point, according to the historian Thomas Bokenkotter (1977, p. 20), was in the controversy over whether the pagan Gentiles could be admitted to the church simply if they believed, or whether they also had to obey the Jewish law and, in particular, become circumcised:

For [Paul] the very essence of the Gospel was at stake in the controversy over circumcision; to require Gentiles to practice the Jewish Law would be tantamount to saying that faith in the risen Lord Jesus was not enough for salvation; observance of the Law was also necessary. . . . So when Paul heard the traditionalists saying the Gentiles must be circumcised, he insisted "what makes a man righteous is not obedience to the Law, but faith in Jesus Christ. . . . if the Law can justify us, there is no point in the death of Christ. . . . When Christ freed us, he meant for us to remain free. Stand firm, therefore, and do not submit again to the yoke of slavery" (Ph 3:8–9).

Paul's views were ultimately decisive and as a result the church shed its exclusively Jewish character and was enabled to spread the Gospel rapidly to the pagan Gentiles. Belief was sufficient and circumcision was not to be required of them (Bokenkotter 1977, p. 21).

The fundamental nature of Islam can also be interpreted as a contract. The obligations of a Muslim can be understood using the three central concepts of *islam*, *jihad*, and *ummah*. *Islam* denotes that the duty of a Muslim is to surrender (which is what the word *islam* means) himself completely to the Supreme Being. As has often been noted, in the Quranic vision there is no dichotomy between the sacred and the profane, the religious and the political. According to Karen Armstrong (2000b, p. 37),

A Muslim's first duty is to create a just, egalitarian society [the community or *ummah*], where poor and vulnerable people were treated with respect. This demanded a *jihad* . . . on all fronts: spiritual, political, social, personal, military and economic. By ordering the whole of life so that God was given priority and his plans for humanity were fully implemented, Muslims would achieve a personal and social integration that would give them intimations of the unity which was God. To fence off one area of life and declare it to be off-limits to this religious "effort" would be a shocking violation of this principle of unification (*tahwid*) which is the cardinal Islamic virtue.

The second point is that "Muslims, like Jews require orthopraxy, a uniformity of religious practise, and see belief as a secondary issue" (Armstrong 2000a, p. 37). Of course, the practices of a Muslim are very specific: The five "pillars" of Islam are *shehadah:* to declare one's faith in the unity of God and the prophethood of Mohammed, to pray five times daily, to pay a tax (*zakat*) to ensure a fair distribution of wealth in the community, to observe the fast of Ramadan, and to make the *hajj* pilgrimage to Mecca if circumstances allow (Armstrong 2000a, p. 37; Finer 1997, p. 677). These are the minimum obligations, but as Finer notes, "To be fully observant he would have to fulfill a voluminous compendium of the most minutely detailed prescriptions for his daily conduct, even down to its most intimate minutiae. This *corpus* has been built up on the verses of the Quran itself, then on the attested sayings and doings of the Prophet – the *hadith* – and finally on the rescensions and elaborations of all these as made by the learned – the *ulemah* – in the ninth and tenth centuries. The result is the *sharia* law" (Finer 1997, p. 667). Thus Islam closely parallels Judaism in that both regulate daily conduct by a vast network of rules. In Judaism's case these are based on the Pentateuch, the Prophets, and the centuries-long accumulation of rabbinical judgments that make up the *halakha* and the Talmud. Nothing in Christian civilization corresponds to this (Finer 1997, p. 667).

Islamic punishments for transgression can be earthly and sometimes meted out to whole groups (some examples are given in Ruthven 2000, p. 112) but, as in the other monotheistic religions, there is also a Day of Judgment which, as Ruthven puts it "fills in the gaps in the ethical doctrines" (p. 116). The horrors of hell are graphically painted, but what is more unusual is that the joys of heaven are given an extended treatment (p. 117). Thus, again, there is, or there may be interpreted to be, exchange, and any outstanding obligations are resolved on the Day of Judgment.

To fix ideas it is worth mentioning one set of religious beliefs where clearly there is *no* contract. This is Calvinist Protestantism. As interpreted by Weber in *The Protestant Ethic and the Spirit of Capitalism* (1930), this branch of Christianity does *not* involve a contract or an exchange. The doctrine of predestination implies that one is either a member of the elect or one is not. One carries out disciplined activities, hoping to prove to oneself that one is a member of the elect. But either one is or one is not, and there is nothing to be done about it – it has already been decided. Thus there is no exchange between the individual and God. It is distinctly odd, and deserves further study,[1] that the religion most famously associated with the rise of capitalist exchange is the only one of the major monotheisms that cannot be interpreted as involving a contractual exchange with the Supreme Being.

In the other cases discussed, it might appear that the theory of exchange can indeed be extended to cover contracts with God: in (Catholic) Christianity, the obligation on the individual is simply to believe; in Judaism and in Islam, there is a set of required practices to demonstrate faithfulness. An individual fulfills his or her part of the bargain in this manner; in exchange he or she avoids earthly punishment and may ascend to heaven rather than descend to hell.

---

[1] One possible solution is sketched in note 8.

However, there is a problem with this line of thought: all of these contracts would appear to be unenforceable. To see the issue more clearly, let us first consider a related problem: that of credible commitment by an autocrat. Consider a king who has absolute power, in the sense that there are no formal checks on the exercise of his authority. Now consider an exchange with that king – for example, suppose that the king wishes to loan money from a financier in his kingdom. Would the financier be willing to make the loan? The problem facing the financier is the risk that the monarch will renege on the contract. If he does, since he is the king, there is no way in which the lender can force him to repay. This is the "Irony of Absolutism." The more power the king has, the more difficult it is for him to get a loan (North 1981; North and Weingast 1989; and Root 1994).

North and Weingast suggested that this problem gave rise to the Glorious Revolution in England, in which power over the treasury was devolved on Parliament. In this way the king could credibly commit to repay. No such devolution of power occurred in France. The result was that the English king solved the problem of how to raise funds and could finance his army and other expenditures, while the French king did not, leading to the chronic shortage of revenue that was one of the factors leading to the French Revolution.[2]

Now let us take the liberty of applying these simple lessons from the theory of autocracy to religion as contractual exchange. This application of economic reasoning to spiritual matters obviously involves some adjustment to the usual way of thinking about theological issues that some may find offensive, but perhaps the reader can indulge in the exercise for a moment. The Supreme Being was, after all, originally envisioned as the absolute monarch (Finer 1997). The problem with making an exchange with an absolute monarch is that he can always renege on a contract. Earthly monarchs can solve the Irony of Absolutism through the credible devolution of power, as the English king did in the Glorious Revolution. But I know of no way

---

[2] The French Revolution, and the theory of dictatorship, are discussed in more detail in Chapter 7. Here, we should note only that the more general problem, which I labeled "The Dictator's Dilemma" (Wintrobe 1998a) and which has been discussed in works on autocracy as old as the ancient Greek scholar Xenophon's dialogue *Hiero, or Tyrannicus* (1948), is that the more power a ruler has over his people, the more reason they have to fear him; this fear breeds a reluctance on the part of the citizenry to signal displeasure with the ruler's policies. This fear on their part in turn breeds fear *on the part of the dictator*, since, not knowing what the people think of his policies, he has no way of knowing what they are thinking and planning, and of course he suspects that what they are thinking and planning is his assassination. Consequently, long-lasting dictatorships are typically those that do not rule through fear alone but build support among their populations. See Chapter 7 for a more detailed discussion.

a supreme being can do this.[3] *The contracts are unenforceable in principle.* There is no third party to adjudicate and enforce the contract. And there is no way to devolve power credibly onto another agency that would play this function. Of course, various people, agencies, and organizations claim to be God's representatives on earth, but they all face a similar problem: how to make this claim credible.[4]

To illustrate, in ordinary life, producers of high-quality products can solve the problem of making a credible commitment by charging a price premium, or through repetitive advertising (Klein and Leffler 1981). But would it not be more than a stretch to suggest that the repetition of purportedly divine messages can solve the supreme being's problem of credible commitment in the same way that endless television advertising is said to solve this problem for producers of high-quality consumer products? Of course, there are other ways to acquire a reputation. Some of these were outlined in Chapter 2. But if behavior on earth cannot be assuredly attributed to God, how can God acquire a reputation for trustworthiness the way firms and ordinary persons do in these models?

To put it simply, in ordinary contracts with other mortals, there are various ways in which the problem of making a credible commitment in the absence of third-party enforceability can be solved. But if some way were to be found that the supreme being could bind himself to a contract, and if he did so bind himself, he would no longer be supreme. All of the three

---

[3] Thus Raskovich notes that, among the early Jewish people, exclusive belief in the one God Yahweh was held to be enforced by a curse. But those who didn't believe discounted the curse, and so ultimately it had no effect on them. So Raskovich resorts to the institution of the (earthly) group boycott for disbelief introduced under King David to explain why the contract was taken seriously. But while this may enforce behavior, it does not necessarily engender belief. Raskovich also says that the depiction of Yahweh as jealous is vivid and frightening and caused fear, and "fear changed heart to belief" (Exodus 14:31, quoted in Raskovich 1996, p. 461). But clearly it need not have that consequence and could easily have had the opposite one. Does fear result in belief generally? Again, consider some illustrations from absolute rule on earth. Many people feared Stalin (Pinochet) during his reign as dictator of Russia (Chile). Did that lead them to believe in communism (free-market economics)? Would it have been rational for them to do so? And were those people who believed in Yahweh because they felt afraid after what they heard or read rational to believe in him?

[4] Sometimes it is suggested that Pascal's justly celebrated "wager" provides a rational foundation for religious belief. Pascal reasoned that the probability of God's existence may be small but the reward is infinite. Consequently, belief is a rational gamble. This is a profound and justly celebrated idea. It would solve God's problem in compelling behavior because people would reason that the punishment for breaking the contract is so large and the possibility that God would honor his part of it may not be large but it is finite. But the problem with this idea is that it does not work at the margin: *how much* belief or religious practice is justified by a small probability of an infinite reward? Prayer once a week? Once a month? Once a year?

monotheistic religions would seem to be faced with this problem and indeed unenforceability would seem inherent whenever you are making a contract with a supreme being.

Now the problem of credible commitments in its modern form is an extremely sophisticated piece of economic reasoning, but the basic application of the idea here is simple – if God is truly supreme, he can do whatever he likes and therefore cannot be bound by a contract – and it would not be surprising if it was intuited by ordinary people. So it is not surprising to read descriptions of Yahweh by the people of ancient Israel as jealous, capricious, and prone to impulsive rages (Raskovich 1996; Johnson 1995, p. 40), and it is no wonder that the Jews of ancient Israel trembled before him.

Now let us return to the events of 9/11. Take the simplest exchange-based explanation: the suicide bombers committed the act because they believed that they would go to heaven as a result and that waiting there would be seventy to seventy-two virgins. From the point of view of economic theory, the interesting question is, *Is this belief rational?* If God is omnipotent, then while he may promise seventy-two virgins, there is no reason for him to fulfill his part of the bargain. He may promise seventy-two white virgins but actually deliver seventy-two white *raisins*.[5] If the answer is, God does not cheat, then this is tantamount to saying he is not omnipotent. The supreme being cannot be bound by a contract with a mere mortal.

It immediately follows that because the contract cannot bind the supreme being, there is no reason why the earthly party to the contract should fulfill his side of the bargain either. What is the point? The supreme being, being supreme, may punish him even if he fulfills all of his obligations, just to show that he is supreme, or for any other reason. So it would appear that *either* the suicide bombers of 9/11 did *not* commit suicide in exchange for the promise of heavenly rewards, or, if they did, *they were not rational.*

An obvious objection to this line of reasoning is that this just shows the limits of economic reasoning, and how unsuitable it is for addressing matters of faith. To suggest that people cannot rationally believe in the afterlife because they know that it is impossible to lodge a complaint that you were promised an afterlife but didn't receive it is simply to misunderstand the nature of religious belief. Faith is neither rational nor irrational. Such beliefs may not be scientific but that does not mean they are not held,

---

[5] A new scholarly interpretation of the Quran, Christoph Luxenberg's *The Syrom-Aramaic Reading of the Koran* (Berlin: Verlag Das Arabische Buch, 2003), does indeed suggest that *white raisins*, not virgins, are all that is promised Islamic martyrs in the Quran in the first place (as reported in the *New York Herald Tribune*, March 4, 2003, p. 2).

sometimes extraordinarily deeply, or that they cannot form the basis for actions or behavior. Many suicide martyrs appear to believe exactly this: that they are sacrificing themselves in exchange for the rewards of heaven. So all this argument shows is that economics is unsuitable for understanding religious belief, something that may have been obvious to most people to begin with.

Before embracing this conclusion, let me invite the skeptical reader to consider a third possibility: that suicide martyrs do believe that they are sacrificing themselves for the rewards of heaven, and that there is a sense in which this belief is rational, which it must be if we are to analyze it using economic theory. But the foundation of this belief is different than that just considered. It is this: a suicide martyr holds this belief and commits this action out of solidarity with others who hold this belief and with the group whose goals he believes are being advanced by this action. He adopts the beliefs of that group for the same reason that members of other groups adopt the same beliefs of their group according to the model of the preceding chapter: out of a desire for solidarity.

The fact that the belief is extreme and difficult to rationalize on ordinary criteria for rational beliefs is part of its attraction. It immediately marks members of that group off from other people who do not share that belief. The group that shares extreme beliefs can develop a sense of solidarity unknown to groups that share less extreme beliefs.

The suicide martyr in particular shows through his adoption of this belief that he is willing to subject it to the ultimate test. His willingness to commit suicide for the cause in exchange for rewards in heaven is surely the most extreme sacrifice, and no greater proof of the sincerity of belief or solidarity can be asked. Thus the commitment to the belief is entirely credible and correctly "signals" his true solidarity.

Finally, from the point of view of the group's leaders, the fear that such beliefs engender in their enemies is no doubt part of its appeal. As Posen suggested (1993) for ethnic groups, and which is also true of any other group, the internal cohesiveness of a group is part of its fighting strength. An army of would-be suicide martyrs may be the strongest possible weapon in the arsenal of a group that is relatively weak on conventional measures of combat strength.

Although the desire for religious solidarity may imply a logically consistent desire for self-sacrifice, note that this explanation does *not* reduce to what I refer to as the simple "seventy-two virgins" explanation – the trade-off of life for eternal salvation. One way to see this point is to look at the effect of a higher discount rate on the willingness to die for the cause. On the solidarity explanation, the most likely candidates for this role are those with a high discount rate. They will experience the joy of solidarity immediately (at the time of planning and committing the act); after that, who knows? On the other hand, the popular "seventy-two virgins" explanation implies a low discount rate: the rewards for the sacrifice do not occur until after death and may continue forever after. So the solidarity explanation and the "seventy-two virgins" explanation have differing implications for who is likely to be a terrorist. While it is obviously difficult to test this idea, something could be done using data on the typical psychological profile of suicide terrorists, such as those discussed in B. Hoffman (1998), or using new data on would-be martyrs, and comparing the implications for the discount rate of those people to a control group. In this regard, it may be worthwhile to mention that Hoffman describes terrorists as typically "driven by burning impatience coupled with an unswerving belief in the efficacy of violence" (1998, p. 174), which is what the solidarity explanation implies.

Finally, the solidarity explanation can be extended to explain martyrdom even when there is apparently no religious motivation, as is true even for many martyrs in Palestine today (Ricolfi 2005). Thus it provides a unified explanation for suicide martyrdom. Indeed, although religious organizations are important in terrorism today, this was not always the case. For example, in 1968 none of the eleven identifiable international terrorist groups was religious: all were either Marxist-Leninist or nationalist (although the three PLO groups, included among the latter, would seem to be a mixed case), and the first "modern" religious terrorist groups do not appear until 1980 (B. Hoffman 1998, p. 90). The most frequent perpetrators of suicide operations in the world remain the Tamil Tigers of Sri Lanka, proponents of a secular, Marxist-nationalist insurgency (Frey 2004), and as of this writing (September 2005) there are many nonreligious suicide bombings in Iraq.

More generally, in our framework, religious motivation is an important way of generating solidarity, but otherwise there is nothing fundamentally different about religious motivation compared with ethnically or nationally based movements. Thus I reject the argument of Dawkins and others that "the world [can be] a very dangerous place" because "a significant number of people convince themselves, or are convinced by their priests that a martyr's death is equivalent to pressing the hyperspace button and zooming through a wormhole to another universe" (Richard Dawkins, in the *Guardian*, September 15, 2001, quoted in Ruthven 2002, p. 100). The rational reply of a potential suicide bomber who is told by his handler to "just press the button and you will be in paradise" is to respond "why don't *you* press the button?"

6.3 Religion and Solidarity

The explanation of religious belief as a solidarity commitment offered here is not new. Emil Durkheim famously emphasized the importance of solidarity in religious groups:

[A religious group] does not unite men by an exchange and reciprocity of services, a temporal bond of union which permits and even presupposes differences, but which a religious society cannot form. It socializes men only by attaching them completely to an identical body of doctrine and socializes them in proportion as this body of doctrine is extensive and firm. The more numerous the manners of action and thought of a religious character are, which are accordingly removed from free inquiry, the more the idea of God presents itself in all details of existence, and makes individual wills converge to one identical goal. (Durkheim [1897] 1951, p. 159, quoted in Hechter 1987, p. 17)

What is perhaps new in the present argument is the idea of a *religious contract* or *religious exchange*. On this interpretation, this is an implicit contract between an individual and other persons or an organization that, formally at least, claims to represent the supreme being. In this contract, a rational person agrees to believe in or practice the faith. In exchange, he gets solidarity or social cohesion in the manner discussed previously. Obedience to the rituals and sacrifices characteristic of many religious organizations *signals* trustworthiness or reliability in contracting.[6] The "contract" is with the representatives, not with the supreme being. On the other side of the contract, the various religious organizations try to acquire reputations for trustworthiness on earth and thus buttress the credibility of their claim to represent the supreme being. Thus the church prospers when it fulfills its contract by actually providing the social services and cohesion demanded.[7] On the other hand, corruption in religious organizations arises when the church does not fulfill its part of the bargain.

For example, the practice of *simony*, in which the privileges of the church were sold for money instead of for good works and other solidarity-producing projects, and which became infamous in the years prior to the Reformation (Bokenkotter 1977, pp. 178ff.), violated the terms of religious

---

[6] Contrast this with Iannacconne's (1992) interpretation of stigma and sacrifice as devices to raise the value of consumption with other cult members by making it more difficult for them to interact with outsiders. Here, the content of the signal matters as well as the particular beliefs, practices, and codes.

[7] Other mechanisms can fulfill this function as well. For example, Ferrero (2003) analyzes the competition for sainthood as a mechanism that the church uses to preserve its role in society.

exchange and destroyed the trustworthiness that is supposed to be an attribute of the church. Thus both sides can break the contract.[8]

6.4 From Social Cohesion to Terrorism?

One religion may generate greater social cohesion than another for a number of reasons. The three aspects of Islam cited earlier would all seem to imply a greater capacity to stimulate social cohesion than either Judaism or Christianity: First, the all-embracing nature of the Muslim religion implies that there neither is nor can be a separation between church and state. Indeed all of life is potentially holy and one "surrenders" to the religion completely. Second, the original doctrine stressed the concept of the just community (the *ummah*), and social justice is the chief social virtue (Armstrong 2000b, p. 5); while all religions preach social justice, the concept of a just *community* to which one devotes oneself is more associated with Islam than with the other monotheisms. Third, as mentioned earlier, common belief is not the only mechanism for securing solidarity. The other method is struggle (*jihad*) against a common enemy. The Muslim religion was the first to unite these two prime sources of solidarity. As Finer (1997, p. 666) puts it, "Whereas the Christian paradigm is the Suffering Godhead, for the Muslim it is the Armed Prophet."

For all these reasons, it might appear that the Muslim religion is the most *potentially* socially cohesive of the three monotheistic religions. One piece of evidence that supports this idea was the spectacular early success of Muslim armies in conquering other areas with superior weapons. And "the central importance of Islam in the conquests" in the work of even non-Muslim historians (Esposito 1999, p. 30) is often noted.

However, neither the desire for social cohesion nor religiosity is a sufficient condition for terrorist activity. Indeed, many deeply religious people are obviously among the *least* likely candidates for this role. A high level of social cohesion may make the individual member of a group ready to sacrifice himself, but the leader of the group or some other individual with whom one identifies still has to order the individual to commit terrorist acts. None

---

[8] This may explain the confluence of commercial capitalism and Protestantism (in which there is no contract) discussed by Weber: the advent of individualistic capitalism simply mimics the advent of individualistic religion. Which came first is a hotly contested matter, and Weber may not have been right that Protestantism caused capitalism and not the other way round. But what Weber does demonstrate, to my mind, is the similarity in spirit of the two "isms" and the logical criticisms of his work by Samuelsson (1964) simply missed this point.

of the three major monotheistic religions orders its adherents to behave this way, and in particular, although there are passages in the Quran that can be interpreted as advocating violent struggle against the enemies of the religion, much more of it is concerned with justice, mercy, and compassion.

In this and the previous chapters we have dealt only with the supply side of rational suicide bombing – why people are willing to obey instructions to commit suicide for the cause. There is still the demand side – what circumstances give rise to the kind of leaders who demand such sacrifices in the service of destruction? This problem was dealt with in Chapter 4. Here I add some ideas that have to do with the circumstances under which religious leaders in particular might take this route.

One clue to demand is that a *successful* organization usually does not ask such sacrifices of its members: terrorism is, as is often argued, a weapon of the weak. This suggests that it is the *failure* of many Muslim states in the contemporary environment that generates terrorism.

The current problems of Muslim states may have historic roots. The great capacity of the Muslim religion to generate social cohesion was combined in the era of the caliphates with a great weakness: the lack of a succession mechanism. The Dictator's Dilemma[9] is obviously magnified when there is no succession mechanism. The problem is magnified further by the organic quality of the Muslim religion. In the case of Muslim theocracies, like Khomeini's Iran or the Taliban in Afghanistan, this is used to legitimate control over all aspects of the lives of the people. On the other hand, in Muslim states that are not theocracies, the ruler often lacks legitimacy and may have no effective way of generating support. Because there was no succession mechanism under the caliphate, and legitimacy could only be conferred by the religious authorities, but in turn there was no formal procedure for doing this, we have events like the following, beginning shortly after the death of the Prophet: "After Umar's assassination the *shura* appointed as caliph one of the Prophet's sons in law – Uthman – and passed over the claim of Muhammad's cousin and son-in-law Ali. But Uthman was assassinated in turn so that Ali finally succeeded. In the eyes of the ambitious governor of Syria, Muawiya, . . . Ali was less than zealous in pursuing the murderers. Muawiya challenged Ali's title and in the event deposed him and took the throne" (Finer 1997, p. 686).

Finer also describes the early caliphatic states as *despotic* (e.g., p. 693) because the ruler himself was not bound by any set of rules on his conduct:

---

[9] See note 2, and also Chapter 8.

"Despotism refers to the autocrat's capacity, in practice and not just in theory, to take at his personal will the life, the limb, the liberty and the property of any of his subjects without due process of law" (1997, p. 684). Others differ: for example Bernard Lewis (1988, p. 91) insists that the caliphs were *not* despotic because they were bound by the law. So the issue concerns how much these rulers were bound by the law in practice. However, Lewis (1988, p. 99) notes that after the tenth century, a doctrine of obedience to even a tyrannical ruler became accepted among the jurists and theologians of Islam. So the dispute concerns the nature of caliphatic rule, but perhaps not the legacy to modern Islamic governments.

Thus it is not the content of the Islamic religion alone, but also its contribution to the structural weakness of Islamic states, *combined* with the tremendous capacity of the religion to generate social cohesion that causes the problem. Gangster states and weak or failed states that do not provide effective and responsive governments services to their citizens leave many in their populations searching for alternative sources of social cohesion – which can under the circumstances often best be provided by autonomous organizations like charismatic religious sects.[10] In these failed states one expects to see pockets of extreme social cohesion, with charismatic leaders subject to no central control providing solidarity and social services in a sea of unemployment and poverty. At the same time they educate their members that their problems are somehow caused by an external enemy and demand that they take actions to help their fellows against the common threat.

6.5 Conclusion

In this chapter, I first rejected the idea that individuals may become suicide martyrs in exchange for the rewards of heaven: exchanges with God are unenforceable, and such behavior would appear to be not rational in the ordinary economic sense. I then proposed a different model, which starts from the idea that individuals are willing to adopt the beliefs of a group in exchange for solidarity or the feeling of belonging to the group. One profound form of solidarity comes from religious belief, and one interpretation of religious behavior is that it represents precisely this kind of "trade" or implicit "contract."

Other groups besides religious ones, such as youth gangs, political parties, and social movements, can also supply solidarity, and there is nothing unique

---

[10] Note that these states often emerge as the result of the fall of dictatorships. I have detailed an account of their fall elsewhere (Wintrobe 1998a).

about religion in this respect. What may be unusual about religious groups is the depth or the intensity of beliefs participants sometimes share, and this may give rise to a willingness to commit rational suicide for the cause. There are some reasons to believe Islam is more typically capable of generating the intense social cohesion involved in such sacrifices, compared with Judaism or Christianity. But while a high level of social cohesion may characterize a "rational" suicide bomber in part, it is obviously not sufficient and could characterize individuals in pacific groups as well as violent ones.

PART FOUR

REVOLUTIONS, NATIONALISM, AND *JIHAD*

SEVEN

Rational Revolutions

7.1 Introduction

Historically, suicide martyrdom has not been the most important manifestation of extremist activity. This part considers a number of other manifestations of extremism: revolution, nationalism, dictatorship, and global *jihad*. This chapter looks at revolutionary activity, a specter that haunted Europe after the great French Revolution of 1789 and frightened the world after the Russian Revolution.[1]

One thing suicide martyrdom and revolution have in common is that they are both difficult to explain with standard rational choice theory. Thus, it is commonplace in the modern analysis of revolutions to say that rational choice can't explain them. The rational choice approach is identified with the line of thought initiated by Olson (1965) and applied to revolutions in detail by Tullock (1971). They focused on the free-rider problem. Because the benefits of the revolution are a public good, available to every individual whether he participates in revolutionary activity or not, and because the contribution of any one individual to making the revolution happen is usually trivial in any society of reasonable size, no rational person will decide to participate. Hence revolutions cannot occur unless some private benefit, which Olson termed "selective incentives," can be found to motivate participation. In turn, because it is hard to imagine how these could be provided at the mass level, revolutions do not occur.

However, revolutions do occur now and then, and this poses a problem for the theory. Moreover, in many of the classic revolutions such as the French Revolution, as well as in modern revolutions such as those of 1989 in Eastern Europe, there seems to have been a great deal of mass participation, and no

---

[1] Parts of this chapter are taken from Wintrobe (2004).

one, to my knowledge, has suggested that the problem of participation was resolved through the provision of mass selective incentives. Consequently, a number of writers have discarded the rational choice approach, proposing instead that participants were motivated by "norms," or morality (see, e.g., Opp and Ruehl 1990 or Rasler 1996).

Of course, the problem of free-riding occurs in many settings and affects almost all forms of political participation. As we saw in Chapter 2, a number of writers have been preoccupied with problems of participation in social movements, elections, and other forms of collective action. Many of these have stuck to the rational choice approach but incorporated aspects of group behavior and social interactions into the individual calculation of costs and benefits. These do not involve any form of *unselfish* behavior, but consider the individual as a *social* being, that is, in his relationship to other individuals or groups of which he may be a member. As I have emphasized, I believe that this modification of rational choice theory is a most welcome and important departure from theories of the past and should be sharply distinguished from models that incorporate altruistic or "dutiful" behavior as a deus ex machina to be introduced when all other attempts at explanation have failed.

Revolution is qualitatively different from other forms of collective action, such as strikes or protests, in the sense that with a revolution the old "order" is replaced. One can think of two kinds of revolutions: revolutions against dictatorships and revolutions against democracies. As I will elaborate in more detail in the chapter, revolutions occur under dictatorship when the old regime loses its capacity to defend itself. They may occur under democracy when the system is plagued by inaction (as in the rise of the Nazis),[2] because dictators can act when democratic politicians cannot. The main kind of revolution discussed in this chapter is revolution against dictatorships.

In this chapter, therefore, I first ask a different and much more complicated question: are revolutions *collectively* rational? I return to the meaning of this question shortly, but to begin with, the question can be broken down into two subquestions. First, do revolutions occur only or mainly where there are deep problems that the old system cannot solve or are they random and possibly mistaken events? I then suggest that if the answer to this question is yes then, this in turn, provides an important clue to the circumstances under which *individual* participation in revolutions is rational – that is, this is part of the answer to the free-rider problem at the individual level. In doing so, I incorporate the ideas behind much of the recent work on bandwagon effects, leadership, and so forth.

---

[2] The Nazi regime is discussed in Wintrobe (1998), chap. 11.

Second, can the postrevolution society be expected to represent an improvement? Obviously this question is very difficult. The reason for including it is essentially that only if the answer to both this question as well as the first one is yes can revolutions be said to be collectively rational.

To sketch the basic argument, let us begin with the fact that most revolutions occur against dictatorships. Roughly speaking (I will make this more precise later), in any "successful" dictatorship the mechanisms used by the regime to remain in office are sufficient to prevent a revolution from occurring, and it is only if something happens that makes the system incapable of maintaining sufficient power that the regime collapses. To put it differently the old regime, so long as it continues to function well, can always prevent a revolution from occurring. Only when the system does not have sufficient power to keep the people at bay does the regime collapse. To illustrate, as Perrie has argued, "the significant difference between the 1905 and 1917 revolutions in Russia lay not so much in the strength of the revolutionary movement as in the weakness of the state" (Perrie 2000, p. 160).

Thus if something happens to weaken the regime substantially, the conditions for its collapse may appear. Once the regime is weak, then this immediately implies that the conditions for rational participation *by individuals* are partly met. Thus, if the system is weak, clearly it is more likely that a revolution to replace it will succeed. In turn, this motivates individuals to participate in the revolution, both as leaders and followers, and the weaker the regime appears to be, the more likely that a bandwagon effect will occur that brings it down. So if revolutions are collectively "rational" in the first sense – that the existing politico-economic system could no longer function effectively – this helps to explain how they could be *individually* rational as well.

Now let us turn to the second, more difficult question for collective rationality: did the revolution produce, or could it be expected, ex ante, that it would produce, net gains from the point of view of the society – that is, were the people better off after the revolution in some sense than before? I consider various criteria here but end up by suggesting that there is one simple sufficient condition that might command acceptance: if the revolution can be expected to result in democracy, it represents an improvement.

The next section looks at some recent work on the rationality of revolutions. Section 7.3 outlines the basic framework of dictatorship to be used here, based on my model of dictatorship developed elsewhere (Wintrobe 1990, 1998a),[3] and briefly looks at the revolutions in Iran and East Germany

---

[3] An understanding of the basics if not the details of this theory of dictatorship will also be useful for understanding parts of the argument of the next chapter as well.

in the light of these models and a partial equilibrium version of my model of dictatorship. I then go on to sketch the full version of my model of dictatorship (Wintrobe 1998a). Section 7.4 then shows what a rational revolution against dictatorship looks like in this model. Section 7.5 applies this analysis to the French Revolution. Section 7.6 discusses various criteria for "rationality" of replacing the old order. Section 7.7 analyzes some possible revolutionary dynamics in an informal way.

7.2 Some Recent Work on Revolution

A central question in revolutionary theory is the relationship between the level of repression under a regime and the likelihood of revolution. Recently there has been a lot of interesting work on this issue, mainly by sociologists, but also by economists and political scientists. These models are often rational choice in spirit but then incorporate social interactions, both among revolutionary groups and between them and the wider society. Thus the models incorporate bandwagon effects, models of critical mass, information cascades, and critical threshold models. Each of these social interactions describes a chain reaction in which the initial participation of small numbers triggers the participation of much larger numbers over time, sometimes (as in East Germany or Iran) bringing down the government.

To explain how revolutions get started, many of the models begin with the idea that *leadership* of revolutionary groups is not difficult to explain, even on simple, Olsonian, grounds. A good example is Van Belle (1996), who shows that leadership of a revolutionary movement can be rational. He calls the benefits to potential leaders "leadership benefits." These may be selective in nature and include the prestige of leadership, the chances of defining the direction and goals of the group, and the rewards that come with the possibility of becoming one of the leaders of the country. Leadership of a revolutionary movement may be risky, but many of the benefits to be derived therefrom, especially if the revolution succeeds, are purely private. So the participation of leaders is easily explained. However, these benefits drop off rapidly with the number of participants. To explain the participation of others, other factors must be added.

These other factors are in the nature of dynamic processes that involve social interactions. Rasler (1996), in her analysis of the Iranian revolution, summarizes the recent literature on these dynamic collective processes in terms of three types of interactions. The first is the *assurance* that people have about the willingness of others to engage in such actions. Social networks play a big role here because most decisions to protest are made jointly with others. A second factor is the protestors' *success* in achieving governmental concessions. Rasler argues that if the regime adopts conciliatory policies, the result may simply be more protest because successful collective action sustains the involvement of old participants and convinces sideliners to join in. Moreover, concessions may signal a regime's vulnerability. Finally, one factor that is often linked to successful revolution is a "critical" or "triggering" event that represents a turning point and galvanizes large segments of the population (1996, pp. 134–135).

Another strand in the literature concerns the effects of repression on dissidence. Opp and Ruehl (1990) have argued that, while repression clearly has a direct negative effect in impeding protest, it has an indirect effect that may stimulate protest in the longer run if repression leads to micromobilization processes that raise incentives for protest.

Ginkel and Smith (1999) argue that dissident activity is more likely to be successful in motivating large-scale protest when repression is high, because under such conditions those who do protest have more credibility and may be seen as "heroes" by the rest of the population, thus making mobilization more likely. Similarly, Rasler provides some empirical evidence for Opp and Ruehl's argument, showing that increased repression by the shah of Iran had the short-run effect of lowering protest but a long-term escalatory effect. So the Iranian revolution was partly caused by excessive repression. Other scholars (Olivier 1991; Khawaja 1993) distinguish the effects of different levels of repression and find on the basis of studies of collective action in the West Bank and South Africa that only severe levels of repression decrease collective action whereas low to median levels escalate it.

The 1989 revolution in East Germany has been subject to intensive scrutiny on the basis of these theories. With respect to the free-rider problem, Opp and Ruehl (1990) have done important studies on the protests in Leipzig showing, on the basis of detailed interview data, that most East Germans who demonstrated against the regime in 1989 somehow *believed* that their individual actions were important. Looking at these arguments, Thompson (1996) has suggested in his useful survey of the literature on the revolution in East Germany that Opp and Ruehl were attempting to "save" rational choice by incorporating these *beliefs* into people's action, and also incorporating norms and altruistic motives into an individual's calculus. But, he maintains, "without these new assumptions, a rational choice theory of revolution is not only falsifiable, *it has been falsified*" (1996, p. 270; emphasis in original).

Obviously the relationship between repression, dissidence, and the likelihood of revolution is complicated. To sort them out, we need a model.

Thus, many of the assertions that have been discussed here appear inconsistent with each other, such as the idea that repression had a positive effect on protest in Iran while concessions by the regime also had a positive effect (Rasler 1996). The idea that increased repression makes micromobilization more likely ignores the fear the rest of the population may experience as a result of the increased repression. Indeed, it could be argued equally well that mobilization would occur as a response to *decreased* repression, because this is naturally interpreted as a sign that the state is weak.

More generally, there is a central question that is ignored in this literature, which analyzes protests without taking into account what kind of regime is being considered. Basic to the issue of whether mass mobilization is likely is whether the population perceives the state as weak or strong. Thus increased repression, *coupled with the perception that the state is weak*, might have the effect of causing mobilization, but *if the state is perceived as strong*, this effect is unlikely.

To develop these ideas further, we need models of the "strength" of the state and of the rational responses of individuals to changes in the level of repression, and how the two are related. I beg the indulgence of the reader as I briefly outline some aspects of my own model of dictatorship (Wintrobe 1990, 1998a), which provides a clear analytical approach to these issues. I first outline this model and then return to the issues discussed in these papers.

7.3 The Behavior of Dictators

7.3.1 The Dictator's Dilemma

The standard view of the difference between democracy and dictatorship in political science (e.g., Friedrich and Brzezinski 1965) is that dictators can use the tool of repression to stay in power. However, the use of repression creates a problem for the autocrat. This is the Dictator's Dilemma (Wintrobe 1990, 1998a) – the problem facing any ruler of knowing how much support he has among the general population, as well as among smaller groups with the power to depose him. The use of repression breeds fear on the part of a dictator's subjects, and this fear breeds a reluctance on the part of the citizenry to signal displeasure with the dictator's policies. This fear on their part in turn breeds fear *on the part of the dictator*, because, not knowing what the population thinks of his policies, he has no way of knowing what they are thinking and planning, and he suspects that what they are thinking and planning is his assassination. The problem is magnified the more the dictator rules by repression, that is, through fear. The more his repressive apparatus stifles dissent and criticism, the less he knows how much support he really has among the population. Consequently, all dictators seek loyal support as well. In general, the easiest way to overcome the problem of obtaining support is to "overpay" supporters, that is, to give them goods at subsidized prices, subsidize their wages or capital projects, and so on.

In sum, while there is always a class of people who are repressed under a dictatorship, there is also, in any successful dictatorship, another class – *the overpaid*. As far as the people in the middle are concerned, the sad thing is that they can side with either group. The general population may be repressed in that their civil liberties may be taken away, but other aspects of the regime may compensate for this as far as they are concerned.

However, *the use of repression doesn't mean that dictators aren't popular*. Indeed, it sometimes appears from the historical record that the more repressive they were, the more popular they became! All the evidence indicates that Hitler was very popular. Communism was *popular* at one time; when it became unpopular, the regimes fell. Reports in the newspapers suggest that Castro and Saddam Hussein were often popular with their peoples.[4]

That dictatorships use two instruments – repression and loyalty or popularity – to stay in power suggests a useful classification of regimes. Four types can be distinguished: tinpots (low repression and loyalty), tyrants (high repression, low loyalty), totalitarians (high levels of both), and timocrats (low repression, high loyalty). Thus, totalitarian regimes combine high repression with a capacity to generate loyalty. Under tyranny, the regime stays in power through high repression alone, and loyalty is low. A tinpot regime is low on both counts. And timocracy implies that loyalty is high even at low levels of repression. These four types or *images* have tended to recur over and over in the literature on dictatorship.[5]

The interrelationships between repression and loyalty, however, are complex. The main complication is that while loyalty and repression both use up resources (and in that sense are alternative "inputs" into the creation and maintenance of political power), their levels are not independent of one another: the level of repression affects the supply of loyalty. In order to sort out the various relationships involved, I use a simple model of the equilibrium levels of repression and political loyalty.

---

[4] See, for example, John Deutsch, "Options: Good and Bad Ways to Get Rid of Saddam," *New York Herald Tribune*, February 24, 1999, p. 8, on Saddam Hussein's popularity.

[5] For details, see Wintrobe (1998), chap. 1.

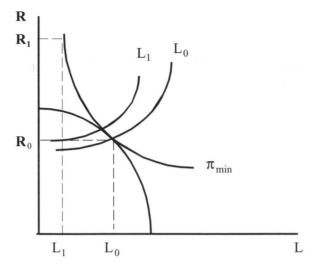

Figure 7.1. Optimal repression and loyalty under a tinpot dictatorship.

7.3.2 Equilibrium Loyalty and Repression

First, I assume that the relationship between the inputs of loyalty and repression and their output (power) can be represented by the production function

$$\pi = \pi(L, R). \tag{7.1}$$

The production function for power (π) is assumed to be "well behaved," that is, π_L, $\pi_R > 0$, $\pi_{LR} > 0$, π_{LL}, $\pi < 0$. These relationships imply diminishing returns in the production of power to the continued use of either instrument alone. This production function is represented by a set of iso-powerlines, where higher iso-powerlines denote higher power. One of these is shown in Figure 7.1.

Second, I assume that the amount of loyalty available to the dictator is, like any capital good, fixed in the short run but variable in the long run. On the other hand, the level of repression is variable in the short as well as in the long run.

Now let us assume the dictator is a tinpot. The objective function of a tinpot dictator is to maximize consumption only. In Figure 7.1, the tinpot dictator seeks no more power over the population than represented by the lowest iso-powerline in the figure, π_{min}. At any lower level of power, the tinpot will be deposed. Should the tinpot obtain more resources than required to attain $\pi = \pi_{min}$ (resource constraints will be discussed shortly), he does not spend them on repression or loyalty, but on his own personal consumption or that of his family. Because the tinpot always remains on π_{min} (as long as he stays in office), it immediately follows that there is an inverse relationship between the amounts of L and R demanded by the tinpot: an increase in R results in a fall in the level of L demanded.

Now consider the supply of loyalty to a tinpot dictator. I assume that while the tinpot may have a monopoly of formal political office, he does not monopolize political power in the country, but faces opposition in the sense of potential alternatives to his government. Citizens and interest groups may establish (possibly covert) ties with these potential opposition leaders. What happens to the supply of loyalty to the tinpot if the level of political repression is increased? To analyze a typical citizen's response, it is useful to assume that loyalty to the government or to opposition leaders is a capital asset that is accumulated in order to facilitate political exchanges. Each citizen may be viewed as accumulating an optimum "portfolio" of these assets, taking into account their expected rates of return and their risk. As in the standard theory of portfolio choice (see, e.g., Arrow 1971 for an exposition), a change in the riskiness or rate of return of any asset will lead the investor to change his desired portfolio, and this change may be decomposed into the usual income and substitution effects.

The increase in repression means that the risks of disloyalty to the citizenry are increased, and its expected rate of return diminished. Consequently the attractiveness of dealing with the opposition decreases, and the relative attractiveness to citizens and interest groups of exchanges with the dictator, or with his representatives, increases. This substitution effect implies that a typical citizen's loyalty – and hence the aggregate supply of loyalty to the dictator – will be positively related to the level of repression. However, there is an income effect that works in the opposite direction: an increase in repression either increases the likelihood for any individual that he will himself be the victim of a sanction or the size of the sanction imposed even if he is for the most part "loyal." This reduces the individual's wealth, and, so long as investments in political loyalty are a normal good, it reduces investments in political loyalty to the regime (as well as to the opposition). At low levels of repression, this effect will be small for most individuals. For example, if, as in the early years of Nazi Germany, repression is directed mainly at obvious opponents of the regime, and at Jews, the loyalty of these groups would obviously be reduced, but persons who fell into neither of these categories could reasonably assume that they would not be the victim of the regime's repressive policies. Consequently, so long as the level of repression is relatively low, it seems reasonable to assume that the substitution effect dominates the income effect for most citizens. If this is the case, the aggregate supply of political loyalty is initially positively related to the level of repression, as depicted by the L curves in Figure 7.1.

In a totalitarian regime on the other hand, I assume that the dictator (Hitler, Stalin, Mao) uses the instruments of repression and loyalty to maximize power over the population under his or her control. The classic historical examples are Nazi Germany and Stalin's Russia in the 1930s. This conception of totalitarian regimes is useful in that it places them at the opposite extreme from tinpots. Most real-world dictatorships undoubtedly lie somewhere in between.

From an economic point of view, the central question is not so much the maximand but the nature of the constraint on the totalitarian leader's maximization of power. Is there any other constraint on the totalitarian leader's maximization of power? So long as the aggregate supply of loyalty curve is upward sloping, the dictator can increase his or her power over the population by increasing the level of repression. Consequently if the supply of loyalty L were upward sloping throughout its range, the only possible equilibrium would be a corner solution involving the perfect repression of the population. However, theoretical considerations suggest that there is a conflict between perfect repression and the maximization of power over the population.

To see this, notice that an increase in repression induces opposing effects on the supply of loyalty to the regime. The substitution effect (the change in the amount of loyalty supplied as a result of a fall in the return or increase in the risk of disloyalty) always favors the regime. On the other hand, an increase in the probability of being discovered for having links to actual or potential opposition movements, or an increase in the sanction imposed for this offense, reduces expected wealth, and this reduction in wealth has an income effect that leads an individual to reduce all investments in political loyalty, including those with the regime. At low levels of repression, it is reasonable to assume that the income effect is small for most people so it is dominated by the substitution effect (as argued earlier in the context of our analysis of tinpot dictatorships). However, as the level of repression increases, the income effect gets larger. In addition, as the level of repression increases, the number and the size of groups that are opposed to the regime become smaller, and at very high levels of repression, opposition to the regime tends to get wiped out. Consequently, the substitution effect becomes vanishingly small as the level of repression becomes very large. Ultimately, then, a point must be reached where the income effect overwhelms the substitution effect for most citizens, causing the aggregate supply of loyalty to the regime to bend backward (not depicted in Figure 7.1).

It follows that to calculate the effects of increased repression on the population, it is crucial to know what type of regime we are dealing with, that is, *whether repression is high or low to begin with.* To look at the Iranian revolution, it seems reasonable to suppose that we are dealing with a tinpot dictator (the shah). Among the indicators of this we may consider that repression was generally low, there was no mass party, and the main purpose of the regime seemed to be to finance the life-style of the shah and his family (see the description in Arjomand 1986 and elsewhere).

Suppose then that there is some exogenous event that reduces the supply of loyalty on the part of the population, which occurred as the economic performance of the regime had deteriorated throughout the 1970s.[6] If the regime is a tinpot, it is in danger of collapsing, as a fall in loyalty will reduce power below the minimum level of power required to stay in office. The shah's optimal response to the deterioration of economic conditions and the emergence of protest was therefore to raise repression in order to stay in office. Thus repression should immediately have been raised to R_1 in Figure 7.1.

In the short run, this is not cost minimizing. In the long run, however, the supply of loyalty will *expand* (along the supply of loyalty curve L_1) and the regime can relax repression and still remain in office. So, as long as the regime is a tinpot, *the optimal response to a fall in loyalty is to expand repression in the short run.*

7.3.3 The East German and Iranian Revolutions

Consequently, the model does not support the analyses of Rasler (1996) and others that the result of increased repression will simply cause a micromobilization of protest and result in regime downfall. Indeed, it is not clear at all that repression did increase, as the measures suggested by Rasler are ambiguous, and even Rasler regards the policies of the regime as at best inconsistent. Others have suggested that, on balance, the shah relaxed repression over this period (Arjomand 1986), and a number of events that occurred and are discussed by Rasler are consistent with this interpretation. Thus, mobilization occurred because the regime appeared weak, and its inconsistent policies on repression in response to the various crises over the period (admirably analyzed by Rasler) reinforced this interpretation.

---

[6] For more details, see Wintrobe (1998), chap. 3.

There is also a general theoretical point to be made. As long as repression is low to begin with, it is difficult to argue that an increase in repression will lower power by so much that it will destroy the regime. This implies that the supply of loyalty is backward bending (negatively sloped) even at low levels of repression. But if that were generally the case, no dictatorship could survive for very long. As soon as repression was raised sufficiently, micromobilization responses implying a fall in loyalty (increase in dissidence) would occur, and the regime would collapse. But there have been many stable and long-lasting dictatorships in the real world.

What about a totalitarian leader? In general, the optimum response to a fall in loyalty here is, from the point of view of *long-run power maximization*, to relax repression.[7] The totalitarian leader is in no immediate danger of being deposed, because power is normally more than sufficient to stay in office. To illustrate, repression had indeed been steadily relaxed in Eastern Europe in response to the collapse in the functioning of the bureaucratic economy[8] and deteriorating economic conditions throughout the 1970s and 1980s without precipitating a revolution.[9]

However, *this analysis ignores the possibility of cascades or bandwagon effects in response to critical events that might be able to bring even a totalitarian dictator down*.[10] Hence I believe that the comments of Przeworski are essentially correct: "The entire event was one single snowball" (quoted in Thompson 1996, p. 273). After the Hungarian regime dismantled its border controls, between June and September 1989, the rebellion in East Germany was, as Thompson puts it, a "'prison revolt' once the Hungarians had organized a huge 'jail break'" (1996, p. 274). So the East German protest was essentially one against a state that had already been fatally weakened, and its collapse part of a chain of collapses. Looked at in that light, there need be nothing irrational about individual participation in the East German demonstrations

---

[7] See Wintrobe (1990, or 1998a, chaps. 3 and 10).

[8] Wintrobe (1998a), chap. 10.

[9] Wintrobe (1998a), chap. 9.

[10] The different responses of the Chinese and the Russian governments are analyzed in my 1998 book, but without reference to the possibility of cascades or bandwagon effects. When this possibility is taken into account, the Chinese response in Tienamen Square of a sudden, sharp increase in repression and subsequent decentralization of power was the correct one, from the point of view of short-run and long-run survival in office. Thus the main change that the possibility of bandwagon effects suggests for my model is that even totalitarians might respond to a short-run fall in loyalty by raising repression (while relaxing it in the long run). The analysis of tinpots is unchanged, and indeed, the conclusion I drew that survival dictates an *increase* in repression is strengthened by the inclusion of the possibility of micromobilization.

in Leipzig. The probability of success was high, because the regime was no longer capable of survival in the long run. Its ultimate collapse was entirely foreseeable by that point, and revolution was only necessary because neither the regime nor the leaders of the various reform movements were willing to recognize that fact and negotiate its demise. And the response of the East German police of not shooting the demonstrators was not, in my view, a mystery or an illustration of an improper totalitarian response to a fall in loyalty, but simple acquiescence in the inevitable collapse of the regime.[11] After all, if the regime did collapse subsequently, what actions could the new, postrevolution regime be expected to take against a police force that did respond in this manner?

To analyze revolutions properly, therefore, it is best to look first at the condition of the state and not at the incentives of individuals within an abstract state. To do this, we need to look at the full model of dictatorship and not at the partial aspect of it depicted in Figure 7.1.

7.3.4 Equilibrium Power and Budget

To proceed, we need to note that Figure 7.1 rests on a simplification. It shows the equilibrium levels of loyalty and repression for a fixed level of the price of loyalty P_L. However, the price of loyalty, P_L, is a variable under the dictator's control. An increase in P_L would bring forth a larger supply of loyalty, L, for any given level of R, that is, it would shift L to the right (not shown).

A second simplification is that the tinpot ruler also represents the special or "corner" solution where the sole aim is to maximize consumption. On the other hand, the leaders of tyrannies and totalitarian regimes represent the opposite extreme of dictators who maximize power.

To generalize the approach, assume first that all dictators have the same utility function, where the arguments are consumption (C) and power (π).

$$U = U(\pi, C). \tag{7.2}$$

Power may be desired either for its own sake, or because dictators wish to impose their ideas of the common good on society.

Combining this utility function with a constraint that shows how money can be converted into power and power into money provides an explanation of the limits to a dictator's power.

---

[11] Nor were the Russian troops signaling any support for a repressive action, as has been pointed out to me by Ekkart Zimmermann.

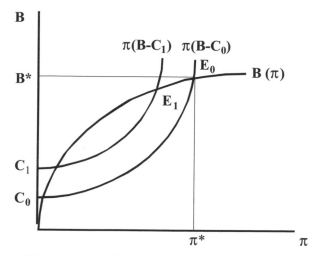

Figure 7.2. Equilibrium power and budget and how they respond to increased consumption by the dictator.

More precisely, the dictator is constrained in two ways. The first constraint – the costs of accumulating power – is governed by the political institutions of the regime, and the second – the capacity to use his power to increase revenue – by the dictator's economy. These constraints are combined in equation

$$B(\pi) = P_\pi \pi(B - C) + C. \tag{7.3}$$

The left-hand side of the constraint in equation 7.3 shows the dictator's budget B as a function of power (π), that is, it shows how the dictator's power may be used (through taxation, regulation, or the provision of public goods) to obtain budgetary resources. The right-hand side shows how the funds are "spent": either on consumption, C, or on accumulating power π via the money-to-power relation $\pi(B - C)$, with each unit of π multiplied by P_π – the "price" of power in terms of money.

These constraints are illustrated in Figures 7.2 and 7.3. In both figures, there is a positive relationship between the resources spent on accumulating power, $(B - C)$, and the level of power (π). This relationship is displayed in Figure 7.2 as the $\pi(B - C)$ curve. This curve in effect shows how the dictator can convert *money* into *power*.

The upward-sloping $\pi(B - C)$ curve in Figure 7.2 thus implies a positive relationship between the amount of money spent accumulating π (the dictator's *total* budget B, minus expenditures on C), and the level of π obtained, with "diminishing returns" to these expenditures.

Of course, diminishing returns to the accumulation of loyalty implies that successive increases in P_L will increase L by less and less. But so long as there is no limit to the dictator's capacity to finance the accumulation of loyalty, there is no obvious limit to the dictator's power, loyalty, or level of repression. In brief, if there is no limit to his resources, there is no limit to his power, because resources can always be transformed into power by the process we have just outlined. Is there any limit to the dictator's resources? It would be arbitrary to specify that the dictator's power is limited by a revenue-maximizing tax. For so long as the dictator has sufficient power, he can raise more funds by imposing new tax bases and by finding other ways to raise money. In short, if there is no limit to his power, there is no limit to his resources either.

It follows that the limits to budgetary resources and to power must be simultaneously determined. We now turn to the dictator's economy, as summarized by the B(π) curve in Figure 7.2. This curve describes the relationship between the exercise of political power, and its consequences for the dictator's budget, that is, the conversion, in effect, of *power* into *money*. Although there are diverse forms of the economy under dictatorship, all of them suggest that this curve, too, displays diminishing (and sometimes negative) returns. The latter case is shown in Figure 7.3

In general, then, the power-to-money curve B(π) may be either positively or negatively sloped. It seems reasonable to assume that, initially, it must be positively sloped: starting from very low (or zero) levels of power, the provision of basic public infrastructure or the imposition of simple taxes at low rates must raise revenue. Beyond this, however, there is little to be said at a general level.

No matter what the slope of B(π), however, equilibrium in Figure 7.2 is at the intersection of the B(π) and π(B $-$ C) curves, or at E_0, implying a (total) budget of B^*, and power equal to π^*.[12]

Note that this equilibrium depends on the dictator's consumption C; if the ruler were willing to reduce this below C_0, for example, the money-into-power curve π(B $-$ C) would shift to the right, implying an equilibrium at the intersection of this new curve with B(π). There is obviously a limit to the extent to which any ruler is willing to reduce consumption. But the dependency of π^* on B^* and on C^* just underlines the fact that, in general,

---

[12] See Wintrobe (1998a), chap. 5, for a proof.

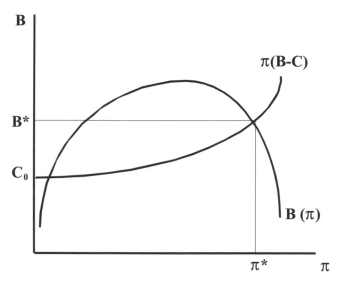

Figure 7.3. Equilibrium power and budget when power decreases budget at the margin.

Figure 7.2 must be considered along with the dictator's utility function. In general, the ruler will choose a combination of C and π, depending on his preferences for the two. So Figure 7.1 and Figure 7.2 or 7.3, combined with the dictator's utility function (equation 7.2) jointly determine the dictator's optimal levels of R^*, L^*, C^*, B^*, and π^*.[13]

7.4 Revolution

To apply this analysis to the problem of revolution against a dictatorship is simple. To begin, note first that, in equilibrium, so long as $\pi > \pi_{min}$, the dictatorship has enough power to remain in office and there is no revolution. The dictator can choose a system of penalties for disobedience of various laws that deter revolutionary action. Thus, penalties will typically be higher for organizing than for participating in revolutionary acts. At the same time, the dictator needs loyalty, as discussed previously. Every "successful" dictatorship solves these problems in a particular way, that is, by choosing a particular mechanism that rewards supporters and another one that punishes disloyalty (sometimes the same system fulfills both functions). In particular, the ruler will want to put in place a mechanism that

---

[13] The first-order conditions for a solution, along with a more comprehensive exposition of the model, can be found in Wintrobe (1998a), chaps. 3 and 5.

"overpays" the army and other forces charged with the task of maintaining order, and he or she may also wish to introduce checks such as competing security systems so that each one acts as a check on the other, as is commonly done in most successful dictatorships. For the rest of the population, the cost-minimizing combination of loyalty and repression will be chosen, but in general the ruler must bear in mind that "winning hearts and minds" will better ensure long-term survival.

However, a change can occur that reduces the effectiveness of the reward or punishment mechanisms. If the change involves a deterioration in the dictator's capacity to accumulate power or to raise resources, this means that the equilibrium budget and power fall. For example, a fall in the capacity to accumulate power lowers the equilibrium budget from B^* to B_1 and equilibrium power from π^* to π_1 in Figure 7.2. If budget and power fall far enough, the system no longer has sufficient power to stay in office, that is, there is a revolution. Such a revolution is "rational" in the sense that the dictatorship no longer has the capacity to defend itself. Thus the essential reason for *collectively* rational revolution is that a change or a series of changes occurs that weakens the state. As we saw earlier, the *leadership* of a revolutionary groups is not difficult to explain, because many of the benefits to leading a successful revolution are purely private. Of course, leading a revolutionary movement can be risky.[14] In turn, the weaker the state becomes, the smaller this risk, and the more that any *individual* potential *follower* or dissident will come to believe that successful revolution is possible. Hence the free-rider problem at the individual level also tends to be solved, because the essential condition for rational participation in rebellion is more likely to be fulfilled when the probability of successful revolution increases. This is the basic (but, as we shall see, not the only) flaw in the traditional emphasis on the free-rider problem.

The fundamental proposition, then, is that the most important predictor of revolutions is the weakness of the state. Goldstone et al. (2004) provides some evidence that supports this proposition. His paper, "It's All about State Structure: New Findings on Revolutionary Origins from Global Data," draws on new research by the State Failure Task Force, which developed a comprehensive list of "state failures," including revolutions but also other severe

---

[14] Kuran (1995) argues that the onset of revolution is unknowable, as people hide their preferences when they are opposed to the regime. From the point of view of the argument of the text, this means that the risks of leading a revolution when it is guessed that the state is weak are amplified. But we would still expect to see entrepreneurship in revolutionary activity when the state is thought to be weak.

political crises from 1955 to 2001. Goldstone et al. found that, surprisingly, factors such as high inflation, excessive government debts, poor economic performance, breakdowns in civil-military relations, and the explosion of ethnic rivalries did not underlie state failures. Rather, "the character of a country's political institutions are the single most important factor shaping the relative risk of state failure" (Goldstone et al. 2004, p. 20). In particular, weakness of the country's political institutions, as measured by its classification as an autocracy with some political competition, weak full democracy, or weak partial democracy, are associated with the greatest increase in relative risk.

7.5 An Illustration: The French Revolution

To illustrate the argument, let us look at the great French Revolution. In his *History of Government*, Samuel Finer refers to the French Revolution as "the most important single event in the history of government" (Finer 1997, p. 1517). He analyzes the origins of the revolution by stressing that three crises occurred simultaneously in France in the years 1787–1789:

1. The king could no longer get loans and the government was "desperate" for new money.
2. There was a constitutional crisis, with the *parlements* seeking to rein in the king, in which they were supported at this stage by the people, who perceived the king's rule as despotic.
3. There was a "violent" economic crisis, with the price of bread soaring at the same time as hundreds of textile workers were being thrown out of employment (Finer 1997, p. 1525). Thus, as Sutherland (2003, p. 41) also emphasizes, "the constitutional crisis coincided with economic calamity."

The first factor has been analyzed by North and Weingast (1989) in their account of the Glorious Revolution in England and was discussed briefly in the preceding chapter. The Glorious Revolution made it possible for the English king to obtain loans as the English parliament controlled the purse and therefore could make the king's promise to repay credible. No such revolution had occurred in France. One interpretation of this "Irony of Absolutism" is that the fewer constraints on the king's power, the less power he may actually have. Interpreted this way, their analysis can be applied to the French monarchy with the help of my Figure 7.4. In order to get loans, it was necessary for the king to devolve power onto an institution with the capacity to enforce repayment, that is, to make the king's promise to repay

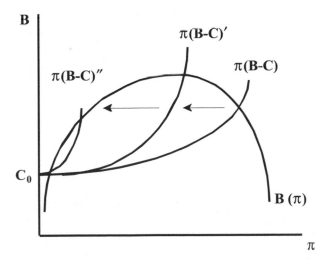

Figure 7.4. The French Revolution.

credible. So the king needed to give up power in order to raise resources, that is, he was on the downward-sloping part of the $B(\pi)$ curve in Figure 7.4 and needed to move up along it to sacrifice power for revenue. This was the reason for the calling of the Estates General in 1788. In brief, the king needed to give up power to get money. This had already been done in the past with the sale of offices (Sutherland 2003, p. 7), but the regime seemed to teeter at the edge of bankruptcy nevertheless by the late 1780s.

The third factor – the rise in the price of bread – can be analyzed in a similar fashion. At that time, bread made up more than 75 percent of the typical person's diet, and a rise in its price could mean starvation. In 1789 this figure had risen to 88 percent for the typical Parisian working man (Sutherland 2003, p. 51). The willingness on the part of the urban mobs and the people in the countryside to demonstrate and to riot in order to restore price controls on bread whenever these were lifted, and the success of these strategies on previous occasions, are well documented (see, e.g., Finer 1997; Sutherland 2003; or Lewis 2000). Consequently, the loyalty of the general population can be thought of as inversely related to the price of bread.

Thus a rise in the price of bread means a leftward shift in the supply of loyalty and therefore a rise in the price of loyalty. This in turn implies a leftward shift in the $\pi(B - C)$ curve, further reducing equilibrium power (and budget, if $B(\pi)$ is upward sloping).

To these three crises we should add a number of other things that amplified the seriousness of the crises. The first is the well-documented incompetence of the king. Finer's (1997, p. 1520) judgment is typical: "The miserable Louis XVI, who acceded in 1774, made the indolent Louis XV looks like a thunderer from heaven: and it is owing to Louis XVI, personally, that the disaffection which unquestionably existed all over France between 1787 and 1789 turned into full blooded revolution."

Other factors in the revolution included the dubious loyalty of the troops (Sutherland 2003, pp. 56–61), some of whom were attracted by revolutionary ideas, and the fact that the war (with Austria and then Prussia) was going badly in 1792 (Finer 1997, p. 1527). And there was obviously considerable resentment and anger in the population toward the Old Regime and its overpaid clients, the church and the nobility.

Less obviously, the communication problems of the regime, amply documented in histories of the revolution, had the effect of amplifying the Dictator's Dilemma. To illustrate, the budget crisis was commonly interpreted by the population as due to the profligacy of the regime. This problem was compounded by the fact that its public finances were a mystery; the fiscal system "was both a mystery and accountable to no one. Indeed the government itself had no idea what its resources or expenditures were" (Sutherland 2003, p. 18). Thus

One of the resentments of the people was how much the court cost. No matter that most of its expenditures were entirely routine: meager sums conferred on widows of military officers and on the relatives of other modest former state servants. No matter that the court budget was so small relative to overall expenditures. *No one knew this at the time.* There were too many spectacular examples of the Crown underwriting the debts of favourites; too many examples of far too much extravagant spending for the acquisition or construction of new chateaux like St Cloud and the Bagatelle for the public to forgive the lush expenditures. After all, the Parlement of Paris itself told the public, in documents that could not be censored, that the source of the public debt was extravagant public spending. (Sutherland 2003, p. 11; emphasis added)

Diagrammatically, larger consumption by the king (C) would shift the $\pi(B - C)$ curve upward from its origin at a point like C_0 to a point like C_1 (not shown in Figure 7.4, but see Figure 7.2). The effect is the same as that of a rise in the price of bread: equilibrium power falls, and equilibrium budget falls if $B(\pi)$ is upward sloping. Even if the king's consumption is not C_1 but C_0, if the population thinks it is C_1, the effect on the *perceived* power of the regime, which is crucial to the revolutionary calculus, is the same.

Other problems amplified the Dictator's Dilemma:

Fantastic rumours were inherent in Old Regime political culture. Partly because communication networks were so primitive and partly because no one in the government thought they had any consistent responsibility to explain themselves to the public, the most amazing urban legends could take on a vivacious life. Thus in the 1740's the rumour went round that the government intended to deport all street urchins to New France.... Thus, people feared the aristocracy and clergy would stop at nothing to retain their privileges. (Sutherland 2003, p. 54)

Later it is suggested that one of the most important factors explaining the peasant rebellion in 1789 was the visit of Louis XVI to Paris after the fall of the Bastille. This was designed to assuage opinion in Paris, "but almost everywhere in the provinces, the King's journey was taken to be an endorsement of popular rebellion. Country people knew that the Third Estate had achieved a great victory and assumed they had the King's sanction to take matters into their own hands.... Most alarming because it was so irrational was the Great Fear, a vast panic which spread over the entire country... between 20 July and 6 August" (Sutherland 2003, pp. 66, 68).

Another important consideration was the multiple directions in which the country headed at various times over the revolutionary years – first right (constitutional monarchy), then far left (the Committee of Public Safety), then middle (the Directory)[15] – as one or another of the different groups involved gained the upper hand.

In all these ways, the communication problems of the regime amplified the Dictator's Dilemma and not only reduced the loyalty of the public but caused the people to participate in revolutionary action as much out of fear about what was going on as dislike of the Old Regime.

In brief, the mechanisms that the regime had used to survive – the privileges of the nobility and the church, price controls on bread to contain the urban mob, and the lack of restrictions on the freedom and secrecy of the crown – had come to haunt it. The king himself remained safe only because it was popularly believed that he supported the revolution. (Sutherland 2003, p. 116). After the flight to Varennes, this idea could no longer be supported, paving the way for the downfall of the monarchy itself (Sutherland 2003, pp. 116, 148–152).

In addition, from standard accounts such as Sutherland's or Perrie's, however, one thing is undeniable; protests, outbreaks of insurrection, rebellions, riots, and every imaginable form of collective action were commonplace, and largely spontaneous, not only in the years leading up to 1789 but from 1789 to 1792 as well. The free-rider problem is not a good starting point for explaining the course of events leading up to or during the French Revolution. On the contrary, *individual* revolutionary (or counterrevolutionary!)

---

[15] Finer (1997), p. 1527.

action may be entirely rational under the circumstances mentioned: the weakness and incompetence of the king, the fact that the regime was essentially financially bankrupt, its vast communication problems, the weak hold of the regime on the loyalty of its troops, the economic and constitutional crisis, and the multiple directions and contradictory programs of the various groups.

A better starting point is the weakness of the state at that time. In Figure 7.4, therefore, the French Revolution may be interpreted as follows. All parties (including the king) wished to move to a new constitution that would put limits on the king's power, that is, to move the $\pi(B - C)$ curve back along the downward-sloping portion of $B(\pi)$ to $\pi(B - C)'$ in Figure 7.4. By giving up power, the king hoped to gain revenue in the same way that the English king had. However, a bandwagon effect developed, possibly due to the constitutional crisis and the economic crisis, amplified by the uncertainties about which direction the regime was moving, and opposition to the regime snowballed. As a result, the $\pi(B-C)$ curve shifted further and further left, reducing both power *and* revenue as it moved along the upward-sloping part of $B(\pi)$ to $\pi(B - C)'$ in Figure 7.4 until the regime collapsed.

7.6 The Rationality of Replacing the Old Order: The Superiority of Democracy

How can we judge whether revolutions produce a "better" society? If a revolution does not, then no matter how "rational" it may be to get rid of the old regime, the whole process cannot be said to be collectively rational, and many revolutions – Cambodia is one example that comes immediately to mind – cannot be said to be rational, at least ex post.

One definition of an improvement is the standard economic compensation test that the gainers could have compensated the losers as a result of the revolution. However, perhaps more than any other political event, revolution involves big winners and big losers. Thus it is even more difficult than usual to apply the standard compensation test criteria. Could the "winners" in the French, Russian, or Nazi revolutions have compensated the losers? To put it starkly, because many of the losers in any of these revolutions were dead as a result of the revolution, the standard criterion would appear to be a bit more difficult (but not impossible!) to apply than usual.

Of course, there are other criteria. One of these is related to the criterion for judging efficient laws in the economics of law. A typical example of an efficient law is the law involving automobile accidents that liability for an accident falls upon the party driving the vehicle that hits another car from behind. This law would obviously appear to be efficient compared with a law that specified that the party hit from behind is liable. If the second law were in force, drivers would spend much of their time gazing in the rear view mirror, rather than at the road in front of them, and the number of accidents might be expected to increase.

The general principle is that liability should be placed on the party who can avoid the damaging interaction at least cost, no matter who may be said to "cause" the accident in some sense. Laws that satisfy this criterion are said to be *efficient* laws. Thus in Coase's (1960) famous example of a railway train that emits sparks and destroys a farmer's crops, liability should nevertheless be placed on the farmer if it is easier for him to relocate than the railroad, even though, obviously, it is the railroad that is "causing" the damages. Thus an *efficient* revolution would be one that replaced inefficient laws with efficient ones in this sense. The French Revolution, governed in part by the Goddess of Reason, attempted to reorganize society on the principle of efficiency (although economic efficiency in the modern sense may not be what the revolutionaries had in mind): hence the abolition of the entire system of the Old Regime and the institution of the ten-day week, the revolutionary calendar, and, most famously, the declaration of the Rights of Man. Some (Tocqueville 1998; Furet 1981) have suggested that the abolition of all the privileges of the old order led directly to the Terror.[16]

Yet another obvious criterion for judging successful revolutions is equality, and undoubtedly one of the great aims of the French and Russian revolutions was to improve equality. This suggests another test of rationality, that the new regime involves more equality than the old. Obviously, these criteria are not identical and conflict in many places. Indeed, some have argued that the fact that the *social question* attained such a central role in the French revolution (which it did not in the American one) is what caused it to turn extreme. This argument is discussed in the next section.

However, there is one simple criterion that might command wide agreement: a revolution that results in more democracy represents an improvement. The reason is simply that democracy gives, if not to all of the people, to more of the people than is typical of nondemocratic systems control over their government. The fundamental requirements of democracy are human rights and genuinely competitive elections. So if a majority does not like

---

[16] However, a more natural interpretation of what happened is that it was the second principle embedded in the Rights of Man, that of the General Will, that was intellectually related to the ideology of the Terror. That is, it was Rousseau, not Voltaire, whose ideas were most amenable to the Terror. This point is discussed further in the next section.

the government, the people can throw it out. On the other hand, if the result of revolution is dictatorship, and the dictatorship does not turn out to be beneficial to the people in the way it might have been thought (e.g., by Marx, Blanqui, Lenin, Pol Pot, and others), then the problem is that the only way to get rid of the new regime is via another revolution, involving much higher "transactions" costs. The advantage of democracy is that it provides a means whereby, if there are efficient laws, more equality, economic policies that pass the compensation test, or any other aspects of a "good" society that are thought desirable, the electorate can always put into power at low cost (compared with any other system of government) a government that promises to implement these policies.[17] Thus revolutions that replace dictatorships with democracies might be termed collectively "rational." This is perhaps the common sense behind Fukuyama's (1992) oft-cited "End of History" argument. Democracy, in some sense, gives the people, or at least more of the people than any other system we know of, control over their own history. Any other system does not.

7.7 Dynamics of Revolution and Extremism

One problem with the argument of the preceding section is that a revolution can promise democracy, but bandwagon effects in the dynamics of revolution mean that anything can happen, including the advent of a more repressive dictatorship. The French Revolution is a good illustration of this point. The initial democratic impulse of the revolution was swept away by the Jacobin Terror and ultimately gave way to the regime of Napoleon Bonaparte. Why did the revolution turn extreme in this way? The question has preoccupied historians for generations. While no definitive answer will be suggested here, it may be worthwhile to look at some of the more famous lines of thought on this question culled from the extensive literature on the French Revolution in the light of modern rational choice theory and group processes discussed in this book. The arguments also illustrate dynamics that are inherent in any revolutionary situation.

7.7.1 Dynamic of the Overthrow of the Ancient Regime
(Tocqueville, Furet)

The French Revolution of 1789 overturned everything except the monarchy. But Tocqueville argued that the French Revolution did not so much mark the

---

[17] This point about democracy is elaborated in Wintrobe (2003).

overthrow of the Ancient Regime as its culmination. By abolishing feudal-ism, guilds, economic regulation, and noble privilege, the French Revolution continued trends that began under the absolute monarchy. Once the noble privileges and institutions were gone, nothing stood between the individual and the all-encompassing power of the state. Francois Furet (1981), follow-ing Tocqueville (1998), argued that these processes in which the intermedi-ate bonds between the citizen and the state were torn away paved the way for the further growth of the state and for more repression. As Furet put it, it "destroyed all the *corps* root and branch in order to leave only individuals confronting the state in their role of citizens" (Furet 1997, p. 82).

The revolution proclaimed the Declaration of the Rights of Man, but these were not enforceable by an independent judiciary (as in the American Constitution). And the Rights of Man contained the principle of the General Will, and there was no provision that this could not override the Rights. Thus, as Finer (1997, p. 1541) put it,

[The Declaration] contains an inherent and lethal contradiction. It states that all authority flows from the general will, but it also declares that man possesses natural and imprescriptable rights, and the two are *not compatible*. That is made more than abundantly clear by the actions of the French revolutionaries themselves; the confiscation of the Church properties, the enforced translation of priests into civil servants, the suspension of all judicial safeguards during the Terror, the procedures used in the judicial murder of Louis XVI – all of these were justified on the grounds that all activities emanated from the general will and that the Assembly embodied it. (emphasis in original)

In brief, the revolution left people without protection from the actions of the state. As Hannah Arendt (1963, pp. 107–108) put it, the revolution tore away the *persona* – the protective mask of a legal personality. The result was a steady reduction in the rights of opponents to the regime as the revolution felt more threatened and the Jacobins took power. Indeed, beginning with the trial of Danton, defense was denied legal counsel (Lucas 1996).

The result was that the overthrow of the Ancient Regime essentially turned into a dynamic of fear: fear that other groups would take power, including most of all the fear of an aristocratic counterrevolution. These fears were bred by competition in revolutionary and counterrevolutionary action. The different contending forces were shown by the multiple directions in which the country headed at various times over the revolutionary years – first right (constitutional monarchy), then far left (the Committee of Public Safety, then middle (the Directory)[18] – as one or another of the different

---

[18] Finer (1997), p. 1527.

groups involved gained the upper hand. These fears were amplified by the communication problems of the regime, discussed in section 7.5, that caused people to participate in revolutionary action as much out of fear about what was going to or could happen as dislike of the Old Regime.

As Tocqueville and Furet argued, in the end the result was more absolutism, and the expansion of the state.[19] This fear of what can happen when the old hierarchy is overturned is a common theme in writings on the French Revolution.[20]

In modern terms, the argument about the effects of the destruction of intermediary bodies is similar to the thesis that "civil society" or "social capital" is what prevents exploitation of the citizen by the state (as discussed by Putnam 2000 and elsewhere, as mentioned in Chapter 2). The intermediary bodies act to protect citizens from the state, and their destruction just makes way for more state repression. However, this argument may not be generally valid, as suggested in our discussion of social capital in Chapter 2. To take the example of the Nazi rise to power discussed there, Weimar Germany was rife with intermediary bodies or social capital, and it was these groups themselves who joined the Nazi party as groups, thus facilitating the rise of the Nazi state rather than slowing it down. So the existence of intermediary bodies or social capital or civil society may simply facilitate the rise of a new repressive apparatus rather than protect the individual from it.

This does not necessarily mean that Tocqueville and Furet were wrong about the French Revolution. But it does suggest at least that the role of intermediary bodies is more complex than they suggested. And if they are not wrong about the French Revolution, the difference between the cases must be explained. One possibility, suggested to me by Pierre Salmon,[21] is that in fact Hitler's and Mussolini's dictatorships were not that repressive with regard to the people belonging to the intermediate groups (the military, the religious, the industrialists, etc.) as they were in other respects. The members of these groups remained thus in a sense protected by the fact that the groups were not destroyed. This could mean that Tocqueville and Furet were right after all. But this implies that in a sense Hitler's and Mussolini's regimes were milder than the first French republic or the Communist regimes, which is a bit hard to swallow (even though it is true that the upheaval in the army and the church was much more radical under the French Revolution and the Communist regimes than under Hitler or Mussolini).

[19] Skopcol (1974) contains a modern version of this thesis.
[20] See, for example, the essays in Best (1988).
[21] This argument was suggested to me in correspondence by Pierre Salmon.

7.7.2 Dynamics of Solidarity

An alternative dynamic of revolution and the turn toward extremism that fits naturally into the themes of this book might be referred to as a "dynamic of solidarity." The idea is simple: in the course of many successful revolutions, including the French Revolution, a bandwagon effect takes place as citizens unite against the common enemy of the old order. However, once the revolution succeeds, and the common enemy is destroyed, so is this basis for solidarity. With the old enemy gone, who or what is to replace it if solidarity is to be maintained? Now, one of the central inspirations of the revolution was Rousseau, who firmly believed that solidarity was only produced by an external enemy. Indeed, his own solution to the vexatious problem of the formation of the General Will, discussed in Chapter 2, was that the external enemy existed *within each person*, that is, in his particular interest, and individuals had to overcome that.

However, there are other ways to produce solidarity, as we have seen in Chapters 2, 5, and 6. Nations also have distinctive methods for creating solidarity, as we will discuss further in Chapter 9. To anticipate that discussion, some examples of these are common welfare programs that protect everyone against poverty, or barriers to entry (immigration), or common belief, as well as the discovery of new external (or internal) enemies. Thus the destruction of the old order need not be accompanied by the search for new enemies if these alternative bases for solidarity could be substituted for the old enemy. However, the first (welfare) was probably impossible in the economic conditions at the time of the French Revolution. Yet relief from poverty is what the people wanted. As Lewis (2000, p. 95) writes," The 'social question' lies at the heart of all modern revolutions, and it first became central to the process of a revolution in France between 1791 and 1792." But though the people demanded relief from poverty, they didn't get it,[22] and the result was the substitution of the other mechanisms along the lines we have discussed: new common beliefs (the principle [Goddess] of Reason) and barriers to entry and exit (nationalism as a cornerstone

---

[22] Arendt (1963) also argues that there was what could be called a "dynamics of Misery" or "dynamics of Rage": When the people are reduced to or have nothing, they only want one thing – bread – and therefore are really one being – *UNE*. Thus poverty or Misery produces one will. However, the argument that poverty produced a single will would seem to be false. As Schumpeter (1950) pointed out, even if everyone agrees on the same goal, they can disagree on the means to get it. Thus one cannot define the General Will even when everyone has the same goal. And it is not obvious from the standpoint of contemporary economic theory that price controls on bread were indeed the correct solution to the problem of the high price of bread.

of postrevolutionary politics). But in addition there did arise the search for enemies, within and without, including the succession of revolutionary wars against the enemies of the new French state and the extremism of the Terror.

This mechanism produced a further, and related, dynamic, which can also be gleaned from Arendt's (1963) essays, and which might be termed the "dynamic of unmasking hypocrisy." It begins with the idea that the revolutionaries themselves were not poor, so in being on the side of the poor they were acting out of compassion (solidarity with the poor), not self-interest. From this point of view, it becomes obvious why hypocrisy became the central vice of the French Revolution. Thus in the end the king was executed not as a tyrant but as a traitor (he "lied to the People"). The dynamic arises for a simple reason: *the search for hypocrisy never ends.* The problem is that "patriotism was a thing of the heart," as Robespierre said (quoted in Arendt 1963, p. 97) and the heart is always full of secrets (to some extent everyone is a hypocrite). As Arendt (1963, p. 110) puts it, "Once the masses found that a constitution was not a panacea for poverty, they turned against the Constituent Assembly as they had turned on the Court of Louis XVI, and they saw in the deliberation of the delegates no less a play of make believe, hypocrisy and bad faith than in the cabals of the monarch. . . . Thus after hypocrisy had been unmasked and suffering been exposed, it was rage and not virtue that appeared."

Nevertheless, out of the country's turmoil came a degree of national solidarity and military strength that enabled France to become "the colossus of the continent" with the victories of Napoleon some years later (Best 1988, p. 105). But this was perhaps not quite what the original revolutionaries had intended.

7.8 Conclusion

This chapter began by asking if a rational choice explanation of revolution is possible and by noting the literature on revolution developed mainly by sociologists with reference to the East German, Iranian, and other contemporary revolutions from this point of view. I then put forth a new approach, which starts by distinguishing between individual and collective rationality. In analyzing revolutions (as distinct from riots, rebellions, or other forms of collective action), I argued that the second type is logically prior to the first, that is, one cannot look at the incentives facing an individual potential leader or follower of a revolutionary movement without considering first what type of state is being faced and whether it is strong or weak. In this chapter, I considered revolutions against dictatorship only, using my model of dictatorship developed previously. The basic condition under which a rational revolution can occur is if the state has been weakened, so that the mechanisms that have sustained the ruler in office no longer function effectively. More precisely, a "weak" regime is one that lacks the power and the revenue to defend itself against insurrection. If the state is weak, then leadership of revolutionary movements will tend to occur spontaneously. And the leader will be more able to successfully stoke resentment against the regime's repression and at its clients ("the overpaid") under these conditions.

In turn, the weakness of the state and the leadership to take action against it tend to make individual participation in revolutionary activity rational, as these are the basic conditions for a bandwagon effect to take place. The likelihood of individual participation in mass actions is further enhanced if the shape of the outcome of a successful revolution is particularly unclear – that is, the "public good" that would result may take various forms, depending on which groups obtain power in the new regime. So individuals who do not participate take the risk that the revolution may occur, but the outcome will favor other groups and not theirs.

These conditions are magnified if the communications problems of the regime, always present in any dictatorship because of the Dictator's Dilemma, are particularly serious. All of these arguments are, I believe, nicely illustrated by the French Revolution.

I then asked if revolution could be collectively rational, not only in the sense that it occurs because the previous state's ability to function had been severely impaired, but in the sense that the regime that replaces it is expected to represent an improvement. I considered various criteria here – economic compensation tests, the efficiency of law, and more equality – and suggested that one criterion may be adequate: that the revolution is expected to result in more democracy. Whether the French Revolution itself meets this test – it did, ultimately, result in more democracy, but only after taking the French people on a tour through various forms of dictatorship – is an interesting question, which I leave to the reader to consider.

The chapter ended with a sketch of some possible revolutionary dynamics, including the dynamic of solidarity. These show some of the possibilities inherent in any revolutionary situation, and why revolutions sometimes turn extreme, as the French Revolution did. A further dynamic is presented in the next chapter, on nationalism. That dynamic was also present in the French Revolution, but the next chapter illustrates it with a different subject, the rise of Slobodan Milosevic out of the ashes of Yugoslavia.

EIGHT

Slobodan Milosevic and the Fire of Nationalism

8.1 Introduction

What did the regime of Slobodan Milosevic in Serbia represent? Was he "radical evil" incarnate, as Susan Sontag (1999) has suggested, or just another Balkan strongman (Djilas 1993)[1] trying to survive? Michael Ignatieff (1999, p. 75) suggested that he "developed a new style of post–Cold War authoritarian populism" just as he had "pioneered ethnic cleansing and the use of refugees as a weapon of war" (p. 74). Of course, Milosevic lost the war with NATO. And perhaps the most appropriate label given to him nowadays is the one originally given and officially sanctioned by Louise Arbour in her capacity as the chief prosecutor for the UN tribunal in the Hague: "War criminal."

The Milosevic episode is a typical example of one of the central dilemmas since the fall of communism: the persistence of dictatorships, or at least of highly imperfect or "ugly" democracies[2] and the problems caused by the interaction and conflict between these regimes and the democracies. The Cold War with communism may have disappeared, but other conflicts with dictatorships have taken its place. The most obvious examples in recent years have been the former Yugoslavia and Iraq, along with the other Middle East dictatorships and the continuing possibility of conflict with China. And there is also the never-ending standoff between Fidel Castro of Cuba and the United States. These frictions and antagonisms continue to cause problems for the world community, even apart from the intertwining of the conflict between dictatorship and democracy into the conflict between the world's democracies and terrorism.

---

[1] As quoted in the *International Herald Tribune,* May 1999.
[2] I am indebted to Mario Ferrero and Vani Borooah for this phrase.

Why do dictatorships cause so many problems? The reason, I suggest, is not just that they are essentially aggressive or warlike, though this characterization is not an unfair description of the behavior of many undemocratic regimes. Insofar as they result in overt war, I contend, the basic problem is the misunderstanding of their nature, that is, of how these regimes work, by the theorists, politicians, and citizens of democratic countries. For example, as discussed in the preceding chapter, while most dictators repress their populations, few survive by repression alone. Typically they also seek to obtain the support of their peoples. To illustrate, consider the case of Slobodan Milosevic.[3] Milosevic was often described as a dictator, but he won elections. The elections hardly measured up to the democratic ideal, but there is little doubt that Milosevic faced real opposition in them. The precise nature of the post-Communist Serbian regime eluded scrutiny. As Robert Thomas (1999, pp. 3–4) put it, "Serbia exists in a classificatory limbo where stunted *democratic* institutions mix uneasily with *authoritarian* structures and both of these elements are overshadowed by the *sultanist* influence of the leader of the ruling party, Slobodan Milosevic."

This chapter is an attempt to understand the behavior of a particular regime, and as well to use that example combined with the model discussed in the preceding chapter to generalize about some new aspects of the behavior of dictators and the reasons for the conflict between dictators and democracies. In particular, I focus on nationalism, ethnic cleansing, and war. These are classic features of the behavior of many autocratic regimes. They were particularly on display in the Milosevic regime. I begin by looking at how he was typically understood both in the popular press and in the light of the most prominent social science theories at that time. I then apply the model of dictatorship partly outlined in the preceding chapter. The basic argument is simple. First, like any dictator, Milosevic needed support in order to survive in office. His provocative and warlike actions toward other groups like the Croatians and the Albanians are best understood, not as the latest round in a centuries-old tradition of ethnic fighting, but as the attempts of a competitive politician trying to survive in a situation where the old basis of power – the Communist system, Titoist version – had disintegrated. Second, in attempting to survive the wave of democratization that swept Eastern Europe after 1989, Milosevic played a wild card – the nationalist card. Nationalism can be wild because, under some circumstances, it is contagious. To revert to the metaphor that is central to this chapter, once the fire of ethnic nationalism has been lit, especially when combined with

---

[3] Much of the material on Milosevic in this chapter first appeared in Wintrobe (2002).

the security dilemma, it can spread uncontrollably and do great damage. So I suggest that, in the end, Milosevic's rule can be viewed as that of a typical totalitarian dictator confronted with the collapse of the original basis of his support (communism), who responded to this collapse by playing with the fire of ethnic nationalism. Ethnic cleansing and war are seen in this light as neither deliberate, coldly planned strategies of brutal repression nor the results of complete miscalculation, but the outcome of a process in which the leadership of the regime was reacting to events that it may have set in motion but did not entirely control.

The next section reviews a number of different points of view that were put forward to explain the recent conflicts in the Balkans. Then section 8.3 outlines the approach taken here and applies it to the Milosevic regime, while section 8.4 extends that approach to understand the contagiousness of ethnic nationalism. Section 8.5 considers the origins and the conduct of the war between NATO and Serbia in this light and in the light of the standard rationalist approach to war.

8.2 Explanations of Milosevic's Strategy

Popular explanations of the conflicts between the Serbs and the Croatians or the Albanians tend to take one of two forms. The conflicts are attributed to either Serbian aggression or ancient hatreds. The appeal of the first explanation is easy to understand. Under Slobodan Milosevic Serbia fought four wars. The aim was obvious – the creation of greater Serbia. So the horrors associated with these conflicts could be blamed on one nation and even one man. In this vein, Susan Sontag (1999) justified NATO's attack on Serbia by referring to the presence of "radical evil" being loosed upon the world. Perhaps a more general pattern had emerged in the post–Cold War period, as Woodward (1995) suggested American policy makers thought, of "rogue or renegade states" headed by "'new Hitlers' such as Saddam Hussein in Iraq and Slobodan Milosevic, who defied all norms of civilized behavior and had to be punished to protect those norms and to protect innocent people" (Woodward, 1995, p. 7).

One difficulty with this view is that, by all accounts, Milosevic appeared to be no ideologue but a simple opportunist.[4] But if Milosevic was simply an

---

[4] Aleksa Djilas (1993, p. 94) describes Milosevic as "essentially an ideological eclectic and a political opportunist." Ignatieff (1994, pp. 37–38) suggests that "few people I meet in Belgrade believe Milosevic himself has any deep nationalist convictions. He merely knows that when he shouts from the podium 'nobody will ever beat the Serbs again!' they applaud him to the rafters."

opportunist, what opportunities or forces was he responding to in these acts of repression? What are the conditions that make such leaders possible? Perhaps, then, the Serbian people were to blame. But what made them different from other peoples? Indeed, on this point, Milovan Djilas, in an interview with Michael Ignaticff, suggests that "the West's greatest mistake . . . is that it has 'satanized' the Serbs" (Ignatieff 1994, p. 38).

The second line of thought was that the Yugoslav and Bosnian conflicts were based on the revival of ancient hatreds or ethnic conflicts after the fall of communism. On this view, Tito provided the strong leadership, backed by the repressive powers of the Communist system to contain the ancient hatreds, which nevertheless continued to simmer under the surface of communism and self-management. When communism disintegrated, they just floated back up to the top. As late as 1990, however, journalists traveling in the region reported that most people seemed to have had no use for the polarizing rhetoric of the minority of extremists. Croats and Serbs lived together in relative contentment, according to Glenny (1992), and many others. Gagnon (1994–1995, pp. 133–134) pointed out that Yugoslavia never saw the kind of religious wars seen in Western and Central Europe; that Serbs and Croats never fought before this century; that intermarriage rates were quite high in those ethnically mixed regions that saw the worst violence; and that sociological polling as late as 1989–1990 showed a high level of tolerance especially in the mixed region.

In one way, then, the central problem with which this chapter is concerned is the sudden emergence of nationalism or the salience of ethnic differences. As Xavier Bougarel has put it, "How is it that a people who voted in one year 74 percent in favor of banning certain kinds of groups voted the second year *for* those groups in exactly the same proportion?"[5] The most commonly accepted answer to this question in social science appears to be the concept of the security dilemma. The problem highlighted in the security dilemma is that a nation's attempt to provide itself with security may be interpreted by another nation as aggressive or threatening, causing that nation to arm in response. A spiral can be set in motion, such as the well-known nuclear arms race, in which each nation's attempt to provide itself with nuclear weapons for defensive purposes causes other nations to arm in return, causing the first nation to feel more insecure, and so on. Posen (1993) was the first to apply the logic of the security dilemma to ethnic conflict. After the collapse of the

---

[5] Xavier Bougarel, "Bosnia and Herzegovina – State and Communitarianism," in David A. Dyker and Ivan Vejvoda, eds., *Yugoslavia and After: A Study in Fragmentation, Despair and Rebirth* (London: Longmans, 1996), pp. 253–254, quoted by Woodward (1997), p. 3.

Soviet system, the different ethnic groups in Yugoslavia were essentially in a situation of "emerging anarchy" analogous to that of the international system that is the normal subject of the security dilemma. Under these conditions each ethnic group naturally sought to protect itself from aggression by other groups, but these actions were interpreted as aggressive by others, and so on.

The difficulty with this line of thought is that, if taken literally, it would seem that ethnic conflicts would be exploding everywhere. Instead, as pointed out by Fearon and Laitin (1996) and by Figueiredo and Weingast (1998), interethnic relations are normally peaceful. Overt ethnic conflict is rare, yet there are many, many situations where ethnic groups formally find themselves in the situation of the security dilemma. One reason for this may be, as Fearon (1998) points out, that it is never made clear why signaling between groups or states cannot be used to reduce the uncertainty about each other's intentions, which is the real source of the security dilemma.

Fearon and Laitin (1996) suggest an alternative model of why ethnic conflict arose after the collapse of communism in Yugoslavia: each ethnic group was unable to credibly commit not to harm the minority within its borders. Thus it is not anarchy per se but the inability to make a credible commitment not to attack the other party that gives rise to the security dilemma (as Kydd 1997 also emphasizes). However, it remains to be explained why this particular commitment problem persisted and even gave rise to war in post-Communist Yugoslavia and not elsewhere in Eastern Europe or in the rest of the world. Figueiredo and Weingast (1998) suggested another condition – "confirming" behavior by the other side – for the security dilemma to hold. Suspicions about the others' behavior require confirmation – some sort of threatening action by the other side – for a spiral to develop. An illustration is the Croatian leader Franco Tudjman's refusal to disavow the symbols of the wartime Ustase regime. This "confirmed" the aggressive nature of the regime toward the Serbs within its borders and made Serbia under Milosevic view any actions by the Croatians with suspicion.[6]

---

[6] A contemporary illustration may be the behavior of China as it rises to economic power vis-à-vis the United States. It is possible that this rise could be entirely peaceful and displays of Chinese nationalism not be seen as threatening. On the other hand, it is easy to imagine that people in the United States could feel threatened by the increased power and nationalism of China, and many in the United States appeared to feel this way when one of China's three largest energy firms, CNOOC Ltd., attempted to take over the American oil company Unocal Corp. The U.S. House of Representatives overwhelmingly approved a resolution urging the Bush administration to block the proposed transaction as a threat to national security. China's Foreign Ministry excoriated Congress for injecting politics into what it characterized as a standard business matter. See the account in the *Washington Post*, July 5, 2005.

In brief, it seems that the security dilemma, like ancient hatreds or Serbian aggression, may be necessary but is insufficient to explain the eruption of nationalism and ethnic conflict in Yugoslavia after the collapse of communism. In the following I essentially argue that the missing link is provided by the explosive quality of nationalism under certain conditions, especially the environment of post-totalitarian politics.

8.3 The Dictator's Dilemma and the Security Dilemma

One aspect of Milosevic's regime that plays no role in the security dilemma analysis is that his regime was often likened to a dictatorship. Perhaps the security dilemma, whether applied to ethnic groups or nations, is altered if one or more of the actors are dictators. What difference does this make? In order to explore this question, we have to ask, first of all, what do we know about dictatorship?

As suggested in the preceding chapter, perhaps the most common notion in political science is the idea that dictators rule by repression alone, as argued by Friedrich and Brzezinski (1965) and many others. The Milosevic regime was certainly repressive, in its control of the secret police and of the major media outlets. But if the Serbs were just a repressed population, why did they fight so hard? And why did they vote for Milosevic, who by all accounts appeared to be popular and indeed won several (more or less free) elections?

Rational choice approaches to dictatorship in public choice are still relatively new. They include Tullock's (1987) early book *Autocracy* and Mancur Olson's (1993) concept of the "stationary bandit." One problem with Olson's model is that it implicitly assumes that the dictator is safely in office. It is this that allows him to set the level of taxes and public goods to maximize his own income. Yet much of Milosevic's career seems to have been spent fending off challenges to his rule. Moreover, if Milosevic simply maximized income, why did he seek to expel the ethnic Albanians from Kosovo, rather than keep them around and subject them to revenue-maximizing taxation? Finally, the result of Milosevic's rule was that he largely destroyed the Yugoslav economy. So if Milosevic was simply a kleptocrat, he was a very bad one.

My own starting point in analyzing dictatorship, as outlined in the preceding chapter, is that the dictator's basic problem is how to stay in power – the Dictator's Dilemma (Wintrobe 1990, 1998). The problem facing any autocrat is that of knowing how much support he has among the general population, as well as among smaller groups with the power to depose him.

It is straightforward to show that this point of view illuminates the working of the Milosevic regime. To review what took place briefly, with the decline of communism everywhere in Eastern Europe in the late 1980s, the Yugoslavian regime was faced with a fall in support. *Why didn't Milosevic simply increase the level of repression in order to stay in power?* Recall that in this model, totalitarian regimes use repression and loyalty to maximize power. If an increase in repression would cause support to increase as well, power would clearly increase. But, if this is the case, the regime would already have increased the level of repression prior to the fall in loyalty. Thus, even though repression and loyalty are positively correlated on the average, at the *margin*, an increase in repression must cause loyalty to *fall*.[7] In other words, in a regime like the Yugoslav one, all the ways in which combinations of repression and loyal support could be used to maximize power were presumably already exhausted prior to the fall in support that occurred in the 1980s. So when support for the regime fell over the 1980s, increasing repression would simply have reduced power further, not increased it. It follows that the regime could only prosper if ways were found to restore loyal support on the part of the population.

The strategies perfected by Milosevic for this purpose have been well documented.[8] In the 1980s Milosevic was a Communist apparatchik. In 1984 he became the head of the Belgrade Communists. He was a party conservative, opposed to the reform movements that were in favor of greater reliance on private enterprise, multiple-candidate elections, and so forth. In 1986 he was elected head of the Serbian party's central committee. According to Robert Thomas (1999, p. 44):

After the famous rally in 1987 at which Milosevic declared to the demonstrators "no one should dare to beat you," a lengthy meeting followed ("The Night of Hard Words") in which Milosevic heard the manifold grievances of the protestors. From that moment he obeyed the nationalist imperative and made the cause of the Kosovo Serbs his own.... [In this way] Milosevic sought to place himself at the head of a mass movement ("the happening of the people") whose aims were ostensibly nationalist, seeking to restore Serbian central control over the provinces, and direct it against the Party establishment ("the anti-bureaucratic revolution").

These meetings were followed by a series of mass demonstrations, organized by Milosevic and his supporters, known as "rallies for truth"

---

[7] This point about totalitarian regimes is demonstrated in Wintrobe (1990) or (1998), chap. 3.

[8] The details of the competitive strategies used in Milosevic's rise to power can be found in any number of historical sources. Here, we rely especially on Dallago and Uvalic (1998), Djilas (1993), Gagnon (1994, 1994–1995), Ramet (1996), and R. Thomas (1999).

(R. Thomas 1999, p. 45). Between July 1998 and the spring of 1999, 100 such meetings took place across Serbia involving an estimated cumulative total of 5 million people. The slogans on placards at meetings were frequently strident and nationalist in tone, such as "In all the places where there are Serbian souls, that is the home and the heart place of my birth" (R. Thomas 1999, p. 45). Milosevic's emphasis on "anti-bureaucratic" reform caught the mood of widespread public anger at the corruption and nepotism that pervaded the party structures.

By 1990, however, communism was disappearing everywhere in Eastern Europe, reformers were coming into power, and the people were demanding freedom in all the former Communist states. In the spring 1990 elections in Slovenia and Croatia, openly antisocialist parties took power in an apparent backlash against Milosevic. The federal prime minister Markovic pushed bills through the federal assembly legalizing a multiparty system and in July 1990 formed a political party to support his reforms. And opposition forces within Serbia itself began organizing and pressuring the regime for multiparty elections, holding massive protest rallies in May (Gagnon 1994, p. 153). Milosevic's response to these challenges in the 1990s was to step up his strategy of ethnic provocation and nationalism and to offer selective incentives (rents) to try and restore the loyalty of key interest groups and the people.

In order to win the 1990 election, the Serbian government printed $2 billion (U.S.) in overdue workers' salaries just before the December elections, the funds illegally taken from the federal treasury (Gagnon 1994–1995, p. 153). Dallago and Uvalic (1998, p. 78) detail the use of other selective incentives: "For firms, the granting of preferential credits, import permits, or postponement of fiscal obligations, while for individuals, privileged access to scarce goods, nomination to high and influential positions in political structures, allocation of flats or houses in the best parts of Belgrade and Zagreb."

Following the 1990 election, the strategy of provoking conflict along ethnic lines was stepped up. The immediate cause appeared to be the massive protest rallies held in Belgrade on March 9 and 10, 1991. Milosevic responded, according to Gagnon, by labeling the protestors "enemies of Serbia" who were working with Albanians, Croats, and Slovenes to destroy Serbia. The result was that the Yugoslav army, despite its promises not to attack Croatia, escalated the conflict in Croatia, and Serbian forces continued their strategy of provoking conflict in Slavonia and on the borders of Krajina, terrorizing civilian populations, destroying Croatian villages in Croat parts of town, bombing cities to drive out the population, and forcing Serbs on threat of death to join them and point out Croat-owned houses. Serbs who openly disagreed with these policies were terrorized and silenced. This policy, by provoking extremists in Croatia into action, in effect became a self-fulfilling prophecy as the Serbian regime pointed to those atrocities as proof of its original charges (Gagnon 1994–1995, p. 160).

At the same time, Serbia also stepped up the pressure on Bosnia. It now portrayed as the ethnic enemy the allegedly fundamentalist Muslim population of Bosnia, who were said to be seeking to impose an Islamic state and to perpetrate genocide against the Bosnian Serbs (Gagnon 1994–1995, p. 161). These strategies would later be repeated against the Albanians in Kosovo.

While these policies of nationalism and provocation to stimulate ethnic loyalty were pursued, Milosevic also engaged in other policies aimed at the party and the government. For example, he gained control of the secret police over the period 1987 to 1990, and the police had, by the end of 1990 (according to R. Thomas 1999, p. 93), "begun to recruit individuals who would unofficially be willing to support the state, and Milosevic's agenda, through the use of extra political methods and physical force." Finally, the standard Communist weapon of securing authority within the party – the purge – was used. According to Aleksa Djilas (1993, p. 89), of the 100 most prominent political figures in Serbia in 1988, by the beginning of 1993, Milosevic had removed all but a handful from power.

The important lesson from our point of view of accounts like those of Djilas, Gagnon, or Thomas is that it seems clear that Milosevic was responding as a competitive politician, faced with a decline in support possibly large enough to keep him from remaining in office. He could not prosper in office simply by increasing repression. Some other key was required to restore the loyalty of the people and that of the bureaucratic functionaries to him so that he could maintain his power at a time when Communist regimes were collapsing everywhere else in Eastern Europe. His provocation of the Croations, Slovenians, the Albanians, and others were driven largely not by ancient hatreds but by domestic politics.

However, still unanswered is the important question, *What made the Serbs so eager to embrace nationalism when they were offered it?* No one seems willing to suggest that Milosevic or the Serbian media were capable of reinvigorating Serbian nationalism in the absence of a receptive public. Thus, the journalist Mark Thompson emphasized that the "[m]edia did not inject their audiences with anti-Muslim prejudice or exploitable fear of

Croatian nationalism. The prejudice and fear were widespread, latently, at least."[9] Aleksa Djilas (1993, p. 87) put it more colorfully:

The mass movement of Kosovo Serbs developed spontaneously. . . . Milosevic only gradually overcame his caution and started supporting it, but he was nonetheless the first leading Communist to do so. With the help of the Party-controlled media and the Party machinery, he soon dominated the movement, discovering in the process that the best way to escape the wrath of the masses was to lead them. It was an act of political cannibalism. The opponent, Serbian nationalism, was devoured and its spirit permeated the eater. Milosevic reinvigorated the Party by forcing it to embrace nationalism.

Why were the nationalist strategies so successful? Are we back to "ancient hatreds" for an explanation? The next section offers an alternative point of view, by developing some of the properties of nationalism in more detail.

8.4 Understanding Nationalism

Nationalism may be defined as a doctrine that "locates the source of individual identity within a 'people' or ethnic group "which is seen as the bearer of sovereignty, the central object of loyalty and the basis of collective solidarity" (Greenfeld 1992, p. 3). Alternatively, according to Smith (1976, p. 2), nationalism is

an ideological movement for the attainment and maintenance of autonomy, cohesion and individuality for a social group deemed by some of its members to constitute an actual or potential nation. In other words, nationalism is both an ideology and a movement, usually a minority one, which aspires to "nationhood" for the chosen group; . . . "nationhood" in turn comprises three basic ideals, autonomy and self-government for the group, often but not always in a sovereign state, solidarity and fraternity of the group in a recognized territory or "home," and third, a distinctive, and preferably unique, culture and history peculiar to the group in question.

Thus, the essence of ethnic nationalism is that it fuses *citizenship* with *ethnicity* and *territory.* All the conflicts arise when one of these three is problematical, for example, if an ethnic group does not possess a distinctive territory, or when there are other, minority, ethnicities located there.

What is so important about ethnicity that singles it out as the criterion by which people select the group that is to govern itself? Why not use some other criterion? For example, one alternative criterion is civic nationalism. "Civic

---

[9] Mark Thompson, *Forging War*, quoted in Snyder and Ballantine (1997).

nationalism" may be defined as the doctrine that "maintains that the nation should be composed of all those – regardless of race, color, creed, gender, language or ethnicity – who subscribe to the nation's political creed. This nationalism is called civic because it envisages the nation as a community of equal, rights-bearing citizens, united in patriotic attachment to a shared set of political practises and values" (Ignatieff 1994, pp. 3–4). For many, civic nationalism is an altogether more agreeable doctrine in that it is inclusive rather than exclusive.

But the exclusivity of ethnic nationalism is precisely what sometimes makes it so attractive from the point of view of a rational individual or ethnic group (if not necessarily that of society).[10] In economic terms, ethnic groups may be said to have a peculiar and unique quality, which is that entry into and, to some extent, exit from them is blocked. To the extent that membership in an ethnic group is based on blood, outsiders cannot enter, and insiders can never completely leave: an Italian who tires of being Italian (say) and wishes to become German cannot do so, and no matter how much he may wish to dispose of his ethnic connections (tell his friends to get lost, never phone his mother again, even on her birthday), he will find it difficult to completely dispose of the "sunk" ethnic capital that he acquired through birth and upbringing.

Now this property of *blocked entry and exit* can sometimes be advantageous. To see this point, it is necessary to drop the assumption often made in economic theory that transactions costs are zero. It follows that in any exchange, economic or social, there is always the possibility of being cheated. Suppose that it is less likely that a person would cheat another person of the same ethnic group than someone unrelated by blood. This could be because the ethnic group has a greater capacity to monitor or punish cheating: for example, the fact that entry and exit are blocked solves the problem of opportunistic entry, and the fact that ethnicity persists through time means that punishment for transgressions in the past is always feasible. So ethnic networks are like capital goods – and the stock may be called "ethnic capital" – in that they persist over time and have economic value in that they permit valuable exchanges to occur.[11]

---

[10] Of course, from a rational choice point of view, one can also think of ethnic nationalism as providing utility directly, by analogy to a consumption good. People could get pleasure directly from the act of identifying with others in the same ethnic group as themselves. For many of the purposes of this chapter, either this view or the investment point of view put forward in the text will suffice, as will be shown in the text where appropriate.

[11] For other rational choice approaches to ethnicity, see Bates (1983), the papers collected in Breton, Galeotti, Salmon, and Wintrobe (1995), and Fearon and Laitin (1996).

On this view, ethnic networks can substitute for other forms of contractual enforcement such as legal contractual enforcement or hierarchical enforcement. Markets, authority, ethnicity, and other institutions such as the family or the firm all provide alternative or substitute means of supporting exchange. So the failure of one of them will mean that people will tend to resort to one or more of the others. It follows that one reason that nationalism increased was that, with the failure of communism in Russia and Eastern Europe, and the fact that markets had not yet been established, ethnic networks provided the main alternative underpinning for people to engage in exchange.

Suppose, then, that the fall of communism combined with Milosevic's "anti-bureaucratic revolution" to result in an increase in cohesion within the Serbian ethnic group. On the investment view, it follows that the transactions costs for a Serb in dealing with other Serbs (the costs of trading with another member of the ethnic group) would be lower than before, essentially because the likelihood of being cheated is less for either public or private transactions. On the consumption view, there is greater ethnic solidarity or identification. From either point of view, then, an increase in cohesion or ethnic solidarity would raise individual utility. However, this is not the end of the story, as there may be other, external effects. One such external effect is the ethnic security dilemma, as already discussed. Among the other effects that may be expected to occur are the following:

1. Increased cohesion tends to help solve the Dictator's Dilemma, if the dictator in office is or can become the leader of the ethnic group. That is, it raises the dictator's security. To put it simply, at the extreme, if everyone who is a Serb supports the Serb leader, and everyone who is not a Serb does not, then it is simple for the Serb leader to know who supports him and who does not. In general, national or ethnic identities tend to divide the world into two groups, "us" and "them," and make it relatively hard to sit on the fence – that is, they force people to choose. Thus the nationalist card is one way to solve the Dictator's Dilemma.

2. The increased cohesion tends to be infectious or to spread *within* the group. That is, nationalism is *contagious:* when some are nationalistic, it tends to make others of the same stripe more nationalistic.

To understand this last point, let us first note that there are two further properties of nationalism, which are of great importance, and which have not been called attention to previously in a precise way. They both follow from the fact that ethnic nationalism, whether looked at as social capital or as identity is intimately involved with tradition and with social interactions.[12] To see what this implies, let the individual's utility function be

$$U(E(t), K(t), x(t)) \tag{8.1}$$

where U is individual utility, t inxes time, E(t) is the individual's level of consumption or investment in ethnic capital today, K is the stock of ethnic capital inherited from one's parents and one's own investments in the past, and x refers to other goods or services that yield utility.

Now let us explore what happens when the stock of (ethnic) nationalistic sentiment (K) increases. The first point is that nationalism tends to be enhanced by tradition or "habitual" in the sense that past consumption or investment enhances the value of experience today:

$$U_{EK} > 0. \tag{8.2}$$

Equation 8.2 states that the larger is an individual's stock of ethnic capital K, the larger is the marginal utility (or marginal productivity, in the case of ethnicity as an investment) of ethnic consumption or investment today. To see this point, assume first that nationalism is a consumption good. For purposes of illustration only, let us look at a person who is of Italian descent but lives in Toronto, Canada, along with 400,000 or so others of Italian descent and 2 million or so non-Italians. Then to say that ethnicity is traditional implies that, for this person, the greater his stock of knowledge of Italian culture, the greater his pleasure in going to some Italian cultural or political event, or reading Italian literature, today. This proposition seems reasonable. It suggests that ethnic traditions are like opera – one needs to have some knowledge and experience in order to get pleasure from them.

Alternatively, nationalism may be looked at as an investment good, as suggested previously. It is valuable because it provides connections with people with whom an individual may wish to trade, either to get a job, a good plumber, a spouse, whatever. In that case, it seems reasonable to assert that the greater the stock of ethnic capital an Italian person (say) has, the larger the *productivity* of the Italian connection, that is, the more transaction costs will be reduced when he or she trades with other Italians rather than with other Canadians. Again, this seems entirely plausible.

Now let us proceed to the second property of ethnic nationalism: *network externality* or *jointness*. Put simply, the value of ethnicity to one individual

[12] Here we are emphasizing the concept of trust or networks as a substitute for law-based exchange, as discussed in Chapter 2. The dynamic properties of social capital are also developed there.

is positively related to that of other individuals. If we look at ethnicity as a consumption good first, this means, to revert to the Italian example, that it is more fun to sing the Italian national anthem with other Italians than to sing it alone, or to read books about the Roman Empire with other Italians than with non-Italians. Alternatively, if ethnicity is looked at as an investment good, jointness implies that investing in ethnicity is more productive when other individuals are doing the same. If, for example, the person in our Italian illustration is Sicilian, it will be more productive to brush up on his Sicilian dialect if other Sicilians are doing the same. Then they can get together and discuss, say, renovating his home in Sicilian dialect.[13] In either case, an individual i's investment or consumption E in period t is positively related to the average level of ethnic consumption, pressure, or investment $\bar{E}^j$ of other individuals. This implies that ethnic nationalism has similar properties as communication networks and other systems with network externalities, as discussed in Chapter 2.

If we assume that nationalism has these two properties, it follows that:

$$E_t^i = f(K, \bar{E}_{t-1}^j) f_k, \ f_{EJ} > 0 \qquad (8.3)$$

where $\bar{E}_{t-1}^j$ = average consumption last period by others, $K = \Sigma^i E_{t-1}$ is the accumulated stock, and both first-order partial derivatives are positive.

If this formulation is accepted, then it turns out that nationalism is contagious, that it tends to be highly elastic with respect to changes in prices or productivity that affect producers or consumers in common, and that it is possibly unstable. To see how this works, let us return to the case of Serbia. It seems reasonable to suppose that, in Yugoslavia after Milosevic came to power, the productivity of ethnic networks increased because of the disappearance of the Communist Party, and the replacement in importance of Communist networks by ethnic networks, as widely advertised by Milosevic's "anti-bureaucratic revolution" of 1987–1989.[14] The immediate or first-period effect (at the beginning of the revolution) of this change on a typical individual's investment or consumption of ethnic nationalism may or may not have been large, but it would have been positive.[15]

---

[13] I owe this illustration to conversations with Isidoro Mazza.

[14] In Russia, they were not so much replaced by ethnic networks as by old connections remaining and strengthening, in the context of a market economy, thus making Russia a "virtual" economy (see Gaddy and Ickes 1998 on this concept) and facilitating links with organized crime.

[15] For the statement in the text to be true, it must technically be assumed that we are looking at an "income-compensated" charge, that is, a pure substitution effect.

It follows that each individual will invest in or consume more ethnic capital. *Next* period, however, every individual will want to invest or consume even more, because the stock inherited from the last period K is now larger and the average level of investment by others ($\overline{E}^j_{t-1}$) has also increased. The same thing will happen next period, and so on. So while in the short run, traditional or habit-based and jointly consumed activities may be inelastic with respect to changes that affect their value, in the long run, they tend to be highly *elastic*. There is also a significant possibility of instability, as the interactions based on traditional behavior and on consumption in common or peer pressure need not dampen out over time but may increase[16]

So far, ethnic nationalism appears just like other activities that tend to be habitual and jointly engaged in, as analyzed by Becker[17] and discussed in Chapter 2. That is, it is like religion (for those who view nationalism positively) or harmful drugs (for those who view it negatively).[18] There is, however, yet a further interaction that makes the likelihood of instability larger than suggested so far and differentiates nationalism from other social interactions. This is the interaction of nationalism with the security dilemma.

To illustrate, suppose there is an increase in nationalistic sentiment or cohesion among the Croatians. As we have already seen, this would stimulate fear on the part of the Serbs because of the security dilemma. The increased fear that every Serb would feel then acts just like a change in the price or the marginal productivity of Serbian cohesion, leading each individual to want to raise his level of ethnic involvement. Again, initially, the change may not be very large. Next period, however, the increase in ethnic capital would lead to still greater consumption or investment via the contagion (network externality and habit) effect. In turn, this stimulates fears on the part of the Croatians because of the security dilemma, again leading to a contagion effect on their part. So the security dilemma and the contagion effects interact with each other in a process of positive feedback, possibly accounting for the kind of explosive changes in nationalist sentiment that we have seen in Yugoslavia.[19]

---

[16] There may be, in addition, a synergistic interaction between peer pressure and habituality (Becker 1996, p. 125).

[17] For models of drug addiction, see Becker (1996). Iannacconne (1988) models religious behavior. For other models of social interactions that derive similar implications on the basis of information rather than social interactions, see Chapter 2.

[18] The reader who views religion negatively and drugs positively can simply transpose these two in the statement in the text.

[19] A similar analysis would explain the "burst" of patriotism expressed by many countries in wartime.

To see these points more precisely, it may be useful to develop a simple diagrammatic apparatus. The phenomenon we are analyzing is dynamic while the diagram is static, but perhaps it will be useful nonetheless. To begin, note first that, from the analysis of nationalism and social interactions, every individual i will have his preferred or desired level of ethnic capital K or desired level of investment E_i. The relationship between the two is just

$$E_i = \dot{K} \tag{8.4}$$

where the dot over the K indicates the rate of depreciation of ethnic capital. If we assume that K is the long-run level of desired ethnic capital, the satisfaction of equation 8.4 simply keeps individual i's level of ethnic capital at that level. The desired level of ethnic capital, in turn, can be derived from the equilibrium desired level of ethnic investment. This depends on the external threat, as described previously: to repeat, an increase in, say, Serb ethnic capital stimulates fear on the part of each Croatian (via the security dilemma). This in turn raises the productivity of Croatian ethnic capital E_c and stimulates each Croatian to accumulate more (via the contagion effects displayed in equation 8.3). But that in turn raises the fear of the Serbs and stimulates each one to accumulate more Serb ethnic capital (increase his investment E_s). But this in turn raises the fears of the Croats again, and so forth. In other words,

$$E_c = h(P_c(F_c(E_s^a))) \tag{8.5}$$

where E_c is Croatian ethnic investment in period t (the time subscripts are omitted for notational simplicity), based on an anticipated Serb investment of E_s^a; F_c is the level of fear experienced by Croatians from Serb cohesion or ethnic investment, and P_c is the productivity of Croatian ethnic capital. A similar relationship exists for Serbian ethnic investment E_s:

$$E_s = g(P_s(F_s(E_c^a))). \tag{8.6}$$

One possible equilibrium is the Nash equilibrium, where anticipated investments are realized or where:

$$E_c = E_c^a \text{ and } E_s = E_s^a. \tag{8.7}$$

This model is depicted in Figure 8.1. Croatian investment in ethnic capital is on the horizontal axis; Serbian investment on the vertical one. The curve C defines Croatian ethnic investments E_c as a function of E_s; similarly, the curve S defines E_s as a function of E_c. The interaction of the security dilemma and nationalism imply that initially there is a region of increasing returns to ethnic investment. Three equilibria are depicted: L, Q, and H.

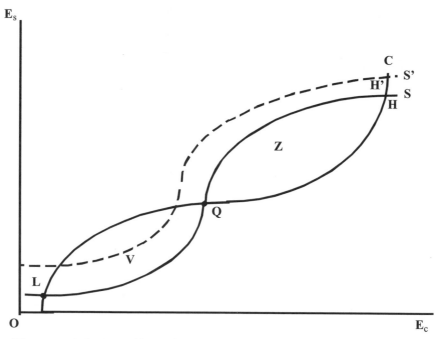

Figure 8.1. Only the equilibria at low (L) and high (H) levels of nationalism are stable.

The equilibrium Q is unstable, however: an initial deviation from it results in a movement up to the point H or downward to L. So there are only two stable Nash equilibria: the "high" level of nationalism as represented by the point H, and the "low" level at L.

Of course, an equilibrium like H need not exist and the "high" level of nationalism could be represented by a corner solution instead. The same is true of L. A sufficient condition for the existence of an interior solution at H is that all the relationships in equations 8.6 and 8.7 are ultimately diminishing or at least nonincreasing. In other words, an increase in anticipated Croat ethnic investment E_c^a ultimately increases the fear of the Serbs F_s by the same or by smaller and smaller amounts; similarly, the effect of F_s on the productivity of Serb ethnic capital P_s and of P_s on Serb investment E_s is also nonincreasing.

To use the model to interpret the rise of Serbian nationalism, suppose that, initially, the equilibrium under Titoist communism was at the "low" level of nationalism represented by L. As the reader can verify, this equilibrium is stable: small deviations from it result in a return to L. In the area V, then, nationalism does not sustain itself; small increases, say, in E_c that do not go beyond the level of Croatian nationalism at Q will simply result in a return to L. In the area Z, on the other hand, each party feels it is *not secure enough*: once past the point Q, the only stable equilibrium is at H. So the area Z may be thought of as the *zone of insecurity*.

Now consider the effect of a large stimulus to nationalistic investment, for example, as we have argued occurred with the collapse of communism and with Milosevic's competitive response to it in the form of his "anti-bureaucratic revolution." These resulted in a large increase in the perceived productivity of ethnic investment E_s to the Serb people at any level of E_c, which in Figure 8.1 is represented by the upward shift in the S curve to S'. The range of points that result in the "high" equilibrium is expanded while the "low" one contracts, and the result may be a movement all the way to the new "high" level of nationalism represented by point H'. Once there, the high level of nationalism and ethnic conflict between Serbs and Croatians is self-sustaining: small disturbances will not change the equilibrium.

Figure 8.1 illustrates the point that two sets of forces produced the explosion of nationalism. First, there are the changes represented by the shift in the S curve – the increase in the return to ethnic capital as a result of the fall in communism combined with Milosevic's leadership in the "anti-bureaucratic revolution." And, second, the potential for ethnic conflict and hatred was always there, as shown by the shapes of the curves S and C, representing the magnitude of the security dilemma between these two groups – for example, the elasticity of F_s with respect to E_c^a – and the marginal productivity of ethnic networks.

Finally, as always in the case of the security dilemma, the spiral depends, especially for its explosive quality, on a lack of communication between nations or a lack of leadership, either of which may dampen down an explosive reaction. As we know, of course, Milosevic did precisely the opposite and practiced the politics of fear. But the analysis also implies that, however malevolent he may have been in setting the fires of nationalism into motion, he did not control them – the contagion property and security dilemma and their interaction imply that the fire has the capacity to spread.

From equations 8.5, 8.6, and 8.7, the most important variables that might give rise to or amplify a spiral are, first, the strength of the security dilemma, that is, the extent to which an increase in Serb ethnic capital stimulates fear on the part of each Croatian (and vice versa); and, second, the marginal productivity of ethnic (Croatian or Serb) capital and the elasticity of its supply. As already suggested, one important factor that affects the magnitude of the security dilemma – for example, the elasticity of F_c with respect to E_s^a – is the structure of communications, both between the two groups and within them. A "happening" of the Serbs, for example, need not necessarily be interpreted as particularly threatening by other ethnic groups. Thus it could be viewed by non-Serbs as a demonstration of solidarity, as an expression of a desire for security, or as a threatening gesture aimed specifically at non-Serbs.[20]

The behavior of the media is one important element in determining which interpretation becomes commonly adopted. For example, contagion can obviously be magnified by the press. Snyder and Ballantyne argued that one situation particularly likely to produce contagion is when a press is newly freed: under these circumstances the press is likely to be oligopolistic and particularly susceptible to outbidding. With respect to Milosevic, it has often been suggested that the press was instrumental in bringing him to power. In particular, it is known that Milosevic chose the television correspondent who would report to Belgrade from Pristina, the capital of Kosovo, and personally phoned the station almost daily to tell the editors what stories to highlight and that "After Milosevic's April 1987 speech in Kosovo, Belgrade TV showed the local Albanian police clubbing the Serbian crowd, and Milosevic saying 'From now on, no one has the right to beat you,' but it left out the pictures of the crowd stoning the police" (Snyder and Ballantine 1997, p. 82). Afterward, Milosevic used the Kosovo issue as a pretext to purge anti-Milosevic sentiment. But he never achieved an absolute monopoly over the Serb media, although he did control the state television station and Belgrade's three major newspapers.[21] Indeed, he appeared to understand the so-called vacuum effect – that is, the idea that people stop believing propaganda if they are given an unrelieved diet of it and, in fact, allowed multiple points of view even on the state-controlled media. Of course, to make sure that no viewpoint other than that of the state gained any particular credibility, he made sure that the opposition was diluted, in part by actively subsidizing new parties.[22]

The second set of variables affecting the likelihood of a spiral is the marginal productivity of ethnic capital and its elasticity of supply: the P_c and P_s functions in equations 8.5 and 8.6. This will tend to be affected by such variables as the productivity of alternative means for supporting exchange (e.g., the legal system, or the Communist Party), the effectiveness of ethnic enforcement (capacity to prevent, monitor, and punish transgressions),

---

[20] For example, in Kydd's (1997) model, states may be of several types: "greedy," "security seekers," "trusting," or "fearful." In the model, security seekers can sometimes take steps to signal their intentions and break out of spirals.

[21] Ignatieff (1999) argues that understanding the role of the media was a particular gift of Milosevic. See also Ramet (1996), chap. 4, and Mark Thomas (1994) on the media.

[22] Gagnon (1994), p. 124.

and the existence of older traditions that can be called on to "mobilize" reinvestment in ethnic capital. One important factor here is the extent to which older traditions have been successfully incorporated into contemporary behavior by the ethnic group. Thus Hagen (1999) argued that the peculiarity of much behavior in the Balkans was due to the fact that blood rituals of revenge were combined with modern nationalism, that is, with the idea that an individual is responsible for the protection of a wider group than his own family and, in particular, of other members of his or her ethnic group. Thus one reason why nationalism did not spread in Slovenia the way it did in Croatia in response to Serbian aggression was simply that there were not many Serbs in Slovenia – hence less fear on the part of the Slovenes that the Serbs would be forced to vanquish them in order to protect their "brothers."[23]

To sum up, I suggest this analysis explains the peculiarly explosive quality of nationalism in Yugoslavia. As Ignatieff (1994) noted, it "spread like wildfire." Or, according to Fearon (1998, p. 114), "ethnic polarization and conflict in this case has the look of 'wildfire' in that the two communities were not nearly so divided only months earlier." Note that, on the investment model, while the ancient hatreds are not sufficient, they do play a role, because the capital so built may have depreciated but still exists, and new "maintenance" operations such as those performed by Milosevic are capable of restoring it to its previous luster. Similarly, Serbian aggression and the security dilemma also play an important role. It is doubtful that any of the wars would have occurred without the leadership of Milosevic, or that his strategies would have been effective without the concerns of the security dilemma. So the security dilemma, Serbian aggression, and the existence of ancient hatreds provided the right background or the necessary conditions for the explosion. Ethnic nationalism provided the detonator.

Finally, this analysis sheds some light on the willingness to partake in "ethnic cleansing," which is so difficult to understand. The essential point is that, as we have seen, with social interactions, a person's actions depend on what others are doing and what she herself did in the past. Consequently, the *morality* of those actions to those persons appears similarly contingent. To put it simply, once others are doing it, it's a lot easier for another person (you?) to do it; it's a lot easier to do it if you have already been doing it

---

[23] Another reason, as Janez Sustersic has argued in a personal communication, was that the political agenda was much more open in Slovenia, so that it was impossible for either the Communists or the emerging opposition to gain support by nationalism only; they had to advocate and carry out real political and economic reforms as well.

in the past;[24] and it is a lot easier to do it if you think others are, or are going to be, doing it to you. From this vantage point, it is not so much the operation of hierarchy and the tendency of individuals to obey authority that is responsible for the commission of evil actions, as argued by Hannah Arendt in her celebrated (1976) analysis of the Nazi functionary Eichmann, but the actions of one's comrades and associates and perhaps of one's ancestors. Indeed, I suspect that the emphasis on obedience to authority that was so paramount in Arendt's line of thought has concealed the importance of peer pressure and contagion in contributing to the willingness to engage in crimes against humanity.

In any case, neither of these considerations (hierarchy[25] or peer pressure) absolves the individuals involved (e.g., the Serbs who actually carried out ethnic cleansing operations) of responsibility for their actions in any way, but it does make their actions, however reprehensible, a lot more understandable.[26] Those who watched and condemned ethnic cleansing from the vantage point of their television sets were correct to do so, but they would have understood the actions better, and possibly felt more capable of doing them themselves, if they recognized the importance of the circumstances of social interactions, habituation, and the security dilemma. Perhaps most important, they might not have felt it necessary to condemn an entire people for what happened, as Stacy Sullivan (1999) came close to doing. Finally, there is a further implication that follows from the contagion properties of ethnic cohesion combined with the security dilemma, if they are understood. Because a small "quantity" of the "virus," that is, another ethnic group loyalty, can spread quickly and result in many others being "infected," some may have thought that it was necessary to uproot it *all*.

8.5 Why the War with NATO?

The analysis of this chapter also sheds some light on why the war with NATO occurred. The central point is that, in the democracies, belief is widespread that dictators rule by repression alone and do not need or seek to obtain

---

[24] The "obedience" experiments of Stanley Milgram (1974) demonstrated the importance of past accommodation to a task in getting people to do things, such as inflict pain on others, that they would otherwise find immoral or distasteful. Akerlof (1991) particularly emphasizes this feature in his model of obedience to authority.

[25] The problems with Arendt's point of view are discussed in Breton and Wintrobe (1986) and Wintrobe (1998).

[26] On the mystery presented by these actions, and by the apparent lack of remorse of the Serbian people, even among those who were uninvolved and who opposed the Milosevic regime, see Harden (1999) and especially Sullivan (1999).

widespread popular support in order to survive. From this point of view (the existence of this misunderstanding), three propositions can be derived.

8.5.1 Why War Occurs So Often between Dictatorships and Democracies and Not between Democracies

War is a puzzle for economic theory. The puzzle is that, so long as there are other means of settling a conflict, two powers should never go to war with each other because, as long as they both estimate the outcome correctly, that is, their expectations as to the likely winner are unbiased, wars are irrational. The reason is that there is nothing that can be settled by war that cannot be settled by cheaper, more peaceful means. So, if the likely outcome and its probability are agreed on by both parties in exactly the same way, why not settle in a peaceful manner and save the costs of the conflict?[27]

To illustrate, look briefly at the dispute between Milosevic and NATO. While they did not know exactly which side will win, there is no reason to believe that they disagreed on the main points. On the one hand it was obvious that little Serbia was no match for nineteen of the most powerful nations in the world, led by the most powerful one, the United States. This led NATO to be certain of the verdict of war. Was not this outcome equally obvious to the Serbs? If so, why did they fight? Serbia, on the other hand, presumably knew that power alone does not win wars. There has to be the will to use it. However big a problem this can be for one nation, it is multiplied many times over when nineteen nations are involved. Its leadership counted on this problem among the nations of NATO to mean that NATO could not prosecute a war properly.

NATO knew this as well. Suppose then that the two sides agreed, more or less, on the probable outcome of the conflict. Then why bother to fight? The war itself merely wastes resources and does not change anything. In brief, so long as the same information on relative strengths is available to both sides of the conflict, there is no reason for them to disagree on the probable outcome of the conflict. Therefore, they should be able to come to some agreement without war.

The implication is that there has to be some systematic basis for misunderstanding (or, alternatively, some other difficulty of reaching or enforcing a bargain) for war to occur. In the case of war between democracies and dictatorships, I suggest that one basis for this misunderstanding is the idea,

---

[27] Fearon (1995) provides a persuasive discussion of the war puzzle from the rational choice point of view.

common in democracy, that dictators are typically not supported by their people and rule by repression alone. In this way, the democracies underestimate the capacity of dictatorships to make war. This, in turn, explains why democracies and dictators go to war with each other. Why did war break out between Serbia and NATO?[28] NATO decision makers wanted Milosevic to sign the Rambouillet accords and thought that, because Milosevic was not supported by his people, he was in a weak position to resist this type of pressure.[29] By the same token, NATO also failed to understand that for Milosevic to accept the terms of Rambouillet would, by threatening Serbia with the loss of Kosovo, undermine the very basis of his support.[30]

So part of the reason that the war started was because of the assumption in the West that Milosevic had no support and could easily be brought to heel.[31] Once the war began, and this turned out not to be the case, the bombing and the logic for escalation acquired a completely different rationale, which was, roughly speaking, that "NATO could not afford to lose to a small-time dictator and maintain its reputation." On this line of thought, the logic of the war completely changed once it began, and it began to go badly for the West.

8.5.2 Which Type of Dictatorship Do Democracies Most Often Go to War With?

The order (frequency of expected armed conflict) is predicted to be: totalitarians first, followed by tyrants, and then tinpots. The ordering is paradoxical in that it implies that democracies go to war most often with those dictatorships with the most support, that is, with totalitarian regimes. Note that the argument, often made within the democracies, that by launching sanctions or going to war with dictatorships, the democracies are only

---

[28] The extension of the argument to the wars with Saddam Hussein is fairly obvious: The first war was based on the misunderstanding that Saddam thought he had a "green light" to invade Kuwait. The second one appears, at this writing, to have been based on the misunderstanding about weapons of mass destruction.

[29] Michael Ignatieff (1999) makes the point in his analysis of the war that the initial bombing campaign was very light. And recall the declaration by Clinton that he would never use ground troops. Both are hard to understand on the ordinary way of thinking. But our line of thought suggests that these actions were consistent with the rational but mistaken belief that Milosevic, being a dictator, lacked deep political support and therefore was in a weak fighting position.

[30] See Hagen (1999), p. 59.

[31] Errors like these are not meant to imply that the parties to the conflict were irrational. People in democracies often simply do not understand that dictators, like democratic politicians, need support to stay in power and do not rule by repression alone.

causing suffering among innocent people is also weakest here. But it is with totalitarian regimes that the misunderstanding on the part of the West is greatest.

8.5.3 Why Waging an Effective Campaign against a Dictator Is Difficult

For example in the Serbian conflict, NATO justified each attack on the grounds that they were only attacking the dictator's power base, which were held to be just the instruments of his repression. The most interesting issue that arose within NATO and was publicly aired was whether it was permissible to attack Serbian television stations. The idea was that it was only permissible, morally, to attack Milosevic's instruments of repression, and it was implicitly held that the only thing that kept Milosevic in power was repression. The notion that his popular support was his most important power base was never aired during the war, nor was the implication ever derived that, if it was only permissible to attack his power base, the people of Serbia could be legitimate targets of war. Accordingly, the idea that dictators rule by repression alone also made it harder for NATO to wage an effective military campaign against Milosevic. In the same way, it has commonly been asserted that only innocent people were harmed by the sanctions imposed against Saddam Hussein and Milosevic.

For all these reasons, bombing a dictatorship can have the effect of solidifying a dictator's hold on power, as long as it stops short of actually removing him. So it has been argued that Milosevic essentially invited NATO's bombing.

At the same time, there was a belief in the West that Milosevic could be useful to the West – "better than anarchy," in the common phrase. In the same way, it was sometimes thought that Saddam Hussein was useful, or the leaders of Communist China. All these dictators are or were thought to be "better than anarchy" in the same way that Olson's "stationary" bandit is said to be better than roving bandits. Consequently, it was suggested that the war against Milosevic was not to be too intensive, so that he would remain in power afterward, in the same way that it was often argued that the goal of the first war in Iraq was not to remove Hussein from power but to "discipline" him. It is arguable that only the indictment by the UN Tribunal in the Hague closed off this approach to Milosevic. The indictment made it difficult for U.S. and European leaders (and Russian leaders needing IMF assistance) to be seen negotiating deals with him and to contemplate resurrecting his image in a positive light once he had learned his lesson.

8.6 Conclusion

In this chapter I have sought to understand the workings of the Milosevic regime and associated phenomena, such as the outburst of Serbian nationalism, war, and ethnic cleansing, all from a rational choice point of view. I found Milosevic's behavior comprehensible as the typical response of a totalitarian leader faced with a decline in support and the possible collapse of his regime: he needed to revive support and stimulated ethnic nationalism in order to survive in power. However, the eruption of ethnic conflict is partly the result of the fact that nationalism is contagious and, especially when combined with the security dilemma, can spread uncontrollably. So Milosevic may have initiated events, but he did not control them and was himself burned by the fire of nationalism that he lit in order to shore up his regime.

The leaders of NATO systematically misunderstood the regime. They appeared to believe that Milosevic could sign the Rambouillet accords (and therefore was in complete control of his people) and, on the other hand, that, as a dictator, he ruled by repression and was therefore unsupported by his people, and hence could be easily beaten by NATO. This misunderstanding of the regime partly explains why the war occurred and why initially things went very badly for NATO.

Among the implications of the reasoning in this chapter about Western policy toward dictators are the following:

1. Nationalism is volatile, especially in conditions when security is at stake. Therefore one should be very careful about doing things that may help ignite it.
2. The indictment of Milosevic by the Hague appeared to hasten peace.
3. Policy makers should not play with dictators, thinking they can be useful or are a stabilizing force that is better than anarchy. The basic reason why conflict arose with Milosevic was because of the imperfection of democracy there. In the long run, the best policy for the promotion of human rights and the avoidance of ethnic cleansing and war is to strengthen democracy and strengthen the international tribunal for human rights.

NINE

Jihad vs. McWorld Revisited

9.1 Introduction

Is there a connection between extremism and the introduction or spread of markets? Has the spread of markets around the world – what is often referred to as "globalization"– fostered or retarded extremism?

One way to begin making the connection is via the concept of "transparency." The fall in the costs of acquiring and transmitting information and of transacting across borders generally is often said to require a global world order in which countries specialize according to comparative advantage and the international division of labor is as complete as possible. In order to facilitate this outcome, economic relations should become as *transparent* as possible, because greater transparency implies lower transactions costs. A larger global division of labor means an expansion of world trade, and greater transparency facilitates this expansion. Democracy, too, thrives on transparency, and dictatorship on obfuscation. Consequently, on this point of view, it is obvious that the new global world order must be governed by the most transparent systems possible, both to promote democracy and economic efficiency.[1]

To some extent, transparency and globalization go together in that both are the result of the information revolution. Of course, transparency is not exactly the same thing as globalization. Indeed, sometimes people associated with the *anti*globalization movement have been demanding "greater transparency" from organizations such as the IMF, the World Bank, and the World Trade Organization (WTO). All of these organizations that "manage"

---

[1] I conjecture that many, perhaps a majority of economists would subscribe to these views. Among the more well-known advocates are Barro (1998), Bhagwati (2004), and Sachs (1999).

the international order have been accused of lack of transparency, perhaps most notably by Stiglitz (2002) in his indictment of their operation. But with this qualification, transparency and globalization obviously belong together: both are the result of new technologies that reduce the costs of transmitting information via fax, email, Internet, and so on.

Another possibility is that while real transparency would indeed be nice, transparency as we know it is often an illusion. The surrealist painters knew that transparency could be illusory, as shown by the painting *The Key to the Fields* (1936) by Rene Magritte. The painting shows a window that is shattered, with the shattered pieces of glass lying around on the floor. On the shattered pieces of glass, there are sections of a painting that looks exactly like the landscape behind the window. Thus, before the window was broken, the glass appeared transparent but it was actually opaque and therefore, in one sense, it revealed nothing. In another sense, the glass "reflected" the landscape perfectly, because the painting on the glass and the landscape behind it were identical. So there is no mystery. Or is there?

Another, less poetic illustration of the sometimes illusory quality of transparency is shown by the recent corporate accounting scandals in the United States and elsewhere in which billions of dollars in expenses somehow did not show up on the balance sheet as costs to the companies, and so the profits of the companies were considerably overstated. And what could be more surreal than the sight of powerful American CEO's being led off to jail in handcuffs?

Nevertheless, many popular commentators have suggested that the American system of political and corporate governance is the most transparent system, and, partly for that reason, it is the system of the future and the one to which the world is going to converge (e.g., D'Souza 2002; Friedman 1999). Other systems of production, such as the Italian solidarity system, the German social democratic model, and East Asian systems like that in Japan and South Korea and that in China appear less transparent than the American way, but they have also been successful in terms of generating economic growth. These are sometimes lumped together (apart from the Chinese system, which is really a special case)[2] as "stakeholder" systems in contrast to the American "shareholder" system, and I follow this practice. The stakeholder system appears to combine economic progress with a greater capacity to spread the wealth and to cushion the risks inherent in the market. Put simply, there seems to be a greater capacity to generate solidarity in this type of system. Perhaps it is worth discarding a little

---

[2] The Chinese system is discussed in section 9.5.

transparency in exchange for more solidarity? On the other hand, economic growth in many European countries, especially Italy and Germany,[3] has stalled in recent years. And while some Asian countries with stakeholder-type systems have had spectacular growth, this sometimes seems to be either accompanied by corruption (South Korea) or authoritarianism (Singapore), or both (China). Indeed, in the most spectacular case of growth (China), it appears that growth is being pursued in part by "liquidating" solidarity.

The main question to be pursued here is the relationship between globalization and extremism. One prophetic analysis of this issue has been that of the sociologist Benjamin Barber in his 1995 book, *Jihad vs. McWorld*. In that book, globalization, there identified as the forces of McWorld, is increasingly pitted against another powerful force, *jihad*. However, the book also contains a surprising proposition: sometimes globalization (McWorld) promotes *jihad*. How can this be? This question is the main subject of this chapter.

In the next section I discuss several different meanings and contexts of the word "transparency." I then focus on one context: transparency in the system of political economy or political and corporate governance. I look at this issue using Barber's framework, *Jihad vs. McWorld*. Section 9.3 outlines this conflict in a more prosaic manner by identifying two broad systems, the shareholder and stakeholder systems, and suggests that the shareholder system is superior in terms of transparency. Section 9.4 explains why the stakeholder system is better at generating and promoting solidarity and uses this analysis to present a simple rational choice explanation of Barber's most obscure proposition – how McWorld actually stimulates *jihad*. Section 9.5 turns to the solidary system and suggests that it, too, has a characteristic flaw – the potential for corruption. This has been an issue particularly with respect to the Korean and Chinese systems, where there appears to have been both spectacular growth and a great deal of corruption. This raises a number of questions: if growth is what is desired, is corruption necessary for that growth, especially in the stakeholder system? Is this price worth paying? And is the shareholder system, on the surface so transparent, free from this flaw?

9.2 The Meaning of Transparency and Its Role in Economic Systems

Dictionary definitions of transparency stress clarity and visibility: thus Webster's defines it as "easily seen through, recognized, or detected." Typical synonyms include "clear, open," or "visible." In economic policy,

---

[3] See Sinn (2002) for a discussion of the German case.

transparency became a "buzz" word after the 1997–1998 East Asian crisis. The term usually refers to the quality of information. Thus, Vishwanath and Kaufman (2001) suggest that transparency has a number of dimensions, such as the level of access to information, its comprehensiveness, relevance, quality, and reliability. In political economy, it often refers to "the absence of perceived corruption," which is what is measured by the Transparency International index (see, e.g., Lambsdorff 2000). Clearly, it is possible to have a lack of transparency in the first sense – obscurity – without necessarily implying its absence in the second – corruption. One oft-used illustration (e.g., Furman and Stiglitz 1998) of lack of transparency in the sense of obscurity is the difficulty of reading the balance sheet of a Korean *chaebol*.[4] However, there have recently been spectacular revelations of corruption there (as discussed in section 9.5). Still the two concepts should be separated in principle.

Even in the first sense of the word, it is surprisingly easy to think of examples where greater transparency is not necessarily desirable.

1. In simple theoretical models, an increase in transparency is just as likely to increase the volatility of prices as to decrease it (Furman and Stiglitz 1998).
2. Politicians are typically not transparent, even in democracies. This is not just a common observation, but is easily demonstrated theoretically: in models of democratic political competition where politicians can choose between ambiguity and transparency, the strategy of ambiguity tends to be preferred.[5]
3. Redistribution may sometimes be possible only with *lack* of transparency. Thus one reason for universal medicare that is often mentioned is that only in this way can the poor be effectively insured. More generally, the desire to obfuscate the true level of redistribution is one reason why redistribution often takes place in kind and not in money.

Yet another meaning of transparency arises from the fact that in many quarters the promotion of transparency is believed to be really a code word or Trojan horse for what I shall call, following Benjamin Barber, "McWorld." McWorld is shorthand for global, U.S.-style capitalism, its signature products like MTV, Coca-Cola, and Hollywood cinema ("McWorld's storyteller"), and most of all its way of life. Barber's book *Jihad vs. McWorld*, which appeared in 1995, seems to have foreseen the future as we are now experiencing it better than more famous prognosticators like Samuel

---

[4] But see section 9.4.
[5] See, for example, Glazer (1990) or Alesina and Cukierman (1990).

Huntington and Francis Fukuyama. Barber (1995, p. 4) saw a world increasingly pit between two alternatives:

The first scenario . . . holds out the grim prospect of a retribalization of large swaths of humankind by war and bloodshed: a threatened balkanization of nation-states in which culture is pitted against culture, people against people, tribe against tribe, a Jihad in the name of a hundred narrowly conceived faiths against every kind of interdependence, every kind of artificial social cooperation and mutuality. . . . The second paints that future in *shimmering* pastels, a busy portrait of onrushing economic, technological, and ecological forces that demand *integration* and *uniformity* and that mesmerizes peoples everywhere with *fast* music, *fast* computers, and *fast* food – MTV, Macintosh, and McDonald's – pressing nations into one *homogeneous* global theme park, one McWorld tied together by communications, information, entertainment, and commerce. Caught between Babel and Disneyland, the planet is falling precipitously apart and coming reluctantly together at the very same moment. (emphasis added)

It is safe to say that the conflict between the two poles was not seen by economists. For example, things like tribalism, nationalism, or *jihad* play either little or no role in economic theory or policy. Indeed, it is not obvious at all what the implications of nationalism or *jihad* are for economic theory or economics policy.

With respect to McWorld, note that I have italicized all the phrases in the quoted passage from Barber that refer to its transparency. For example: (1) transparency requires *standardization* of inputs and outputs: this is what allows everything to be *fast*; (2) transparency was not part of the original Washington Consensus, but it is safe to assume it is part of the current one:[6] many have blamed lack of transparency, if not for the onset, at least for the depth of the 1997–1998 East Asian crisis; (3) its illusory quality: thus McDonald's food is not really good; members of the cast of "Friends" are not really representative of everyday American life nor will emulating them necessarily make you happy; and if a man buys a Lexus, he will not find beautiful women jumping into the front seat beside him when he stops at a red light.

The more general point is that the forces of McWorld *promote* transparency, that is, the more transparent the relationship the closer it gets to the kind of relationship characteristic of McWorld. Thomas Friedman (1999)

---

[6] See Williamson (2000). The other major change in the ideas that make up the consensus is probably the idea, supported by people as diverse as Bhagwati, Krugman, and Sachs, that there is a fundamental difference between goods markets and capital markets and that the latter always need careful regulation (including the possibility of controls on international capital movements) whereas the former may not.

sees economic transparency and political democratization being promoted through the globalization of capital markets, a process he calls "globalution." He suggests that the "Electronic Herd" of international investors insist on transparency before they will invest in a country (Friedman 1999, p. 147) – especially since the East Asian crisis of 1997–1998. The conventional interpretation of the role of transparency in that crisis seems to be that while it is difficult to understand how lack of transparency could have *initiated* the crisis (Furman and Stiglitz 1998), there is evidence that the crisis lasted longer and was deeper in less transparent countries (Vishwanath and Kaufman 2001).

Jihad and McWorld are opposites in many respects, but in others they are similar. Both aspects are illustrated by the story Barber cites from a *New Republic* report by Slavenka Drakulic of Admira and Bosko, two young star-crossed lovers from Sarajevo:

They were born in the 1960s. They watched Spielberg movies; they listened to Iggy Pop; they read John Le Carre; they went to a disco every Saturday night and fantasized about travelling to Paris or London. Longing for safety, it seems they finally negotiated with all sides for safe passage, and readied their departure from Sarajevo. Before they could cross the magical border that separates their impoverished land from the seeming sanctuary of McWorld, Jihad caught up to them. Their bodies lay along the river bank, riddled with bullets from anonymous snipers for whom safe passage signalled an invitation for target practise. The murdered young lovers, as befits emigres to McWorld, were clothed in jeans and sneakers. So, too, one imagines, were their murderers. (Barber 1995, p. 19)

Jihad and McWorld have other things in common besides blue jeans and sneakers: for one thing, *both forces are antidemocratic.* We know from public choice theory that the "consumers" of McWorld don't make good citizens. *Jihad* is political but demands the subservience of individual values to a common, often authoritarian, cause. And to some extent, it is McWorld that makes *jihad* possible, which for some was the true meaning of September 11th.[7] It is not just that McWorld facilitates *jihad* by providing the means for messages to be exchanged or broadcast worldwide and for terrorists to pick their targets around the world (or for the fact that their targets, that is, the people they see as their enemies, *are* around the world – what Barber refers to as *jihad versus* McWorld), though that is also important. The point is deeper: *McWorld stimulates* jihad.

---

[7] For others (e.g., Ajami 2003), 9/11 was just a fight *within* Islam, which had really nothing to do with the United States except insofar as it insulted the religion and interfered with the expansion of Islamic religious rule, for example, by stationing troops in the holy cities of Mecca and Medina.

It is difficult to understand exactly why this might be so from Barber's dialectical arguments and poetic metaphors, but the essence of his argument seems to be that McWorld empties the body of its soul, which then craves *jihad* in order to restore it. I return to this point later in the less poetic language of rational choice. But some things are obvious. McWorld tends to destroy local relationships and particularity along with many sources of social cohesion like common pensions and welfare programs. This leaves the population, especially its less mobile elements, vulnerable to extremist groups.[8]

McWorld's effects on economics can be summarized in terms of production and consumption. In production, McWorld creates wealth through specialization by comparative advantage, which is one of its attractions.[9] But it also dictates the substitution of general for specific human capital, thus obviating the need for implicit contracts or trust relationships within the firm. In consumption, Gertrude Stein's famous aphorism is perhaps never more true than of a (any) McDonalds's restaurant: there is (indeed, by design!) no "there" there.

But how does that create *jihad*? The answer is not obvious and is the main subject of this chapter. One way to approach it is to start by thinking of different national systems of production.

9.3 Shareholder versus Stakeholder Systems

A contrast is often drawn between two types of systems – the American or shareholder system and a "stakeholder" system, characteristic of much of Europe and especially Japan and South Korea.[10] In the shareholder system, the objective of the firm is said to be to the maximization of the value of the firm. However, such firms are often widely held, with no shareholder maintaining a controlling ownership and so there is considerable room for managerial objectives to enter the system. In the stakeholder systems, by contrast, capital is typically raised through an affiliated bank, and the objectives of the firm are more complex, involving the interests of various stakeholders such as the bank and the firm's employees.

---

[8] McWorld also makes many other kinds of relationships possible, such as email or relationships within transatlantic groups, such as the noted Villa Colombella Group.

[9] However, there is no evidence that increased wealth will reduce terrorism, as we saw in Chapter 5.

[10] Sometimes three systems are distinguished; for example, Gilpin (2001) classifies systems into the American, the Japanese, and the German models. Of course, many classifications are possible, depending on the purpose at hand.

The two systems can be compared on three dimensions: industrial relations, corporate governance, and the role of the government. To consider industrial relations first, the simplest way to derive the existence of the two types of system is via efficiency wage theory (Shapiro and Stiglitz 1984; Bulow and Summers 1986).[11] In this line of thought, the productivity of employees is assumed to be difficult to measure. Firms are therefore faced with a potential shirking problem. A firm can deter employees from shirking basically in one of two ways: by monitoring them more closely or by paying them higher wages. Thus firms face a choice between relatively low pay combined with high monitoring, or high pay and low monitoring. Gordon (1996) suggested that the industrial relations characteristic of different countries fall into these two types. For example, he contrasts the low-wage, high-monitoring system used especially in the shareholder systems of the United States and Canada with the high-wage, low-monitoring "stakeholder" system in much of Europe and Asia (Gordon 1996, p. 85). To give some illustrations of magnitude, in 1980 the supervisory ratio in the United States was about 11.5 percent, while real wages were virtually flat over the period 1973 to 1989; in Germany the supervisory ratio was about 3 percent and real wages increased over the period in question by about 3 percent per annum. Looking at a cross section of twelve countries, they do seem to cluster into the two types and, as predicted, the average annual real wage change for production workers in manufacturing over the period 1973 to 1989 is negatively related to a measure of supervision – what Gordon calls the "bureaucratic burden" – the percentage of total nonfarm employment working in administrative and managerial occupations in 1980.

Like Americans, many Europeans are proud of their system and many European politicians especially in France and Germany are adamant that they do not wish to adopt the American system of industrial relations. The main problem that is often alluded to with respect to the European system is that growth has been stagnating there recently. However, many countries in Europe seem to be extremely reluctant to part with the solidarity features of the system. The history of recent labor market reforms in Germany illustrates this point,[12] as does continued opposition to a more "flexible" system in France[13] and the recent struggle over the modification of Article 18 in Italy (which provides that an employee who is found to have been fired unjustly is entitled, not merely to compensation, but to have his job back).

---

[11] See the discussion of this theory in Chapter 2, section 2.4.
[12] See, for example, the discussion in the *New York Herald Tribune*, August 17, 2002.
[13] See S. Hoffman (2002).

The second difference between the two systems is the system of corporate governance. Under the stakeholder system, managers bear some responsibility toward their employees and to the affiliated bank that provides the firm with the capital. Both of these stakeholders often have a say in how the corporation is run. Under the U.S. system, the manager or CEO is charged with the task of maximizing the value of the firm (as expressed by the share price) and is responsible only to its board of directors. However, the CEO is typically not the owner of the firm and so, as has been recognized ever since the work of Berle and Means in the 1930s, the manager may pursue his own, so-called managerial objectives such as hiring excess staff or building luxurious headquarters at the expense of those of the shareholders. This is perhaps the weakest point of the system, as members of the board are often alleged to be "in the pocket" of the manager (i.e., the manager and the board constitute a solidary group), or at least not sufficiently independent, well informed, and active enough to police his activity credibly. One indication of this is that managers in the United States are hardly ever fired (Murphy 1999, p. 2543).

There are corrective mechanisms in the shareholder system, including incentives like stock ownership or options that are supposed to align the interests of the manager with the owners of the firm, and the possibility of hostile takeovers (the so-called market for corporate control). One consequence of the first is that the pay of American executives, which is partly set by the executives themselves, is larger by an order of magnitude than compensation in Europe or Asia (Murphy 1999). The takeover mechanism is also deeply flawed on both theoretical and empirical grounds, as a substantial literature has now demonstrated.[14]

Finally, the third difference between the two systems is the role of the government. In Europe and most especially in some Asian countries like Japan and South Korea, the government takes a very active role in deciding matters of corporate policy, such as where investments are to be made, whereas in

[14] The basic theoretical problem with the market for corporate control, first pointed out by Grossman and Hart (1980), is that, for a hostile takeover bid to be successful, the firm's current shareholders would have to be induced to sell their shares to a group that is bidding for the firm with the aim of raising the value of those shares once the takeover is complete. So why would the current shareholders sell, unless the bidder offers them the entire value of the prospective improvement? But, if that is what has to be offered, what motive is there left for the bidder to take over the firm? Empirical evidence does bear out the prediction of these models that a substantial premium must be offered to the firm's existing shareholders (see, e.g., Bradley 1980 or Roll 1986). Other predictions of the models are more controversial. For a range of views, see, for example, the papers in the *Journal of Perspectives* symposium on this subject (Varian 1988).

the shareholder system, intervention by the government is, by comparison, highly limited.[15] In addition, democracy is more typically associated with the shareholder system than with at least some variants of the stakeholder system.

What does this have to do with transparency? It seems that in all three aspects, the American or shareholder system is more transparent. To take the industrial relations aspect first, the U.S. system pays employees relatively low wages and monitors them intensively. Gordon's "bureaucratic burden" is highest in the United States. Now, monitoring obviously requires transparency while higher wages do not.[16] The shareholder system therefore promotes transparency within the company partly in order to monitor the activities of employees more easily. In terms of the second aspect mentioned – corporate governance – the actions of corporate executives are said to be transparently reflected in the share price of the corporation, an easily observable number. By contrast, the competence of the CEO and the value of enterprises under the stakeholder system is much more difficult to ascertain. Finally, the third variable – the greater role of the government in stakeholder systems – obviously muddies their transparency still further, as it is less obvious in the stakeholder system whether a policy or strategy was the business's idea or was mandated by the government.

So in all three dimensions the shareholder system appears more transparent than the stakeholder system. The next section turns to the role of solidarity in the two systems, and derives our central proposition – how McWorld stimulates *jihad*.

9.4 How McWorld Stimulates *Jihad*

No organization runs on formal relations alone, and all rely to a considerable extent on informal organization that enables them to function relatively

---

[15] Johnson (1982) and Wade (1990) are the classic sources for the argument that the increased role of the government has helped economic performance in the Asian countries. There is also a large literature to the contrary: a good representative example is Bhagwati (2004).

[16] One might try to rationalize the combination of low pay for employees with enormous executive compensation packages if the actions of the CEO were harder to monitor by an order of magnitude than other employees, and his actions had a relatively large effect on the firm's performance. However, if it is the CEO who is to be held responsible for the performance of the firm as measured by its stock price, then these two points cannot both be true as this variable is easily observable. On the other hand, if the CEO is not the determining factor of the firm's value, why pay such high compensation?

smoothly.[17] As we have seen, this point can be expressed in various ways. One is that, in addition to monitoring and compensation, employees within both the shareholder and the stakeholder systems are members of *networks*, or will have accumulated *social capital* within the firm. Alternatively, as I suggest here, an element of *solidarity* – a particular type of network or form of social capital – is retained in both the shareholder and stakeholder systems. These bring a capacity to operate without constant formal instruction and approval, without which any organization will drown in red tape.

Nations also can employ a number of institutional mechanisms to produce solidarity among their citizens. One of these is programs that *ensure equality among the group*, such as common pensions and universal medicare. The more everyone within a group receives exactly the same treatment, the less energy an individual in the group will put into trying to increase his or her own advantage at the expense of the group and the more will be put into seeking benefits for the group. Of course, there is a free-rider problem: each individual's attempt to maintain group solidarity benefits not just himself but everyone in the group. If the group is large, free-riding will limit the extent to which individuals will work for the group's advantage. However, as a substantial literature now demonstrates, there are various ways to overcome the free-rider problem, including not only the classic Olsonian selective incentives but mobilization through networks and social ties (Opp and Hartmann 1989), and group leadership and the promise of rewards from successful action (Uhlaner 1989; Morton 1991; and Chong 1991). Given a constant level of these incentives, more equality of treatment within the group means more effort directed at group goals.

Group solidarity will also be larger, the larger the *barriers to entry and exit* from the group. The reasoning is similar: the harder it is to leave the group, the more members will be motivated to take measures that take care of it. The more membership is restricted, the less it will be felt that any improvement in the group's fortunes will be dissipated through opportunistic entry. To illustrate, the peculiar solidarity of ethnic groups comes from the fact that entry to and exit from the group are essentially blocked, as discussed in the preceding chapter. Other groups find other ways to limit entry: among these must be included obfuscating the way the group works to outsiders, for example, by using ingroup rituals and practices and ingroup signals and

---

[17] As discussed in Chapter 2, Breton and Wintrobe (1982) developed the role of social capital networks in production, emphasizing that some networks or kinds of trust increase productivity while others reduce it. Here I am taking a simpler point of view.

symbolism. Groups also use stigma to raise the marginal rate of substitution of within-group consumption (as argued by Iannacconne 1992 for sects). Such practices make it more difficult for members of the group to interact pleasurably with outsiders and raise the value of ingroup interaction.

Finally, and most obviously, group solidarity is most famously built through *jihad* against an external enemy, whether another nation, ethnic group, or civilization. The larger the perceived threat to individuals in the group from outside, the greater the solidarity of the group. There are several possible reasons for this. It may be a biological trait inherited from the time when men banded together in the face of an external threat (Rubin 2002). Another possibility is that the more any individual believes that the threat is directed at him or her personally because of his or her membership in the group, the greater the tendency to invest in group solidarity.

As discussed in Chapter 2, barriers to entry and exit, mechanisms to ensure equality, a set of unique and common beliefs, and the struggle against an external enemy are alternative methods to raise solidarity. It follows that if some of the mechanisms become more costly to use, the others will be substituted for it. One implication is that it would be particularly important for the European Union, for example, in which historic enmities among the member countries have been forgone, to continue to subsidize the welfare state and labor market regulation if solidarity is to be maintained there.

What happens to the shareholder and stakeholder systems as the result of increased globalization (McWorld)? First, globalization tends to encourage the adoption of the shareholder system over the stakeholder system. The fall in transportation and information costs makes it more feasible for companies to diversify production internationally. Globalization implies an increase in the elasticity of demand for labor as firms can increasingly substitute foreign for domestic labor (Bhagwati 2000; Rodrik 1997). This substitution is obviously easier in the shareholder system, in which workers do not have "rights" to jobs and need not be compensated for their losses if terminated. Moreover, globalization insists on transparency, and this favors the expansion of the shareholder system as well. So, on both these grounds, globalization tends to favor the shareholder system over the stakeholder system.[18]

Globalization also changes the nature of both shareholder and stakeholder systems in that it reduces their demand for solidarity. There are a

---

[18] Some (e.g., Gilpin 2001)) assert that greater transparency in Germany, along with increasingly high labor costs is pushing it toward the shareholder system. West Germany currently has the highest real wages in manufacturing worldwide (Sinn 2002, p. 8).

number of reasons for this. Globalization detaches the CEO from relations within the firm and gives the firm a greater incentive to substitute nonspecific for specific human capital (Cerny 1995). Globalization also tends to inflate executive salaries in the shareholder system[19] and this makes it more difficult for social capital to be created or maintained within the firm as it is more difficult to have exchanges between parties when they are very unequal (Zingales and Rajan 2000). The increased transparency demanded by McWorld also reduces solidarity to the extent that social cohesion rests on equality and therefore requires that obvious inequalities be obfuscated. Finally, globalization has two effects on common beliefs: on the one hand, it means lower costs of information everywhere, thus making it more difficult to sustain a unique set of common beliefs within a group that are different from those held by other groups; on the other hand, it makes it easier for extreme or unusual groups to find like-minded members around the world (perhaps the most frightening example of this is the blossoming of Internet sites for groups like pedophiles). In all these ways, then, it would seem that globalization reduces the capacity of nations to maintain solidarity (while increasing the capacity for individuals to enjoy diversity).

To summarize, globalization reduces the capacity of either system to generate solidarity via the mechanisms of equality of treatment within the firm, raising barriers to entry and exit, or maintaining a unique set of common beliefs. It follows that the demand for solidarity via struggle against some external enemy is increased.[20] *Here, then, in broad rational choice terms, is how McWorld stimulates* jihad.

Actually, it is not quite that simple, and we need to construct this argument more carefully. To develop the connection between globalization and extremism, suppose that every nation has some extremist groups within it.

---

[19] Over the past thirty years the average annual salary in the United States expressed in 1998 dollars rose about 10 percent (from $32,522 to $35, 864). Over the same period the average real compensation of the top 100 CEOs in the United States went from $1.3 million (39 times the pay of an ordinary worker) to $37.5 million, more than 1,000 times the pay of ordinary workers (Krugman 2002, p. 64).

[20] It may be objected that there are always a variety of possible institutions for any purpose, and there must be other ways to create solidarity besides the four mentioned, so that if the first three become more costly, others besides the fourth can be substituted. However, while this is surely true, the ones mentioned are not examples of institutions but mechanisms, and they cover many of the institutions that can play this role. The easiest way to think about the proposition in the text is by analogy to the proposition in standard theory that an increase in the price of capital will raise the demand for labor. No doubt other factors of production could be substituted for capital as well, including some that are not usually mentioned in standard theory (entrepreneurship, organization?), and others which have yet to be discovered. But the demand for labor will still increase.

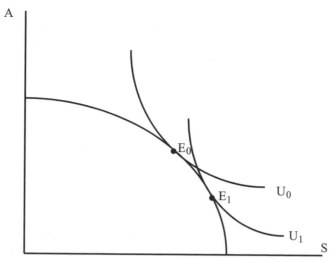

Figure 9.1a. How globalization breeds extremism. Globalization reduces the alternative bases for solidarity (barriers to entry and exit, common social programs), increasing the value of solidarity to some individuals from extremist groups. The typical member of such a group moves from E_0 to E_1. Figure is based on Figure 5.1.

One attraction of these groups is that they provide solidarity, as discussed particularly in Chapter 5. Now look at Figure 9.1a. The figure displays the indifference curves (choice between autonomy and solidarity) of an individual member of an extremist group, and the position and slope of the constraint is governed by the group's technology for developing solidarity among its members. As suggested previously, globalization reduces the nation's alternative bases for the supply of solidarity such as barriers to entry and exit, common social programs, and common beliefs. Consequently, the spread of markets deprives individuals of these sources of solidarity. So they will be more willing to join extremist groups in order to get solidarity, and those individuals who are already members of such groups will want more solidarity with them than before. So the typical individual member of an extremist group chooses E_1 rather than E_0, implying greater solidarity with the group.

Figure 9.1b shows the effect of this choice on the group's capacity to produce pressure. Because there is greater solidarity within the group, the organization can now produce more pressure for any given level of resources K and L and organizational technology O. So, at any given level of risk (e.g., σ_0^2 in Figure 9.1b), the amount of expected pressure increases (e.g., from P_0 to P_1). Because solidarity is more important for extremist methods of pressure than for moderate methods, the capacity of the group to produce

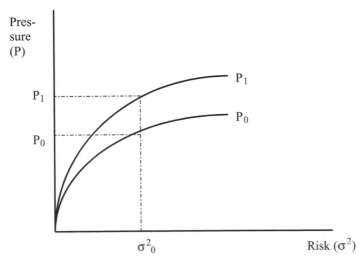

Figure 9.1b. Globalization and extremism 2. The extremist group can now produce more pressure for any given level of resources K, L, and O, because the members of the organization have chosen more solidarity than before. Figure is based on Figure 5.4.

pressure increases more the higher the level of risk taken, as shown also in Figure 9.1b.

Figure 9.1c shows the effect of this change on the group leader's choice between moderate and extreme methods of pressure. As discussed previously (in Chapter 4), this can be represented as the choice between a riskless asset (moderate methods of pressure) and a risky one (extreme methods). Because expected pressure increases for any given level of risk, so does the capacity to achieve the goal of the organization (Z). In Figure 9.1c, the relationship between risk and return (EZ) therefore shifts up (from EZ_0 to EZ_1). The increase in return for any given level of risk implies a substitution effect that favors risk taking. As well, there is an "income" or "wealth" effect due to the increase in the organization's capacity to produce pressure. The wealth effect also favors risk taking if the leader's coefficient of relative risk aversion decreases with wealth. If this is true, both effects favor increased risk taking, that is, a larger proportion of the organization's resources will be used in extremist as opposed to moderate activity. On the other hand, if the coefficient of relative risk aversion increases with wealth, the wealth effect is opposed to risk taking, and the conclusion depends on whether the substitution effect dominates the wealth effect.[21] Thus, *whether the degree of extremism increases or not depends crucially on the extremist leader's attitude*

---

[21] See any modern text on portfolio choice theory, for example, Elton and Gruber (2003).

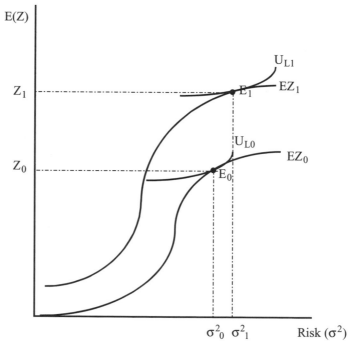

Figure 9.1c. Globalization and extremism 3. The increase in return for any given risk shown by the upward shift in EZ implies that the group leader wishes to take more risk (make more extensive use of extreme methods), so long as either relative risk aversion is constant or decreasing with wealth, or, if it is increasing, it is still dominated by the substitution effect. In those cases, the leader moves from a point like E_0 to one like E_1. Figure is adapted from Figure 5.5.

to risk. Provided either that the substitution effect dominates the wealth effect, or that the wealth effect is either neutral with respect to risk (constant relative risk aversion) or favors it (decreasing relative risk aversion), the leader chooses more extremism as a result of this change. If either of these qualifications hold, *McWorld stimulates* jihad.

This process is not the only way in which McWorld stimulates *jihad.* Another is described by the French Islamic specialist Olivier Roy (2004), with respect to the effect of globalization on Islamic radical religious groups, or what he calls "neofundamentalist" Islam. Neofundamentalist Islam provides a code of conduct that functions in a similar manner in any part of the world, and is thus "a perfect tool of globalization":

[Neofundamentalist] religion, conceived as a detextualized set of norms, can be adapted to any society, precisely because it has severed its links with a given culture and allows people to live in a sort of virtual, deterritorialized community that includes any believer. The religious community is decoupled from real societies and, in this sense neofundamentalism acknowledges the secularization that affects them. It nevertheless maintains the usual fundamentalist claims that in Islam there is no separation between religion and state, and that Islam is an all encompassing religion. But it does that simply by ignoring the real world and building an abstract community where it is for the individual to experience, in his or her self, a totality that no longer exists. *Wherever the true believer is, he remains in touch with the virtual community by sharing the same portable kit of norms, adapted to any social context.* The internet is also a perfect paradigm and tool of this virtual community. (Roy 2004, p. 271; emphasis added)

The advent of neofundamentalist Islam leads to more extremism. Roy's argument can also be made more precise with our diagrammatic apparatus (and is subject to the same qualification about risk taking). In Figure 9.1a, the neofundamentalist innovation whereby radical Islam is decoupled from a specific nation and made portable –"deterritorialized" – could be represented as an upward shift in the technology for producing Islamic solidarity in non-Islamic nations and other places where it could not have thrived before (not shown). As in the previous analysis, this would lead the typical individual to take more solidarity than before. This change then feeds into Figures 9.1b and 9.1c in exactly the same way as in the previous analysis, and leads to exactly the same conclusion (with the same qualification about attitudes toward risk): the group becomes more extreme.

One difference between this argument, based on Roy and the one I outlined first is that the second argument refers to the effects of globalization on extremism (Islamic radicalism) anywhere in the world, not just in the nation where markets have penetrated more fully.

Yet a third argument can be made along these lines, deriving from globalization's capacity to increase market opportunities in countries where these were scarce previously. This mechanism, which is implicit in Berman (2003),[22] is that globalization means greater outside opportunities for individual members of religious or other socially cohesive groups, and may cause some individuals to leave groups in which they previously may have been enthusiastic participants. In order to prevent dilution of the group's quality, group leaders will tend to raise the sacrifice or level of prohibitions necessary to remain within the group in order to avoid dilution of the quality of the group's experiences. In other words, they tend to become more extreme.[23]

---

[22] I owe this point to a taped discussion with Eli Berman, part of the program *Extremism,* (Wintrobe, December 2004).

[23] A related process of increasing group extremism is discussed in Ferrero (2002b). Here, increased extremism is a way in which groups prevent the dissipation of rents that might otherwise occur as a result of successful political action. The increase in extremism is meant to drive out less extreme members, leaving the rents from group pressure to be shared among a smaller number of members.

It is worth emphasizing some of the implications of these arguments. For example, the European welfare states build solidarity by providing pensions, medicare, unemployment insurance, and so forth. The American-style system has fewer of these and considerably more inequality and "real poverty" (Alesina, Glaeser, and Sacerdote 2001). The process of globalization, which to some extent spreads American-style values (Friedman 1999) of small government and flexible labor markets makes it more difficult for other countries to sustain different systems. If they do lose them, they may find that, if their citizens have a real demand for solidarity, as I am suggesting in this chapter, *jihad* might have to take the place of these other mechanisms. Indeed, on this line of reasoning, it may be no accident that the previous peak of globalization occurred just before World War I.

Similarly, it may be no accident that the United States administration headed by George W. Bush made war abroad at the same time as domestically it created further opportunities and tax breaks for the relatively rich.[24] In the absence of *jihad* against an external enemy, opposition to inequality-enhancing policies might spell their defeat. At the same time, the idea that competition against an external adversary can substitute for other solidarity-producing mechanisms explains how it can be that American conformism, noted since Tocqueville, can go hand in hand with the equally oft-noted competitiveness of American society.

The mechanisms of equality, barriers to entry and exit, common belief, and *jihad* operate in all countries. Politicians, firms, and religious leaders everywhere compete to satisfy their citizens' demands for solidarity. Dictatorships no less than democracies are interested in building support through this mechanism.[25] It follows that politicians everywhere are more eager to embrace the principle of *jihad* in a more globalized world. In turn, the interests of firms and governments in potentially opposing sets of countries intertwine. The "security dilemma" operates equally well with solidarity instead of armaments. Increased solidarity in one country therefore can be threatening to other countries if they see themselves as potential victims of aggression.

---

[24] Many analysts have noted that standard economic theories of the factors generating income inequality (skill-biased technical change, and increased international trade) cannot explain the recent increase in inequality in the United States (e.g., Krugman 2002). So, even if the present analysis is wrong, there is still a big problem that requires explanation.

[25] Whether dictatorships do this more or less than democracies is an interesting question. Dictatorships are more capable of imposing barriers to entry and exit from their societies. On this ground, their leaders should be less interested in *jihad*. But inequality tends to be greater under dictatorship, leading to the opposite prediction.

In this way of thinking, the "Clash of Civilizations" discussed in Huntington's celebrated (1996) book of that title is not an inevitable outcome of differences among peoples but of political processes that have at their root a desire on the part of their citizens for solidarity. This desire is frustrated by the destruction to equality-enhancing processes, unique common beliefs, and barriers to entry and exit caused by increased globalization, leaving only *jihad* to satisfy it. Similarly, people's needs for solidarity and what the exploitation of these can lead to may be what is left out of the optimistic predictions of an "End of History" and the triumph of liberal democracy, or, more generally, for a world increasingly characterized by democracy, human rights, free markets, and the peaceful resolution of conflicts by international institutions.

The ideas in *Jihad vs. McWorld* are reinforced by considering the ideology put forward by some of the thinkers behind the contemporary radical Islamic *jihad* movement. Buruma and Margalit's *Occidentalism* (2004) examines the strands of hostility to the West in the thought of radical Islamic thinkers such as Sayyid Qutb and Sayyid Muhamud Taleqani. These are the dreams and stereotypes of the Western world that fuel hatred in the hearts of Al Qaeda and like-minded organizations. Buruma and Margalit (2004, p. 11) suggest that "[t]he strands [of hostility] are linked . . . to form a chain of hostility – hostility to the City, with its image of rootless, arrogant, greedy, decadent, frivolous cosmopolitanism; to the mind of the West, manifested in science and reason; to the settled bourgeois, whose existence is the antithesis of the self-sacrificing hero; and to the infidel, who must be crushed to make way for a world of pure faith."

What do all of the notions in the paragraph just quoted have in common? I suggest that *all of the "enemies" of radical Islam are manifestations of threats to and destroyers of Islamic solidarity:* the city is a place inhabited by rootless individuals who are free of traditional constraints; science and reason are independent sources of knowledge and authority that challenge the hegemony of religious authority; self-interest is opposed to the common interest; and the infidel is an apostate.

Buruma and Margalit also show that many of the ideas common to radical Islam actually have their roots in Western extremist thought. The sources for them can be found in the Counter-Reformation and the Counter-Enlightenment in Europe, in the many varieties of fascism and national socialism in East and West, and in the thought of anticapitalist and antiglobalization thinkers. For example, Engels was repulsed by "the lack of solidarity in this society of 'atomized' individuals, each going after his own 'selfish' interests" (Buruma and Margalit 2004, p. 25). The Nazis wanted to overturn the French Revolution. And so on. Thus "today's suicide bombers don't suffer from some unique pathology but are fired by ideas that have a history" (p. 12). In this way of thinking, the 9/11 attack on America played into an ancient myth – the myth of the destruction of the sinful city.

Of course, from a different point of view, globalization and the West that sponsors it – even the Western city – isn't all bad. Specialization and the division of labor increase wealth and, on many accounts, have reduced poverty worldwide. Even the destruction of solidarity has its virtues: Individualism thrives in a rootless atmosphere. The city is a great place for the nonconformist. Capitalism, too, promotes the individual and frees people from the links and bonds to society that are characteristic of more-tradition-based societies. Globalization extends the reach of these tradition-destroying processes around the world. *Solidarity requires conformity*, as discussed at length in Chapters 2 and 5. But if the bohemian or the intellectual (or the capitalist entrepreneur) can live without solidarity, that doesn't mean he is free of its pressures. Believing so was the weakness of the Weimar Republic. The bohemian – the nonconformist person, the pure individualist – is the first victim of *jihad*, whether from within the society or without.

9.5 Asian Growth through Corruption: A Fourth Way?

9.5.1 Corrupt Tigers

In section 9.3, I suggested that two of the dynamic features of the American system – its openness and its relative absence of a social safety net – come at a cost: a reduction in solidarity. The social welfare states of Europe do not face this problem to the same degree. However, they face a different problem: corruption. The analysis so far has been developed without reference to corruption, as is standard in the literature. But it is time to introduce it.

Tanzi (1995, p. 167) defines corruption as "the intentional noncompliance with the arm's-length principle aimed at deriving some advantage for oneself or for related individuals from this behavior." He points out that the word "corruption" comes from the Latin verb *rumpere*, meaning "to break." The implication is that something – a rule, moral code, a promise – is broken in a corrupt act.

Corruption also often means doing a favor for someone. In the stakeholder system, exchanges are often made and enforced along network lines, in contrast to law-backed exchanges characteristic of the shareholder system. Network exchanges are often made in secret and enforced by informal mechanisms, and these kinds of exchanges lend themselves most easily to corruption. In societies with high levels of social capital (solidarity), networks or connections among family and friends tend to be more extensive. Consequently, such societies are especially prone to corruption.

To illustrate, among countries with extensive high-growth experience since World War II, the Italian economy has, somewhat surprisingly, been a standout in Europe, and per capita growth there is now suggested to have been the largest in Europe during the fifty years or so since the end of the war. In the past few years, growth there has stalled. But even during its period of rapid growth, Italy also had many problems with corruption, as illustrated by the extensive scandals opened up by the "mani pulite" (clean hands) investigations of the 1990s.[26]

Of course, the countries with the best growth performance over the past two decades or so are the Asian "tigers." At one time it was said that these countries grew quickly because there was less rent seeking there, thanks in some cases at least to the presence of authoritarian but efficiency-minded dictatorships (Haggard 1990; Bardhan 1997). Bureaucrats in these countries were lauded for their neutrality, and it was said (e.g., by Barro 1998) that authoritarianism eliminated or at least reduced the rent seeking to be found in the corrupt democracies in the West. However, this idea seems to have come under a cloud recently. For example, while Singapore may indeed be the closest approximation to the myth, here is Lee Kwan Yew himself, responding to a 1996 report that his son, Deputy Minister Lee Hsien Loong, accepted discounts of more than $700,000 in a soft sale of condominiums conducted before bids were opened to the public: "I am me. It's not a level playing field" (quoted in Hutchcroft 1997, p. 223).

With respect to South Korea in particular, David Kang's detailed investigations (2002a and b) have exploded the idea that Korea grew because its bureaucrats were neutral. His study shows that, as he puts it, "Corruption was rampant, and the Korean state intervened in the way it did because doing so was in the interests of a small group of business and political elites" (Kang 2002a, p. 178). The high-growth era is thought to have started with the Park regime. Kang's account of the process is straightforward: "The basic process was simple: Business and political elites exchanged bribes for political favours. . . . Businessmen used the rents from cheap capital to expand as rapidly as possible, thus ensuring their continued political and economic importance. Development and money politics proceeded hand in hand" (Kang 2002a, p. 185).

---

[26] See Della Porta and Vanucci (1997) on corruption in Italy.

The extent of the corruption of the political process as documented in detail by Kang appears remarkable. Leading members of the Democratic Republican Party took massive donations from the *chaebol* in return for loans and deals. If businessmen did not provide sufficient funds when asked, the Bank of Korea called in their loans, or they suffered a tax audit, or their subsidy application was denied (Kang 2002a, pp. 186–187). But politicians did not dominate the process. Rather, business and the state were partners. The result was a massive expansion of industrial capacity.

How could such rent seeking account for what is certainly one of the biggest success stories among the Asian tigers? If one thinks about it, it is not hard to understand why economic growth could have been high at the same time as the state was handing out contracts in exchange for bribes. Growth benefits capital owners (producers) more than labor because the increased value of assets in the future implied by economic growth can be immediately capitalized into the price of capital assets today, whereas the increased value of labor or other assets such as a cleaner or safer environment can be realized only over time. Thus, if investment decisions by the government are based on bribes, it is to be expected that business groups will offer the most compared with labor or environmental groups, and it is no accident that such a system, while corrupt, can result in a high rate of investment and growth.

Economists have been somewhat blind to this possibility because they have focused on the costs of "rent seeking." But in South Korea this process was well controlled under the authoritarian regimes and centralized in the highest offices of the party. Thus there was no unseemly rent seeking in the classic sense of wasteful expenditure on lawyers and lobbyists to get the ear of the government: the bribes were coming from the six or seven top *chaebols* and no other group need have bothered to bid. Second, because it was all cash, there was technically no waste in the economic sense, just a transfer from one party to another. And, third, because the firms providing the bribes were doing so in order to obtain investment funds, the process may have stimulated growth.

Campos and Root (1996) explain the performance of the "tigers" in general by the idea that growth in these countries is shared, and in general I suspect that there is a great deal of truth to this view. There is no doubt, for example, that real wages in South Korea have increased enormously over the past forty years or so (see the figures in Sachs and Radelet 1998). This sharing is what makes the solidary system so attractive. But the exposure of the corruption casts a shadow both on the idea that sharing was chiefly responsible for the spectacular growth performance and, in general, on the desirability of at least the East Asian version of stakeholder capitalism. And it is not comforting that the amount of corruption seems to have multiplied with the turn to democracy (Kang 2002b, p. 196).

9.5.2 Corrupt Communist Chinese Capitalists

Perhaps the most remarkable story of growth over the past twenty years or so has been that of mainland China. Here there is no hidden corruption to be exposed: China has been consistently ranked one of the most corrupt countries in the world since the indexes were begun. Yet its growth rate over that period has been spectacular. How is this to be explained? China's policies certainly do not conform to the prescriptions of the Washington Consensus. And one cannot assert that the Communist Chinese bureaucrats, who still seem to control the political system even though central planning is dead and the state enterprises are in steep decline, are immune to offers of bribes or favors in exchange for rents. The system is *based* on the exchange of bribes and favors for rents.[27]

One explanation is that, possibly even more than South Korea, China has a powerful and authoritarian government that controls the corruption process. In bribery, monopoly is better than competition (Shleifer and Vishny 1993). Under competition, so many bribes may be required that no investment project goes through. Perhaps the typical outcome of competitive bribery is illustrated by Peru, where competition in corruption has produced "dead" capital, as discussed by De Soto (2000). So part of the explanation of how corruption works to promote growth in China is that the corruption is still tightly controlled by the party.

Another piece of the puzzle is the increased prevalence of illegal asset stripping, in which managers "appropriate" the assets of SOEs (state-owned enterprises) for their private use (Chen 2000, p. 43). In this way state assets are privatized, but the process destroys trust and solidarity. In describing the process, Chen (2000) notes that labor protests increased in the 1990s by "quantum leaps," involving more than 3.6 million workers in 1998 alone; in prereform China, the crucial dimension of state-labor relations was an "all-encompassing dependency of labor on the state enterprise," in which workers receive medical care, housing, pensions, and other benefits from the firm (what Andrew Walder [1986] calls "neo-traditionalism"). The 1987 "Optimal Combination" reform, designed to reduce the excess work force in state enterprises, gave managers the power to dismiss workers, but also insisted that a minimal living allowance be given to those laid off (Chen

---

[27] A comprehensive picture of the process is presented in Lin (2001).

2000, p. 46). However, in the 1990s many firms reneged on this obligation, and indeed many began to withhold the pay of the workers still employed by the firm and to stop funding workers' pensions, claiming they had to reduce costs in order to be competitive in the market. At the same time, in many of these factories, managerial asset stripping became extensive. This takes various forms:

In some cases, managers transfer the most profitable activities of the SOE's to their own businesses, leaving the debts with the parent enterprise, which eventually has to close down. In others, managers spend enterprise funds without restraint on luxury housing, extravagant entertaining, free overseas travel, and so on. . . . Many managers become wealthy while their employees are close to liquidation. They are, in a phrase used by workers, "rich Buddhist abbots in poor temples." (Chen 2000, p. 51)

Chen's study found that the circumstances that were particularly likely to give rise to protests were the combination of managers' reneging on obligations to the workers along with evidence of managerial asset stripping. In many cases, the party has to intervene to prevent the demonstrations from getting out of control. A worker from Jianxi province told an interviewer:

How pitiful we workers are! But how about the cadres? They are gambling, womanizing, living in luxury houses, and driving fancy cars. Where does that money come from? They cannot possibly earn that amount of money even in ten thousand years. . . . What do we workers hope for? We hope that there will be another cultural revolution and all those corrupt cadres will be killed! (in Chen 2000 p. 51)

Analyses and stories of asset stripping abound in recent issues of Chinese economic journals (e.g., Wang 2002; Ding 1999, and especially He Qinglian's monumental "China's Descent into a Quagmire," serialized in three parts in the *Chinese Economy,* 2000–2001). He Qinglian traces the rise of asset stripping to the introduction of "shareholding" into state enterprises. The story, with its accompanying naiveté about the workings of corporate governance in shareholder systems, will be familiar to those who followed the privatization process in Russia:[28]

This system was seen by its creators as the "ruby slippers" (*fabao*) that would bring about a magical transformation in state-owned enterprises. The traditional role of "shareholding" for raising capital was, in the eyes of both officials and economists in China, of only secondary consideration. . . . government officials and economists optimistically forecast that once shareholders gained the relevant property rights as owners, the management, development, and distribution of wealth generated

---

[28] I have discussed the case of Russia elsewhere (Wintrobe 1998b).

by the entire enterprise would be under strict supervision by the newly created shareholders, thereby making management responsible to both its superiors (the board of directors) and its subordinates (employees). The latter in particular would become the new "masters" of the enterprise as their buying and selling of shares in the market would lead to constant supervision and monitoring of enterprise efficiency. (Qinglian 2001, p. 35)

Instead, what seems to have happened is the liquidation of debts and of trust within the party, as exemplified by the actions of the manager in Chen's labor protest story. Workers who labored for many years, accumulating debts within the party by receiving wages below their marginal productivity, expected that in their senior years they would be compensated for this in the form of a pension and care in their old age, courtesy of the "neotraditional" paternalistic factory system. Instead, it appears that many managers are in effect appropriating the employees' firm-specific capital. Unlike the Russian case, in the Chinese case there is economic growth to accompany the corruption. Even in the Chinese case, however, it seems that this growth may not benefit the workers. A proper "growth accounting" story would factor in the loss of trust or solidarity in the process of asset stripping, losses as real from the economic point of view as the loss of a building or any other capital asset, as Shleifer and Summers (1988) have pointed out. Thus to the extent that the growth has taken place via what might be called the *liquidation of solidarity*, it may not be real.

Finally, growth in China may be sowing the seeds of *jihad*. The individuals have been stripped of their solidarity and trust assets, and they cannot recover them by the old mechanisms of barriers to entry, common welfare programs, and other features of the neotraditional system. This leaves the option of *jihad*. Indeed some observers claim that nationalism in China appears to be growing extremely rapidly (e.g., Copper 2002, p. 25).

9.5.3 Pitfalls in the Analysis

The argument of section 9.5.1 could be interpreted by some as suggesting that if a country wants growth, why not try corruption? Before embracing this formula, however, it might be worthwhile to look at some pitfalls. The first is that measured growth via corruption is not necessarily real growth once the losses to the economy from the liquidation of trust or solidarity are factored in. And the distributional consequences are likely to be particularly unfavorable with this style of growth. The stories about what is happening to many employees of state-owned enterprises in China provide sobering illustrations of these points.

Second, there is an alternative possibility about corruption: that it takes place, and the economy doesn't grow at all, or even declines. Many Middle Eastern and African countries are the most outstanding examples. They are famously corrupt, but they do not have any impressive growth record to show for it – quite the contrary. Apart from some of the suggestive ideas referred to in the previous section, no one knows why some corrupt countries grow while others do not. Mauro's oft-cited (1995) evidence is that, on balance, corruption is inimical to growth.[29]

The other possibility is that corruption severely impairs the society that permits it. In this connection, Lambsdorff (2002) suggests that corruption may be more costly than rent seeking, in that it can motivate the creation of monopolies and regulations to obtain bribes. The capacity for people to cheat each other as corruption grows in China is, on some accounts, growing by leaps and bounds. One possibility is that China is getting stuck in an equilibrium corruption trap. Another is that the practices there are laying the ground for Chinese *jihad*.

9.6 Conclusion

Economic systems can grow, or not, in a variety of ways. The shareholder-transparent system favored by McWorld and the stakeholder system are two of these. The stakeholder system appears superior in that there is some commitment to equality of treatment, which builds solidarity, and therefore reduces the potential for *jihad*. The main danger with the solidarity system is that it may retard growth. The system also has greater potential for corruption, because network exchange tends to be secret and informally enforced. Moreover, under either system, one group of actors can appropriate the capital value of mutual trust and destroy the trust in the process. Arguably, this is what took place in the United States under the "downsizing" phenomenon in the 1980s and with the privatization process in Russia in the 1990s,[30] and appears to be happening now with the process of asset stripping in China. In the United States, downsizing allowed the executives of firms to raise their own salaries by firing their employees. In Russia, the privatization of state assets before proper institutions were in place allowed insiders to buy control of the firms at bargain prices and strip them of their assets. In

---

[29] Some questions about the magnitude, though not the direction, of Mauro's numbers has been raised by Li, Xu, and Zou (2000).

[30] For details on this view of downsizing in the United States, see Wintrobe (2000). My account of the Russian privatization process is Wintrobe (1998b).

China, the same process of asset stripping appears to be going on, but the result is growth partly because the Communist Party retains overall control over the process. However, there is some informal evidence that corruption is reaching new heights in the process.

Globalization demands transparency and thus favors the expansion of the more transparent shareholder system. The problem is that the greater penetration of markets as a result of globalization can stimulate *jihad*. I described three ways in which this can happen: in the first, globalization reduces such bases of solidarity as barriers to entry and exit, common welfare and other programs, and common beliefs, leaving only the mechanism of *jihad* to satisfy the demand for solidarity. So individuals will be tempted to join extremist groups in order to get the solidarity they lack from other sources, and those who are already members will want more from these groups. This typically (not always, as discussed) leads extremist group leaders to become more extreme. In the second, globalization leads to the creation of what Olivier Roy (2004) calls "deterritorialized" religious communities that allow radical groups to operate worldwide without any connection to the societies in which their members live. Again this usually leads to the use of more extremist policies by group leaders. And in the third, described by Berman (2003), the increased market opportunities provided by globalization lead groups to step up their extremism in order to avoid dilution of the quality of solidarity within them. These three mechanisms provide a rational choice foundation for Benjamin Barber's proposition that McWorld stimulates *jihad*.

The challenge facing the solidarity system is to find ways to promote growth that do not involve corruption. The challenges facing the transparent system are to show that its transparency is not illusory, and to find ways of promoting solidarity within the system apart from the promotion of external enemies. The challenge facing proponents of globalization is to find ways to accommodate the desires for solidarity and community that are thwarted by globalization. Otherwise the forces of *jihad* may not be contained.

PART FIVE

CONCLUSION

Summary of Propositions and Policy Implications

10.1 Summary of Propositions in the Book

In this book I have tried to understand political extremism on the assumption that the participants in extremist movements – both leaders and followers – are rational. But I added a twist to the standard rational choice approach: people are completely rational and selfish, but they are social and desire social interaction. They want solidarity, usually with a group. As these concepts are sometimes used loosely, I provided precise mathematical definitions of solidarity and related concepts like social capital in the appendix to Chapter 2 of the book.

In the first part of the book I sketched how this idea could be applied to problems such as crime, poverty, and international finance. The second part focused on using the model to explain varieties of extremist behavior in politics, such as the proclivity of leaders with extremist ideas to use violence to achieve their goals, how seemingly rational people can be led to commit suicide for a cause, and specific phenomena like nationalism, *jihad,* and revolution. Chapters on the great French Revolution, the explosion of nationalism under Yugoslavia under Milosevic, the phenomenon of suicide terrorism, and the rise of Islamic radicalism along with globalization illustrated these ideas.

For easy reference, I present a summary list of the main propositions in the book. Sometimes I add a brief comment as well as providing the chapter source.

I. The desire for group solidarity or social interactions is a fundamental feature of people's preferences or behavior (Chapter 2).

The outcome of this preference for group solidarity or responsiveness to social pressure is the accumulation of stocks of social capital, solidarity, trust, or networks. Solidarity is a concept most often associated with sociology but its essence has been used in economics. For example, the "rotten-kid theorem" in the economic theory of the family originated by Gary Becker is essentially a demonstration of the conditions under which the members of the family demonstrate perfect solidarity. They act to maximize the income of the group (the family unit) and would not take actions that raised their own incomes at the expense of the group's. In economic policy, this desire for solidarity is typically left out of recipes for economic development like the so-called Washington Consensus or predictions about "The End of History." So when these policies are applied, there are predictable problems. For example, an outburst of nationalism is commonly associated with the penetration of markets, especially by "foreigners" or minorities (Chua 2004). At the same time, individuals are often aware of the benefits of markets and will be responsive to governments that find ways of promoting solidarity that interfere less with the operation of markets. In politics, the desire to be part of a group or a winning movement explains participation in collective action, including revolutionary activity.

Individuals may also be "bound" to a group not because of any desire to associate with other people but because the incentive structure of the organization has this effect. For example, with so-called efficiency wages, the individual is better off purely in terms of wage income by being loyal to the organization. Successful terrorist activity requires intense loyalty, and terrorist organizations employ organizational structures that promote loyalty such as the "cell" form of organization.

I also discussed other ways besides incentives in which solidarity can be created:

II. Solidarity can be accumulated and maintained through barriers to entry and exit, common programs, common belief and *jihad* (Chapter 2).

The most important conclusion of this way of thinking is given in proposition III.

III. Participation in groups changes the individual's behavior (Chapters 2 and 3).

For many people, life isn't solely or even mainly about consumption with one's family. Social interactions are a big part of it. This implies that the observer cannot just look at a person's preferences and their income constraints to see what that person will do because group membership and social interactions change what she decides to do. Further, once social interactions are included, the kinds of behavior that are often labeled "extremist" become more plausible.

IV. From the rational point of view, the essential difference between moderate and extremist methods of political competition is that extremist methods are more risky (Chapter 4).

What is striking about this proposition is not simply that extremist methods are more risky, but the implicit point that from the rational point of view, this is the *only* relevant difference between extremist and moderate methods of competition. That is, there are no moral constraints or "norms" that might constrain the use of violence to achieve political ends. In turn, this implies that individuals who are less averse to risk are more likely to use extremist methods. But even more interesting is proposition V.

V. Groups with indivisible objectives are more likely to use extremist methods (Chapter 4) and to be rigid and intractable in their thinking (Chapter 5).

Big ideas, grand visions, and utopian vistas are central to the extremist mind-set. The more extreme (and far-reaching) the position of a group, the more likely it is to adopt extremist methods. In turn, groups with far-reaching or extreme objectives are likely to provide more solidarity. The terrorist (as opposed to the extremist) combines indivisible objectives with what Hoffman has described as a "burning impatience." Violence is also more likely to be used when movements do not have to build a mass base. At the same time, not all or even most extremist groups use violence, and "extremist" ideas are invaluable to the functioning of democracy. Many new ideas are labeled extremist when they are first put forward, and to stifle nonconformism from its outset is the surest way to destroy democracy. This suggests not a cost-benefit analysis of the control of extremism by sacrificing freedom of speech, but the preservation of it combined with a firm emphasis on the control of violent methods of political action.

VI. People who join an organization for solidarity, or who decide they wish more solidarity, end up taking more solidarity than they originally intended (the "solidarity multiplier") (Chapter 5).

A person who wishes more solidarity accepts or will find that this implies more conformity to the beliefs of the organization. Solidarity means adopting the beliefs of the group. But with this adoption of beliefs, the person will find that he or she wants more solidarity than before. Further, when people adopt beliefs partly because others hold these beliefs, they are naturally more "rigid" or dogmatic than when beliefs are adopted on scientific grounds and they are relatively immune to new information or rational argument. If beliefs are held because others hold them, they will change only when others change them. The "Group Mind" oft-noted with respect to extremist and terrorist activity is the consequence, not the cause, of joining and participating in an extremist group.

VII. Rational people will be willing to become suicide martyrs when they are at or near a corner implying complete solidarity with the group (Chapter 5).

Either incentives or desires can explain solidarity but only the solidarity multiplier can explain how an individual can become completely loyal, or lose his identification completely, as implied by this corner solution. Altruism cannot explain suicide martyrdom because of the free-rider problem. Nor does a belief in the afterlife, because one cannot make enforceable exchanges with a supreme being (see propositions X and XI).

VIII. The poor and the uneducated are not necessarily more likely to choose suicide martyrdom if the demand for solidarity is elastic with respect to income and education levels (Chapter 5).

The "cost" of suicide martyrdom is the value of life forgone, leading to the prediction that relatively poor and uneducated people are more likely to engage in this activity. But if the "benefit" is solidarity with the cause, and if more educated and richer individuals value this more, this simple and popular prediction is not an implication of the rational choice approach. Nor is it supported by the evidence to this date.

IX. An increase in the capacity of the organization to convert autonomy into solidarity implies a switch to more extreme methods.

The leader of an organization whose members exhibit a high degree of solidarity can direct them toward relatively extreme methods with less fear of their defection. This makes extreme methods more attractive to the leader.

X. Rational people do not commit suicide bombing in exchange for the rewards of heaven (Chapter 6).

People may choose to have faith in God, or believe in the afterlife, and such beliefs are neither rational nor irrational. A person may also choose suicide martyrdom in order to please God, and this is not necessarily irrational. But the idea that one can make an *exchange* with God in which suicide martyrdom is rewarded with an afterlife is not rational, for the simple reason that there is no way to enforce such a "contract."

XI. Religious groups are natural organizing nodes of solidarity (Chapter 6).

People may rationally believe in the afterlife, not because the belief is itself rational, but out of solidarity with people in groups that promote this belief. The difference between the explanation in proposition X versus that implied by proposition XI is not trivial. And it is possible, in principle, to find out empirically which explanation is correct because they have different implications for the discount rate: on the solidarity explanation, martyrs have a high discount rate (they are impatient), but on the afterlife explanation, a low one. The oft-noted observation that terrorists are driven by impatience suggests that the solidarity explanation is closer to the truth.

XII. The main predictor of revolutions is the weakness of the state (Chapter 7).

If the state is strong, it can withstand setbacks such as a reduction in the rate of economic growth, an increase in inflation, scandals, and so forth, and so these do not by themselves lead to revolution. Only when the mechanisms of the state for staying in power have been weakened do these or other problems pose a threat to the order. Goldstone (2005) provides powerful, systematic evidence for this proposition.

XIII. Successful revolutions, particularly if they do not result in democracy, may set in motion a search for new enemies to maintain solidarity (Chapter 7).

Bandwagon effects in revolutionary activity make the revolution possible but also make its future uncertain. The loss of the external enemy inherent in successful revolutions leads to the continuous search for enemies to maintain solidarity. Moreover, the loss of the old "order," however unjust, means the loss of solidarity inherent in the old order, and this too gives rise to the search for new sources of solidarity.

XIV. Ethnic groups are natural organizing nodes of solidarity because they have natural barriers to entry and exit (Chapter 8).

XV. Nationalism can be explosive, especially combined with the ethnic security dilemma (Chapter 8).

All forms of social capital are contagious, as with any network externality. But in the case of nationalism, this contagion is augmented by the security dilemma, as greater social cohesion among one nation is potentially threatening to other nations.

XVI. Among regime types, war occurs most frequently between dictatorships and democracies, and among types of dictatorship, between totalitarian dictatorships and democracies (Chapter 8).

Wars are always the result of misunderstanding. Leaders and citizens of democracies typically misunderstand dictatorship in that they think dictators rule by repression alone and not through support. This misunderstanding is greatest with totalitarian dictatorship.

XVII. Globalization breeds extremism by reducing the capacity to create solidarity via barriers to entry and exit, unique common beliefs, or common programs (Chapter 9).

There are three main ways in which this occurs. First, globalization strips countries of their capacity to build and maintain solidarity via barriers to entry and exit, common programs that ensure equality of treatment, common beliefs, and other traditional bases, thus encouraging *jihad,* the only mechanism remaining to get solidarity. Second, globalization leads to convergence among mainstream political groups, leading to the isolation and radicalization of extreme groups, as happened in Italy in the 1970s, in Germany in the 1980s, and, as Roy (2004) argues, is happening now in the Middle East. Third, as Berman has argued (2003), globalization leads to increased market opportunities for some, leading extremist groups to raise the sacrifice or level of prohibitions necessary to remain in order to avoid dilution of the quality of group services and experiences.

XVIII. The more important the social interactions in a particular policy area, the less effective policies based on changing prices are likely to be (Chapters 2 and 10).

The best way to understand this proposition is to look at Table 10.1.

Chapter 3 discussed the structure of the table and illustrated this with the first five items: the family, the army, poverty/microfinance, crime, and international finance. Here the table is extended to cover aspects of extremism, including extremist groups, nationalism, revolution, and the effects of globalization. The same structure is once again present in all the new cases. In each instance the table summarizes the arguments made in the book, and most of the table is self-explanatory. The main item that requires more explanation is the last column, on policy implications. However, before turning to those, note that something new is learned from the table about the stepwise interactions we first noted in Chapter 3, listed in the next-to-last column. Thus, in the cases concerning aspects of extremism, as in the five discussed previously, there is a second dynamic at work besides the contagion property. This second dynamic occurs within the individual or group, but is a consequence of group participation. The dynamic takes various forms: the solidarity multiplier that characterizes the suicide martyr; increasing returns that characterize the relationship the group leader believes exists between the intermediate and ultimate goals of the group; the "traditional" or "habitual" aspect of nationalism that implies that current nationalistic feelings depend on how nationalistic one was in the past and the "security dilemma" that results from increases in nationalism; the ratcheting upward of the search for enemies after a successful revolution; or the stepping up of extremist ideas and policies within extremist groups as a result of globalization that leads to political convergence among more mainstream groups (as described by Roy 2004) and thus to the isolation and radicalization of more extreme groups. Globalization also provides members of extreme groups with new outside market opportunities. This threatens to dilute the loyalty of people within the group, which responds by tightening its extremism (as described by Berman 2003).

Note that in every case, this second dynamic amplifies the contagion property of social interactions and makes them more unstable.

The next section expands on the policy implications implicit in the last column of the table.

10.2 Extremism: Policy Implications

The last four items in Table 10.1 are all concerned with extremism and its various manifestations: terrorism, nationalism, revolution, globalization, and *jihad*. We focus on extremism and terrorism first. Policy on these issues has also been discussed at various points in the text, notably in Chapters 4, 5, and 9. This is a good place to sum things up.

One way to approach the subject of policy with respect to extremism and terrorism is via the "carrot versus stick" debate that characterizes much of the policy debate over how to deal with terrorism. We first looked at this issue in Chapter 5, but it is worth revisiting from the point of view of Table 10.1. To begin with, those who take the "carrot" position argue that we should look at the root causes of terror and offer potential terrorists an alternative path. Frey (2004) argues strongly that deterrence does not work with respect to terror and proposes the "carrot" policy. On the other hand, the U.S. government since 9/11 has more or less exclusively followed a "stick" policy.

As suggested earlier, the substitution effect tends to be in the same direction with either policy. Moreover, the substitution effect is in the desired direction, and there is indeed evidence of this substitution effect at work (Landes 1978; Sandler and Lapan 1988). But this conclusion neglects the income or wealth effect. While the substitution effect is in the right direction

Table 10.1. *Nine Issues (including Extremism) Where Social Interactions, Not Prices, Are Central to Understanding and Policy*

Issue	What Makes Them a Group?	Social Interaction (Contagion)	Structure/ Hierarchy	Problem or Poison W: without hierarchy H: due to it	Stepwise Interaction	Policy P: price SI: nonprice
Family relations	The family	The rotten-kid theorem (solidarity is contagious)	The family needs a head	W: powerlessness of other members H: authoritarianism breeds disincentives, the Samaritan's dilemma	Repeated interaction	P: price incentives create division SI: automaticity of gifts breeds solidarity
Military power	Army unit	Sacrifices by leaders breed solidarity (solidarity is contagious)	Formal discipline, informal leadership by example	W: panic, disintegration H: excess conformity breeds stupidity	Marching	P: discipline alone does not create a strong army SI: solidarity conquers fear
Crime	Criminals: gangs Citizens: community	Neighborhood deterioration demonstrates to criminals that the neighborhood is "safe" for crime, to people that it is unsafe	Subway "station manager"; community involvement on the side of the police	Gangs: W: dead end H: boss takes the cream Community: W: vulnerable to gangs H: racial profiling	Smaller offenses lead to bigger ones	P: price: p↑ or f↑ SI: Maintain order and police small offenses/community involvement
Poverty/ microfinance	Know each other well	They can get loans together but not separately	Structure of mutual monitoring, /leadership by the bank	W: no loans or repayment H: moral hazard	Dynamic small repayment incentives	P: raise interest rate, adverse selection SI: subsidize/group liability
International finance (the Asian crisis)	2 groups: 1/ alliance capitalism (cronies) 2/ the electronic herd	1/ conformity, corruption 2/ buy or sell because others are buying/selling	1/ Asian hierarchies: Japanese firm, chaebol, guanxi 2/ Federal Reserve/ IMF	(IMF) W: vulnerability, panic H: moral hazard	Stepwise adjustment in interest rates difficult in a panic	P: interest rates ↑→ bankruptcy SI: property rights, general trust

Extremism and terrorism	Common belief that society is against them/ unjust	Conformity to beliefs that are common within, extreme viewed from without breeds solidarity	Utopian or charismatic leadership	W: dissent, heresy destroy solidarity H: conformity is the price of solidarity	Increasing returns (leaders) solidarity multiplier (followers)	P: sanction, isolate, restrictions on freedom of speech SI: engagement, inclusion, make the indivisible divisible
Nationalism	Same ethnic group or "nation"; barriers to entry and exit	Explosive, especially when combined with the security dilemma and uncertain rights	Ethnic leadership	W: no trades possible H: conflict, "us" vs. "them"	Nationalism is traditional or "habitual," security dilemma	P: sanctions SI: trade, inclusion
Revolution	Dissatisfaction with government	Participation externalities, bandwagon effect	Weak state makes revolution possible Leadership of revolution occurs spontaneously	W: free rider H: successful revolution needs new enemy, asset stripping breeds counterrevolution	The search for hypocrisy and enemies of the revolution never ends	P: repression SI: improved communication to find out what people want, distribution of rents to create loyalty
Globalization and *jihad*	Nations	Globalization spreads the shareholder system and markets	National governments weakened by globalization; globalized Islam strengthened	W: Globalization reduces traditional bases of solidarity, and thus increases the demand for *jihad* from extremist groups H: *jihad* from government itself	Political convergence leads to isolation and radicalization of extremist groups; increased market opportunities leads to groups stepping up their extremism to maintain loyalty	P: markets SI: find ways other than *jihad* (e.g., universal health or welfare programs) to maintain solidarity

with either policy, the wealth effect may not be. And the wealth effect implicit in many antiterrorist policies is obviously very large.

Thus, with deterrence or "stick" policies, the wealth effect is in the wrong direction if extremists' relative risk aversion increases with wealth. With "carrot" policies, the income effect is in the wrong direction in the opposite case (if relative risk aversion decreases with wealth). In that case, terrorist leaders are more inclined to use violent methods as their organizational capacity increases. The critical variable for assessing the direction of the wealth effect is the behavior of the coefficient of relative risk aversion as wealth changes, not an easily discoverable number about anyone, let alone terrorist leaders. Consequently, the only policy that is guaranteed to be in the right direction (though not, of course, necessarily effective) is a policy of "carrot *and* stick." To the extent that the wealth effect is neutralized, no matter what the attitude toward risk of potential terrorists, the policy is guaranteed to be in the right direction.

In practice, one can see everywhere the failures of the stick policy alone, from the continuing Israeli-Palestinian problem to the difficulties in Iraq. Demonizing terrorists as "evil" and setting out simply to destroy them often just adds to their base of support. On the other hand, the idea that, after a murderous attack like 9/11 or 7/7, the population will be in a mood to listen to the grievances of those who share the goals of the perpetrators is a nonstarter. Policy has to understand these responses (note that they are both solidarity-based) and take them into account. Combining the "carrot and stick" policies can do this. Recall also that the provision of the "carrot" along with the "stick" tends to solve some of the difficulties with deterrence originally discussed in Chapter 4. For these reasons the policy of "carrot and stick" is superior to either policy tried alone.

Earlier I suggested an important reason why deterrence policies may be ineffective: the indivisibility of the goals of extremist leaders. It is not that the leaders are irrational. Rather, it is, because their goals are so large and the distance from them so great. So the cost of the punishment pales in comparison. The same difficulty would appear to apply to the "carrot" solution or to the combination of "carrot and stick." It is not obvious what kind of "carrots" can be offered to the truly millenarian. *The more millenarian the group, the less effective are counterterrorist policies of either the "carrot" or the "stick."* This is the common sense behind the idea that it is impossible to appease someone like Osama bin Laden, whose goals appear to be the restoration of the caliphate and theocratic rule. As to followers, millenarian groups and other very extreme groups are particularly likely to have members who are characterized by the "all-solidarity" corner solution described in Chapter 5. Such individuals are unlikely to be very responsive to either penalties or rewards offered by people coming from outside the group.

But to be effective, policy does not have to appeal to or deter the truly committed – it can be effective if it appeals to or deters people who are on the margin of joining terrorist groups. From this point of view, the problem with many deterrence policies used alone is that they have an effect on the social cohesion of the terrorists. It contributes to their isolation, and in this way reduces the attention that members of the group pay to sources of information that are associated with the policy of punishment and isolation. And it provides them with a natural external enemy. For both of these reasons, deterrence policies used alone are particularly likely to get us into the region where price policies don't work but social interaction policies might.

This brings us to an alternative way of classifying policies, that which is implicit in Table 10.1. The classification there is not by "carrot versus stick" but by policies that operate as price incentives on individuals and those which take into account the social interactions of individuals with others. Many "carrot" policies are indeed social-interaction-based.

Throughout this book I have suggested three kinds of policies along these lines:

1. Perhaps the most important is to *make the indivisible divisible.* Such policies (discussed in Chapter 4) may not affect or convince the leaders of violent extremist groups, but they can offer alternatives to potential supporters of them.
2. The strengthening, not weakening, of human rights can act to weaken the hold of extremist groups over individuals.
3. Recognize that the root appeal of extremist groups is the desire for solidarity and try to provide alternative sources of social cohesion.

To sum up, the policy implications of the models in this book with respect to the control of terrorism include deterrent policies against the use of violent political methods combined with "carrot" policies to offer alternatives to isolated and dissatisfied members of society, and the three policies just listed that explicitly recognize the social interactions that are the heart of the appeal of many forms of terrorism.

The other policy implications listed in Table 10.1 concerning nationalism, revolution, and globalization and *jihad* can be considered in the context of two events: the end of the Soviet Union, or, as it was labeled around that time, the "triumph of liberal democracy and the end of history" (Fukuyama

1992), and 9/11. At the end of the Cold War, commentators were full of optimistic pronouncements for a global order based on liberal capitalism and democracy (e.g., Friedman 1999). In 1989 Francis Fukuyama famously announced the end of history, "not just the end of the Cold War, or the passing of a particular period of history, but the end of history as such: that is, the end point of mankind's ideological evolution and the universalization of Western liberal democracy as the final form of human government" (1992, p. 2).

What happened? In the view of many, the answer is simple: the world changed on 9/11. But where did 9/11 come from? And what does it represent? Norman Podhoretz saw in it the beginning of World War IV (in his article entitled: "World War IV: How It Started, What It Means, and Why We Have to Win" [2004]). An alternative view is that

> The U.S. Government has greatly *overreacted* to the terrorist threat to Americans, creating "a false sense of insecurity." . . . Over the past decade, fewer than 400 Americans a year have died as a consequence of domestic and foreign terrorism, about the same number who drown from using a bathtub and less than one percent of the number who die from traffic accidents. (William Niskanen forthcoming)

Does the current conflict with radical Islam represent a temporary blip on the road to the end of history, or can we consign the latter concept to the wastebasket? While I will not of course attempt a definitive answer to this question, there are three things that particularly emerge from the arguments and models of this book that are relevant to this question. Moreover, the policy implications about revolution and nationalism in Table 10.1 follow from these.

1. The end of (most) Soviet-style totalitarian systems did not mean the end of dictatorship, and in fact other forms of dictatorship such as tyranny are more likely to engender terrorism. In a globalized world, terrorist acts are also increasingly likely to be directed against countries in the West to the extent that they are seen as supporting tyrannies.
2. Globalization itself carries with it the seeds of *jihad* (the last item in Table 10.1)
3. Extremism is in a sense always with us, and the particular manifestations of it that we see today in the form of radical Islam was itself a response to the convergence observed at the end of the Cold War, a response that could have been foreseen.

Let us elaborate on these points.

10.2.1 The End of Totalitarianism and the Rise of Tyranny Implics an Upsurge in Terrorism

Tyrannies are more likely to engender terrorism than totalitarian regimes or democracies. To see this point, recall that what distinguishes tyranny from totalitarianism is that loyalty to tyrannical regimes is relatively low. For example, most of the regimes in the Middle East, especially Egypt, Syria, and Saudi Arabia, would be classified as tyrannies. Such regimes typically simply repress dissent, and so they do not fulfill their citizens' demands for public goods and for solidarity. Thus there are typically no organizations propagandizing the citizens of the regime, and there is little or no provision of clubs, social services, medicare, and the like under tyrannies. These regimes can be effective at stamping out moderate methods of dissent by simply banning demonstrations, disloyal news media, and other forms of opposition to the regime, and by hunting down and neutralizing potential sources of opposition. But they do not satisfy the demand for solidarity, as the Milosevic regime tried to do and the Chinese regime does with nationalism, or as the former Soviet Union did with communism and later nationalism as an ideology and way of life, and with an array of social and welfare services delivered, if not equally, at least relatively unequally, to all. So, if we look at the model from the supply side, under tyrannies people are left seeking ways to have their demands for solidarity fulfilled.

Like totalitarian regimes, democracies can provide social cohesion. But unlike totalitarian regimes, there are typically many competitive suppliers of solidarity in modern democracies like those in North America and Europe, including churches and other religious groups, youth gangs, unions, firms, and so on. So people do not have to turn to extremist groups in democracies to fulfill their desires for solidarity. To sum up, on the supply side, it seems that the most natural places for extremist groups to prosper is under tyrannies.

If we consider demand, democracies provide the freedom for extreme groups and their leaders to organize, to publicize their cause, and to participate in democratic elections if they wish to, so long as they do not engage in violence. Typically democracies also find ways to satisfy at least some of the demands of even those who are deeply opposed to the government. That is one reason why communist and fascist parties have lost most of their appeal in Western democracies. Totalitarian regimes provide no such freedom, and because of their centralization of power do not feature institutions such as federalism or the division of powers that unbundle the indivisibility that is central to the programs of extremist groups. But, so long as they remain strong, totalitarian regimes are capable of wiping out dissent. For example, there was no breakaway movement in Chechnya under the old Soviet system. Again, therefore, we expect that the demand for terror is most likely to occur under tyrannies, or at least weak totalitarian regimes.

So, on balance it would appear that both the demand for and the supply of terror will be largest under tyrannies or weak totalitarian regimes.

What does this mean for policy? One implication is that the United States, in subsidizing tyrannies like those in Saudi Arabia, Egypt, and Pakistan, is, in a world of globalized terror, effectively subsidizing the production of terror against itself. Indeed, it is interesting that many of the "outposts of tyranny" identified as such by U.S. Secretary of State Condoleeza Rice in 2005, and therefore not entitled to subsidies[1] – North Korea, Cuba, Zimbabwe, Belarus, and Myanmar – are in fact totalitarian regimes, which typically do not engender terror.

The political scientist (and former ambassador to the United Nations) Jeanne Kirkpatrick (1982) did make the distinction between the two types of regimes. She argued that the attempt to overthrow what she called a "traditional autocracy" (tinpot or tyrant, in my language) often simply resulted in the replacement of the regime by a totalitarian one, as she argued happened in Iran and increasingly looks to be the long-run outcome of U.S. policy in Iraq.

So with the fall of the Soviet system and the rise of globalized markets, the main terrorist threat to countries in the West arose in tyrannies. The fact that the United States, in funding the *mujahadeen* in an attempt to undermine the Soviet system, itself gave the terrorists the training they needed was an additional reason to expect trouble but this is a separate and ad hoc point, whereas the conclusion I have just drawn is systematic.

Totalitarian regimes did not disappear with the fall of the Soviet system, but the ones that remained, or aspired to that status, like the Milosevic regime, now lacked the overarching ideology that had been provided by communism. Such dictators are particularly tempted to use nationalism and *jihad* as a way of solving the dictator's dilemma, and building support for their regimes, and it is no accident that Milosevic launched four wars in his quest for Greater Serbia. The misunderstanding of his aims by democratic leaders in the West, who typically did not then and do not now understand that dictators cannot survive in office by simply repressing their populations,

---

[1] The remarks of Rice are discussed in the *International Herald Tribune,* August 14, 2005. On implementing this the classification of regimes empirically, see the independent attempt to do so and the evidence that they do indeed fall into distinct types by Islam and Winer (2004).

makes war particularly likely between democracies and dictatorships, especially totalitarian ones.[2] But nationalism is contagious, and it is particularly likely to spread through its interaction with the security dilemma, and because of this we do not know how much of the process remained under Milosevic's control, however guilty he was to play with fire in the first place. Such dynamic processes are typical of social interactions. In turn, the "evil" that was perpetrated in the name of ethnic cleansing arose partly from this contagiousness.

10.2.2 Globalization Itself Causes *Jihad*

At the same time as the fall in information costs was making transatlantic communication possible as never before and spinning businessmen around the world in search of opportunities and transporting academics to exotic locations for conferences, it also made obsolete the old dreams of communism and fascism based on insular communities. The reaction against these developments in the form of the "no-global" movement was predictable. But at the same time it made possible new global communities to satisfy the demands for solidarity. For example, for popular music lovers, globalization made possible the advent of "world music." Other forms of communities more suited to the information age include globalized religious communities, including global radical Islam. In addition, the lure of markets that tends to pull people out of communities where the demands of the group on the individual are intense threatened to dilute the quality of those groups, and they in turn became more radical to keep up their appeal. And one way for clubs, groups, and nations to satisfy the wants for solidarity of their peoples was to launch *jihad*. Milosevic was no ideologue but an opportunist: he simply found that when he spoke the words "No one will beat you again!" people applauded from the rafters. In the same way, all of the "extremists" we have considered in this book were, in part, responding to opportunities.

10.2.3 Convergence Causes Extremism

To my knowledge, Kitschelt (1997) was the first to point out that a move toward convergence on the part of mainstream political groupings leaves those on the extremes with less reason to negotiate with centrist groups, and

---

[2] It is possible that misunderstanding of the nature of dictatorship also led to the second Iraq war, but in this case there are explanations which seem more obvious, and which have been put forth in many places. The misunderstanding certainly contributed to the problems in the aftermath of the war.

so they tend to turn more extreme. This is one way to explain the extremism of the Red Brigades in Italy and the Baader-Meinhof Gang in Germany in the 1970s. Roy (2004) has made a similar argument with respect to the contemporary Middle East. The movement to the center of many regimes in the Middle East, and the failure of the religious theocratic option in Iran, implies the forces of moderation have come to the fore. But where does that leave the people who don't like the policies of the center? So the upsurge of radical Islam can be analyzed in the same way as the earlier bouts of terrorism in Italy and Germany. Once again, the centrifugal forces of globalization leading to convergence gave rise to a contrary, centripetal movement that was entirely predictable.

10.2.4 Concluding Remarks

Finally, it is worth emphasizing that policy should not throw out the baby with the bathwater. Extremism has to be considered separately from terrorism, and is a much broader category than that, or even than particular manifestations of extremism like extreme nationalism, revolution, or *jihad*. Extremists are innovators, and the fruits of their innovation often invigorate society. Freedom of speech is the lifeblood of democracy. Many new ideas appear extreme when they are first uttered, and serious curbs on freedom of speech will destroy democratic life. At the same time, the basic model of extremist groups in this book implies that extremist groups will naturally find violence a temptation. So policy should draw a line that divides the advocacy of new ideas and solutions from "hate" speech and the advocacy of violence. Such laws can be consistent with democracy.

Extremists, including revolutionaries, nationalists, religious extremists who dream of "Global Islam," or people who long for a homeland, are dreamers. In rational choice terms, in their dreams they identify the "missing factor" for making their dreams a reality. For Gandhi this was independence from the British, for King equal rights for American blacks, for Milosevic Greater Serbia, for Osama bin Laden a new *ummah*. Sometimes their dreams turn into nightmares for the rest of us. But a society that tries to stamp out extremism is trying to stamp out its capacity to dream.

References

Ajami, Fouad, *The Arab Predicament: Arab Political Thought and Practise since 1967*. Cambridge: Cambridge University Press, 1981.

Ajami, Fouad, "Iraq and the Arabs' Future," *Foreign Affairs* (January–February 2003).

Akerlof, George A., *An Economic Theorist's Book of Tales*. Cambridge: Cambridge University Press, 1984.

Akerlof, George A., "Procrastination and Obedience," *American Economic Review* 81 (1991), 1–19.

Akerlof, George A., and Janet Yellen, "Gang Behaviour, Law Enforcement and Community Behaviour," in H. J. Aaron, T. E. Mann, and T. Taylor, *Values and Public Policy*. Washington, D.C.: The Brookings Institution, 1994.

Alesina, A., and Alex Cukierman, "The Politics of Ambiguity," *Quarterly Journal of Economics* 105 (1990), 829–850.

Alesina, A., Edward Glaeser, and Bruce Sacerdote, "Why Doesn't the United States Have a European-Style Welfare State? *Brookings Papers on Economic Activity*, no. 2 (2001), 187–279.

Alesina, A., Edward Glaeser, Bruce Sacerdote, and Romain Wacziarg, "The Economics of Civic Trust," in Susan Pharr and Robert Putnam, eds., *Disaffected Democracies*. Princeton, N.J.: Princeton University Press, 2000.

Andreoni, James, "Criminal Deterrence in the Reduced Form: A New Perspective on Ehrlich's Seminal Study," *Economic Inquiry* 33 (1995), 476–483.

Appleby, R. Scott, ed., *Spokesmen for the Despised: Fundamentalist Leaders of the Middle East*. Chicago: University of Chicago Press, 1997.

Arblaster, Anthony, *Democracy*. Minneapolis: University of Minnesota Press, 1987.

Arendt, Hannah, *The Origins of Totalitarianism*. 2nd ed. New York: Harcourt Brace Jovanovich, 1951, 1973.

Arendt, Hannah, *On Revolution*. Harmondsworth: Penguin, 1963.

Arendt, Hannah, *Eichmann in Jerusalem: A Report on the Banality of Evil*. Rev. ed. New York: Penguin, 1976.

Arjomand, S. A., "Iran's Islamic Revolution in Comparative Perspective," *World Politics* 38 (1986), 383–414.

Armstrong, Karen, *The Battle for God*. New York: Ballantine, 2000a.

Armstrong, Karen, *Islam: A Short History.* London: Weidenfeld and Nicholson, 2000b.

Arrow, K. J., "The Theory of Risk Aversion," in K. J. Arrow, *Essays in the Theory of Risk Bearing.* Chicago: Markham, 1971.

Austin Smith, David, "Interest Groups: Money, Information and Influence," in D. C. Mueller, ed., *Perspectives on Public Choice: A Handbook.* Cambridge: Cambridge 1997.

Azzam, Jean-Paul, "Suicide Bombing as Intergenerational Investment," *Public Choice,* forthcoming.

Banerjee, Abhijit V., "A Simple Model of Herd Behavior," *Quarterly Journal of Economics* 107, no. 3 (1992), 797–817.

Banerjee, Abhijit, Timothy Besley, and Timothy Guinnane, "Thy Neighbour's Keeper: The Design of a Credit Cooperative with Theory and a Test," *Quarterly Journal of Economics* 109 (1994), 491–515.

Barber, Benjamin, *Jihad vs. McWorld: How Globalism and Tribalism Are Reshaping the World.* New York: Ballantine, 1995.

Bardhan, Pranab, "Corruption and Development: A Review of Issues," *Journal of Economic Literature* 35 (1997), 1320–1346.

Barro, Robert J., "Democracy and Growth," *Journal of Economic Growth* 1 (1996), 1–27.

Barro, Robert J., *Getting It Right: Markets and Choices in a Free Society.* Cambridge: MIT Press, 1998.

Bates, Robert H., "Modernization, Ethnic Competition, and the Rationality of Politics in Contemporary Africa," in Donald Rothschild and Viktor A. Olorunsola, eds., *State versus Ethnic Claims.* Boulder, Colo.: Westview Press, 1983.

Becker, Gary S., "Crime and Punishment: An Economic Approach," *Journal of Political Economy* 76 (1968), 169–217.

Becker, Gary S., "A Theory of Social Interactions," *Journal of Political Economy* 82 (1974), 1063–1091.

Becker, Gary S., *Accounting for Tastes.* Cambridge: Harvard University Press, 1996.

Becker, Gary, and Kevin M. Murphy, *Social Economics: Market Behavior in a Social Environment.* Cambridge: Harvard University Press, 2000.

Berman, Eli, "Sect, Subsidy and Sacrifice: An Economist's View of Ultra Orthodox Jews," *Quarterly Journal of Economics* 115 (2000), 905–953.

Berman, Eli, "Hamas, Taliban and the Jewish Underground: An Economist's View of Radical Religious Militias," NBER Working Paper 10004, 2003.

Berman, Eli, and David Laitin, "Rational Martyrs vs. Hard Targets: Evidence on the Tactical Use of Suicide Attacks," in Eva Myersson Milgrom, ed., *Suicide Bombing from an Interdisciplinary Perspective.* Princeton, N.J.: Princeton University Press, forthcoming.

Bergstrom, Theodore C., "A Fresh Look at the Rotten Kid Theorem," *Journal of Political Economy* 97 (1989), 1138–1159.

Bergstrom, Theodore C., "Evolution of Social Behaviour: Individual and Group Selection," *Journal of Economic Perspectives* 16 (2002), 67–88.

Bernheim, B. Douglas, "A Theory of Conformity," *Journal of Political Economy* 102 (1994), 841–877.

Besley, Timothy, and Stephen Coate, "Group Lending, Repayment Incentives and Social Collateral," *Journal of Development Economics* 46 (1995), 1–18.

Best, Geoffrey, ed., *The Permanent Revolution: The French Revolution and Its Legacy.* London: Fontana Press, 1988.

Bhagwati, Jagdish, *The Wind of the Hundred Days: How Washington Mismanaged Globalization.* Cambridge: MIT Press, 2000.

Bhagwati, Jagdish, *In Defense of Globalization.* Oxford: Oxford University Press, 2004.

Bikchandani, Sushil, David Hirshleifer, and Ivo Welch, "A Theory of Fads, Fashions, Custom, and Cultural Change as Informational Cascades," *Journal of Political Economy* 100 (1992), 992–1026.

Black, Anthony, *The History of Islamic Political Thought.* New York: Routledge, 2001.

Bloom, Mia, *Dying To Kill: The Allure of Suicide Terror.* New York: Columbia University Press, 2005.

Bokenkotter, Thomas, *A Concise History of the Catholic Church.* New York: Doubleday, 1977.

Borooah, Vani, "Racial Bias in Police Stops and Searches: An Economic Analysis," paper delivered at the 2000 EPCS meetings.

Bradley, Michael, "Interfirm Tender Offers and the Market for Corporate Control," *Journal of Business* 53 (1980), 345–376.

Brennan, Geoffrey, "Some Democratic Propensities for Extremist Results," in Albert Breton, Gianluigi Galeotti, Pierre Salmon, and Ronald Wintrobe, eds., *Political Extremism and Rationality.* Cambridge: Cambridge University Press, 2002.

Breton, Albert, Gianluigi Galeotti, Pierre Salmon, and Ronald Wintrobe, eds., *Nationalism and Rationality.* Cambridge: Cambridge University Press, 1995.

Breton, Albert, Gianluigi Galeotti, Pierre Salmon, and Ronald Wintrobe, eds., *Political Extremism and Rationality.* Cambridge: Cambridge University Press, 2002.

Breton, Albert, and Ronald Wintrobe, *The Logic of Bureaucratic Conduct.* Cambridge: Cambridge University Press, 1982.

Breton, Albert, and Ronald Wintrobe, "The Bureaucracy of Murder Revisited," *Journal of Political Economy* 94 (1986), 905–926.

Brown, Donald E., *Human Universals.* New York: McGraw Hill, 1991.

Buchanan, James, "The Samaritan's Dilemma," in J. Buchanan, *Freedom in Constitutional Contract.* College Station: Texas A&M University Press, 1977.

Bulow, Jeremy, and Lawrence Summers, "A Theory of Dual Labor Markets with Applications to Industrial Policy, Discrimination, and Keynesian Unemployment," *Journal of Labor Economics* 4 (1986), 376–414.

Buruma, Ian, and Avishai Margalit, *Occidentalism: The West in the Eyes of Its Enemies.* New York: Penguin Press, 2004.

Byman, Daniel, Kenneth Pollock, and Gideon Rose, "The Rollback Fantasy," *Foreign Affairs* (January–February 1999), 24–41.

Campos, Edward, and Hilton Root, *The Key to the Asian Miracle: Making Shared Growth Credible.* Washington, D.C.: The Brookings Institution, 1996.

Cassidy, John, "The Ringleader: How Grover Norquist Keeps the Conservative Movement Together," *New Yorker*, January 8, 2005, 46.

Cerny, Philip, "Globalization and the Changing Logic of Collective Action," *International Organization* 4 (1995), 595–625.

Chen, Feng, "Subsistence Crises, Managerial Corruption, and Labour Protests in China," *China Journal* 44 (2000), 41–63.

Chong, Dennis, *Collective Action and the Civil Rights Movement*. Chicago: University of Chicago Press, 1991.

Chua, Amy, *World on Fire: How Exporting Free Market Democracy Breeds Ethnic Hatred and Global Instability*. New York: Anchor Books, 2004.

Cohen, Jean, "Trust, Voluntary Association and Workable Democracy: The Contemporary American Discourse of Civil Society," in Mark E. Warren, *Democracy and Trust*. Cambridge: Cambridge University Press, 1999.

Coleman, James S., *Foundations of Social Theory*. Cambridge: Harvard University Press, 1990.

Condorcet, Marquis, "Essay on the Application of Mathematics to the Theory of Decision Making," in K. Baker, ed., *Condorcet, Selected Writings*. Indianapolis: Bobbs-Merrill, 1976.

Copper, John, "The 'Glue' That Holds China Together," *The World and I* 17, no. 7, 20–25. Washington, D.C.: Washington Times Corporation, 2002.

Corman, Hope, and Naci Mocan, "Carrots, Sticks and Broken Windows," *Journal of Law and Economics* 48 (April 2005), 235–266.

Crenshaw, Martha, "The Logic of Terrorism," in Walter Reich, ed., *Origins of Terrorism: Psychologies, Ideologies, Theologies, States of Mind*. Cambridge: Cambridge University Press, 1990.

Dawson, Lorne L., *Cults in Context: Readings in the Study of New Religious Movements*. Toronto: Canadian Scholars Press, 1996.

Dallago, Bruno, and Milica Uvalic, "The Distributive Consequences of Nationalism: The Case of Former Yugoslavia," *Europe-Asia Studies* 50 (1998), 71–90.

Della Porta, Donatella, and Alberto Vanucci, "The Perverse Effects of Political Corruption," in Paul Heywood, ed., *Political Corruption*. Oxford: Blackwell, 1997.

Della Porta, Donatella, "Social Capital, Beliefs in Government and Political Corruption," in Susan Pharr and Robert Putnam, eds., *Disaffected Democracies*. Princeton, N.J.: Princeton University Press, 2000.

De Soto, Hernando, *The Mystery of Capital*. New York: Basic Books, 2000.

Diamond, Douglas, and Philip H. Dybvig, "Bank Runs, Deposit Insurance, and Liquidity," *Journal of Political Economy* 91 (1983): 401–419.

Ding, X. L., "The Illicit Asset-Stripping of Chinese State Firms," *China Journal* (1999), 1–28.

Djilas, Aleksa, "A Profile of Slobodan Milosevic," *Foreign Affairs* (1993), 81–96.

Drake, R., *The Aldo Moro Murder Case*. Cambridge: Harvard University Press, 1995.

D'Souza, Dinesh, *Culture and Prosperity*. Washington, D.C.: Regnery Publishing, 2002.

Duffy, Eamon, *Saints and Sinners: A History of the Popes*. New Haven: Yale University Press, 1997.

Elster, John, *Alchemies of the Mind: Rationality and the Emotions*. Cambridge: Cambridge University Press, 1999.

Enders, Walter, and Todd Sandler, "What Do We Know about the Substitution Effect in Transnational Terrorism?" unpublished manuscript, University of Southern California, April 2003.

Esposito, John L., *The Islamic Threat, Myth or Reality?* 3d ed. Oxford: Oxford University Press, 1999.

Fanon, Franz, *The Wretched of the Earth*. Translated by Constance Farrington. New York: Grove Press, 1963.

Farmer, Roger, *The Macroeconomics of Self-Fulfilling Prophecies.* 2d ed. Cambridge: MIT Press, 1999.

Fearon, James D., "Rationalist Explanations for War," *International Organization* 49 (1995), 379–414.

Fearon, James D., "Commitment Problems and the Spread of Ethnic Conflict," in David A. Lake and Donald Rothchild, eds., *The International Spread of Ethnic Conflict: Fear, Diffusion, and Escalation.* Princeton, N.J.: Princeton University Press, 1998.

Fearon, James D., and David D. Laitin, "Explaining Inter-Ethnic Cooperation," *American Political Science Review* 90 (1996), 715–735.

Fehr, E., "The Neural Basis of Altruistic Punishment," *Science* 305 (August 27, 2004), 1254–1258.

Ferrero, Mario, "Competition for Sainthood and the Millenial Church," *Kyklos* 55 (2002a), 335–360.

Ferrero, Mario, "The Political Life Cycle of Extremist Organizations," in Albert Breton, Gianluigi Galeotti, Pierre Salmon, and Ronald Wintrobe, eds., *Political Extremism and Rationality.* Cambridge: Cambridge University Press, 2002b.

Ferrero, Mario, "Martyrdom Contracts," unpublished manuscript, University of Eastern Piedmont, Italy, 2003.

Figueiredo, Ruij P., Jr., and Barry R. Weingast, "The Rationality of Fear: Political Opportunism and Ethnic Conflict," draft, Stanford University, January–June 1998.

Finer, S. E., *The History of Government from the Earliest Times.* 3 vols. Oxford: Oxford University Press, 1997–1999.

Fo, Dario, *Accidental Death of an Anarchist.* London: Methuen, 2003.

Frank, Robert H., *Passion within Reason.* New York: W. W. Norton, 1988.

Frey, Bruno, *Dealing with Terrorism – Stick or Carrot?* Cheltenham: Edward Elgar, 2004.

Friedman, Thomas, *The Lexus and the Olive Tree.* New York: Farrar, Strauss and Giroux, 1999.

Friedrich, K., and Z. Brzezinski, *Totalitarian Dictatorship and Autocracy.* Cambridge: Harvard University Press, 1965.

Fukuyama, F., *The End of History and the Last Man.* New York: Harper Collins, 1992.

Fukuyama, F., *Trust: The Social Virtues and the Creation of Prosperity.* London: Hamish Hamilton, 1995.

Furet, F., *Interpreting the French Revolution.* Translated by Elborg Forster. Cambridge: Cambridge University Press, 1981.

Furet, F., "The French Revolution Revisited," in G. Kates, ed., *The French Revolution: Recent Debates and New Controversies.* London: Routledge, 1997.

Furman, Jason, and Joseph E. Stiglitz, "Economic Crises: Evidence and Insights from East Asia," *Brookings Papers on Economic Activity* 2 (1998), 1–137.

Gaddy, Clifford G., and Barry W. Ickes, *Russia's Virtual Economy.* Washington, D.C.: Brookings Institution Press, 2002.

Gagnon, V. P., Jr., "Serbia's Road to War," in Larry Diamond and Marc F. Plattner, *Nationalism, Ethnic Conflict and Democracy.* Baltimore: Johns Hopkins University Press, 1994.

Gagnon, V. P., Jr., "Ethnic Nationalism and International Conflict: The Case of Serbia," *International Security* 19 (1994–1995), 130–137. Reprinted in Michael

E. Brown, Owen R. Coté Jr., Sean M. Lynn-Jones, and Steven E. Miller, eds., *Nationalism and Ethnic Conflict.* Cambridge: MIT Press, 1997.

Galanter, Marc, *Cults: Faith, Healing and Coercion.* New York: Oxford University Press, 1989.

Galeotti, Gianluigi, "At the Outskirts of the Constitution," in Albert Breton, Gianluigi Galeotti, Pierre Salmon, and Ronald Wintrobe, eds., *Political Extremism and Rationality.* Cambridge: Cambridge University Press, 2002.

Gambetta, Diego, *The Sicilian Mafia: The Business of Private Protection.* Cambridge: Harvard University Press, 1993.

Geertz, Clifford, "Which Way to Mecca," *New York Review of Books,* July 3, 2003.

Ghatak, Maitreesh, "Group Lending, Local Information and Peer Selection," *Journal of Development Economics* 60 (1999), 27–50.

Ghatak, Maitreesh, and T. W. Guinnane, "The Economics of Lending with Joint Liability: Theory and Practise," *Journal of Development Economics* 60 (1999), 195–228.

Gilbert, D. T., Susan Fiske, and G. Lindzey, *The Handbook of Social Psychology.* Boston: McGraw-Hill, 1998.

Gilpin, Robert, *Global Political Economy.* Princeton, N.J. Princeton University Press, 2001.

Ginkel, J., and A. Smith, "So You Want a Revolution: A Game Theoretic Explanation of Revolution in Repressive Regimes," *Journal of Conflict Resolution* 43 (1999), 291–316.

Ginsborg, Paul, *A History of Contemporary Italy, 1943–80.* London: Penguin, 2003.

Giorgio, *Memoirs of an Italian Terrorist.* Translated with an introduction by Antony Shugaar. New York: Carroll and Graf, 2003. Originally published as *Memorie dalla clandestinita un terrorista non pentito si racconta,* SEMIR, Italy, 1981.

Giurato, Luisa, and Maria Cristina Molinari, "Rationally Violent Tactics: Evidence from Modern Islamic Fundamentalism," in Albert Breton, Gianluigi Galeotti, Pierre Salmon, and Ronald Wintrobe, eds., *Political Extremism and Rationality.* Cambridge: Cambridge University Press, 2002.

Glaeser, Edward, and Bruce Sacerdote, "Education and Religion," unpublished manuscript, Harvard University, 2002.

Glaeser, Edward, Bruce Sacerdote, and Jose A. Scheinkman, "Crime and Social Interactions," *Quarterly Journal of Economics* 111 (1996), 507–548.

Glazer, A., "The Strategy of Candidate Ambiguity," *American Political Science Review* 84 (1990), 237–242.

Glazer, Nathan, "On Subway Graffiti in New York," *Public Interest,* Winter 1979.

Glenny, Misha, *The Fall of Yugoslavia.* New York: Penguin Books, 1992.

Gold, Riger V., "Revenge as Sanction and Solidarity Display: An Analysis of Vendettas in 19th Century Costa Rica," *American Sociological Review* 65 (2000), 682–704.

Goldstone, Jack, Ted Gurr, Monty G. Marshall, and Jay Ulfelder, "It's All about State Structure: New Findings on Revolutionary Origins from Global Data," *Homo Oeconomicus* 21, no. 2 (2004), 429–455. Special issue on revolutions edited by Mario Ferrero.

Gordon, David, *Fat and Mean.* New York: Free Press, 1996.

Gunaratna, Robin, *Inside Al Qaeda: Global Network of Terror.* New York: Columbia University Press, 2002.

Greenfeld, Liah, *Nationalism: Five Roads to Modernity.* Cambridge: Harvard University Press, 1992.

Gregor, A. James, *The Ideology of Fascism.* New York: Free Press, 1969.

Grofman, Bernard, and Scott L. Feld. "Rousseau's General Will: A Condorcetian Perspective." *American Political Science Review* 82, no. 2 (1988): 567–576.

Grossman, S., and O. Hart, "Takeover Bids, the Free-Rider Problem, and the Theory of the Corporation," *Bell Journal of Economics* 11 (Spring 1980), 42–64.

Hagen, William, "The Balkans' Lethal Nationalisms," *Foreign Affairs* 78 (July–August 1999), 52–64.

Haggard, Stephen, *Pathways from the Periphery: The Politics of Growth in the Newly Industrialized Countries.* Ithaca, N.Y.: Cornell University Press, 1990.

Harden, Blaine, "The Milosevic Generation," *New York Times Magazine,* August 29, 1999, 30–61.

Hardin, Russell, "The Crippled Epistemology of Extremism," in Albert Breton, Gianluigi Galeotti, Pierre Salmon, and Ronald Wintrobe, eds., *Political Extremism and Rationality.* Cambridge: Cambridge University Press, 2002.

Hechter, Michael, *Principles of Group Solidarity.* Berkeley: University of California Press, 1987.

Hess, H., *Mafia and Mafiosi: The Structure of Power.* Lexington, Mass.: Lexington Books, 1973.

Hobsbawm, Eric, *The Age of Extremism: The Short Twentieth Century, 1914–1991.* London: Michael Joseph, 1994.

Hoffman, Bruce, *Inside Terrorism.* New York: Columbia University Press, 1998.

Hoffman, Stanley, "The Clash of Globalizations," *Foreign Affairs* 81 (July–August 2002), 104–115.

Huddy, Leonie, "Group Identity and Political Cohesion," in David O. Sears, Leonie Huddy, and Robert Jervis, eds., *Oxford Handbook of Political Psychology.* Oxford: Oxford University Press, 2003.

Huntington, Samuel, *The Clash of Civilizations and the Remaking of World Order.* New York: Simon and Schuster, 1996.

Huthcroft, Paul, "The Politics of Privilege: Assessing the Impact of Rents, Corruption, and Clientelism on Third World Development," in Paul Heywood, ed., *Political Corruption.* Oxford: Blackwell, 1997

Iannacconne, Lawrence R., "Sacrifice and Stigma: Reducing Free Riding in Cults, Communes and Other Collectives," *Journal of Political Economy* 100 (1992), 271–291.

Iannacconne, Lawrence R., "Introduction to the Economics of Religion," *Journal of Economic Literature* 36 (1998), 1465–1496.

Ignatieff, Michael, *Blood and Belonging: Journeys into the New Nationalism.* London: Vintage Penguin, 1993.

Ignatieff, Michael, "Annals of Diplomacy: Balkan Physics," *New Yorker,* May 10, 1999, 68–80.

Inglehart, Ronald, "Trust, Well-Being and Democracy," in Mark E. Warren, *Democracy and Trust.* Cambridge: Cambridge University Press, 1999.

Islam, Muhammed, and Stanley L. Winer, "Tinpots, Totalitarians (and Democrats): An Empirical Investigation of the Effects of Economic Growth on Civil Liberties and Political Rights," *Public Choice* 118 (2004), 289–323.

Jankowski, Martin Sanchez, *Islands in the Street: Gangs and American Urban Society.* Berkeley: University of California Press, 1991.

Johnson, Chalmers, *MITI and the Japanese Miracle: The Growth of Industrial Policy, 1925–1975.* Stanford, Calif.: Stanford University Press, 1982.

Johnson, Paul, *A History of the Jews.* London: Phoenix, 1995.

Jones, Stephen R. G., *The Economics of Conformism.* Oxford: Basil Blackwell, 1984.

Juergensmeyer, Mark, *Gandhi's Way: A Handbook of Conflict Resolution.* Berkeley: University of California Press, 1992.

Karl, Jonathan, *The Right to Bear Arms: The Rise of America's New Militias.* New York: Harper Paperback, 1995.

Kang, David C., "Bad Loans to Good Friends: Money Politics and the Developmental State in South Korea," *International Organization* 56 (2002a), 177–207.

Kang, David C., *Crony Capitalism: Corruption and Economic Development in South Korea and the Philipines.* Cambridge: Cambridge University Press, 2002b.

Katz, Michael, and Carl Shapiro, "Network Externalities, Competition, and Compatibility," *American Economic Review* 75 (1985), 424–440.

Kean, Thomas H., and Lee H. Hamilton, *The 9/11 Report: The National Commission on Terrorist Attacks on the United States.* With reporting and analysis by the New York Times. New York: St. Martin's Press, 2004.

Keegan, John, *The Face of Battle: A Study of Agincourt, Waterloo and the Somme.* London: Jonathan Cape, 1976.

Kelling, George L., and Catherine M. Coles, *Fixing Broken Windows: Restoring Order and Reducing Crime in Our Communities.* New York: Simon and Schuster, 1996.

Kelling, George L., and James Q. Wilson, "Fixing Broken Windows," *Atlantic Monthly,* 1982.

Khawaja, M., "Repression and Popular Collective Action: Evidence from the West Bank," *Sociological Forum* 8 (1993), 47–71.

Kirkpatrick, Jeanne, *Dictatorship and Double Standards: Rationalism and Realism in Politics.* New York: Simon and Schuster, 1982.

Kitschelt, Herbert, *The Radical Right in Western Europe: A Comparative Analysis.* Ann Arbor: University of Michigan Press, 1997.

Klein, Benjamin, and Keith Leffler, "The Role of Market Forces in Contractual Performance," *Journal of Political Economy* 89 (1981), 615–641.

Knack, Stephen, and Phillip Keefer, "Does Social Capital Have an Economic Payoff?" *Quarterly Journal of Economics* 112 (1997), 1251–1289.

Knoke, David, *Political Networks: The Structural Perspective.* Cambridge: Cambridge University Press, 1990.

Krieger, Joel, *The Oxford Companion to the Politics of the World.* Oxford: Oxford University Press, 1993.

Krueger, Alan B., and Jitka Maleckova, "Education, Poverty, Political Violence and Terrorism: Is There a Causal Connection?" *Journal of Economic Perspectives* 17 (2003), 119–144.

Krugman, Paul, "What Happened to Asia?" unpublished manuscript, MIT, 1998.

Krugman, Paul, *The Return of Depression Economics.* New York: Norton, 1999.

Krugman, Paul, "For Richer: How the Permissive Capitalism of the Boom Destroyed American Equality," *New York Times Magazine,* October 20, 2002.

Krugman, Paul, *The Great Unraveling: Losing Our Way in the New Century.* New York: W. W. Norton, 2003.

Kuran, Timur, *Private Truths, Public Lies: The Social Consequences of Preference Falsification.* Cambridge: Harvard University Press, 1995.

Kydd, Andrew, "Game Theory and the Spiral Model," *World Politics* 49 (1997), 371–400.

Kymlicka, W., *Multicultural Citizenship: A Liberal Theory of Minority Rights.* Oxford: Oxford University Press, 1995.

Lambsdorff, Johann, "Corruption and Rent-Seeking," *Public Choice* 113 (2002), 97–125.

Landes, William M., "An Economic Study of US Aircraft Hijacking, 1961–1976," *Journal of Law and Economics* 21 (1978): 1–32

Lenin, V. I., *What Is to Be Done? Burning Questions of Our Movement.* New York: International Publishers, 1969.

Lesser, Ian O., Bruce Hoffman, John Arquilla, David Ronfeldt, and Michele Zanini, *Countering the New Terrorism.* Santa Monica: Rand, 1999.

Levitt, Steven D., "Understanding Why Crime Rates Fell in the 1990s: Four Factors That Explain the Decline and Six That Do Not," *Journal of Economic Perspectives* 18 (2004), 353–372.

Levitt, Steven D., and Alladi Venkatesh, "An Economic Analysis of a Drug-Selling Gang's Finances," *Quarterly Journal of Economics* 115 (2000), 755–789.

Lewis, Bernard, *The Political Language of Islam.* Chicago: University of Chicago Press, 1988.

Lewis, Bernard, *The Crisis of Islam: Holy War and Unholy Terror.* New York: Random House Modern Library Edition, 2003.

Lewis, Gwynne, "The French Revolution 1789–99," in David Parker, *Revolutions and the Revolutionary Tradition, 1560–1991.* London: Routledge, 2000.

Li, Hongyi, Kixin Colin Xu, and Heng-Fu Zou, "Corruption, Income Distribution and Growth," *Economics and Politics* 12 (2000), 155–182.

Lin, Yi-Min, *Between Politics and Markets: Firms, Competition and Institutional Change in Post-Mao China.* Cambridge: Cambridge University Press, 2001.

Linz, Juan, "Some Notes toward a Comparative Study of Fascism in Sociological Historical Perspective," in Walter Laqueur, *Fascism: A Reader's Guide.* Berkeley: University of California Press, 1976.

Lipset, Seymour Martin, and Earl Rabb, *The Politics of Unreason: Right Wing Extremism in America, 1790–1977.* 2d ed. Chicago: University of Chicago Press, 1970, 1978.

Lochner, Lance, "Individual Perceptions of the Criminal Justice System," unpublished manuscript, University of Western Ontario, 2005.

Loury, Glenn, "A Dynamic Theory of Racial Income Differences," in P. A. Wallace and A. LeMund, eds., *Women, Minorities and Employment Discrimination.* Lexington, Mass.: Lexington Books 1977.

Makiya, Kanan, and Hassan Mneimneh, "The Hijacker's Manual," *New York Review of Books,* January 17, 2002.

Margolis, Howard, *Selfishness, Altruism, and Rationality: A Theory of Social Choice.* Cambridge: Cambridge University Press, 1982.

Massing, Michael, "The Blue Revolution," *New York Review of Books,* November 19, 1998, 32–34.

Mauro, Pablo, "Corruption and Growth," *Quarterly Journal of Economics* 109 (1995), 681–712.

McGarry, J., and B. O'Leary, *The Northern Ireland Conflict: Consociational Engagements.* Oxford: Oxford University Press, 2003.

Meyer, Alfred G., *Leninism.* New York: Praeger, 1962.

Milgram, Stanley, *Obedience to Authority: An Experimental View.* New York: Harper and Row, 1974.

Miller, Geoffrey, "Contracts of Genesis," *Journal of Legal Studies* 22 (1993), 15–45.

Mishkin, Fred, "Understanding Financial Crises: A Developing Country Perspective," NBER WP 5600, 1996.

Morduch, Jonathan, "The Microfinance Promise," *Journal of Economic Literature* 37 (1999), 1569–1614.

Morton, Rebecca, "Groups in Rational Turnout Models," *American Journal of Political Science* 35 (1991), 758–776.

Mueller, Dennis, *Public Choice III.* Cambridge: Cambridge University Press, 2003.

Murphy, Kevin, "Executive Compensation," in Orley Ashenfelter and David Card, eds., *Handbook of Labor Economics,* 3B:2486–2557. Amsterdam: Elsevier, 1999.

Niskanen, William, "The Several Costs of Responding to the Threat of Terrorism," *Public Choice,* special issue on terrorism (forthcoming).

North, Douglass, *Structure and Change in Economic History.* New York: W. W. Norton, 1981.

North, Douglass, and Barry Weingast, "Constitutions and Commitment: The Evolution of Institutions Governing Public Choice in Seventeenth Century England," *Journal of Economic History* 49 (1989), 808–832.

Olivier, J. I., "State Repression and Collective Action in South Africa, 1970–1984," *South African Journal of Sociology* 22 (1991), 109–117.

Olson, Mancur, *The Logic of Collective Action.* Cambridge: Harvard University Press, 1965.

Olson, Mancur, "Dictatorship, Democracy and Development," *American Political Science Review* 87 (1993), 567–575.

Opp, Karl-Dieter, and P. Hartmann, *The Rationality of Political Protest: A Comparative Analysis of Rational Choice Theory.* Boulder, Colo.: Westview Press, 1989.

Opp, Karl-Dieter, and W. Ruehl, "Repression, Micro-Mobilization, and Political Protest," *Social Forces* 69 (1990), 521–547.

Page, Benjamin, and Robert Y. Shapiro, "Restraining the Whims and Passions of the Public," in Bernard Grofman and Donald Wittman, eds., *The Federalist Papers and the New Institutionalism.* New York: Agathon Press, 1989.

Paldam, Martin, and Gert Tinggaard Svendsen, "Missing Social Capital and the Transition in Eastern Europe," *Journal for Institutional Innovation, Development and Transition* (IB Review) 5 (2001; published 2002), 21–34.

Pape, Robert A., "The Strategic Logic of Suicide Terrorism," *American Political Science Review* 97 (2003), 343–361.

Pape, Robert A., *Dying to Win: The Strategic Logic of Suicide Terrorism.* New York: Random House, 2005.

Parker, D., *Revolutions and the Revolutionary Tradition, 1560–1991.* London: Routledge, 2000.

Paxton, Robert O., *The Anatomy of Fascism.* New York: Albert A. Knopf, 2004.

Perrie, M., "The Russian Revolution," in David Parker, *Revolutions and the Revolutionary Tradition, 1560–1991.* London: Routledge, 2000.

Pharr, Susan, and Robert Putnam, *Disaffected Democracies: What's Troubling the Trilateral Countries?* Princeton, N.J.: Princeton University Press, 2000.

Podhoretz, Norman, "World War IV: How It Started, What It Means, and Why We Have to Win," *Commentary* (September 2004), 17–54.

Posen, Barry R., "The Security Dilemma and Ethnic Conflict," *Survival* 35 (1993), 27–47.

Posner, R. A., "The Social Costs of Monopoly and Regulation," *Journal of Political Economy* 83 (1975), 807–827.

Post, Jerrold M., "Terrorist Psycho-Logic: Terrorist Behaviour as a Product of Psychological Forces," in Walter Reich, ed., *Origins of Terrorism: Psychologies, Ideologies, Theologies, States of Mind.* Cambridge: Cambridge University Press, 1990.

Putnam, Robert, *Making Democracy Work.* Princeton, N.J.: Princeton University Press, 1993.

Putnam, Robert, *Bowling Alone: The Collapse and Revival of American Community.* New York: Simon and Schuster, 2000.

Qinglian, He, "China's Descent into a Quagmire," *Chinese Economy,* Part 1, 33 (May–June 2000); Part 2, 34 (March–April 2001); and Part 3, 34 (July–August 2001).

Ramet, Sabrina Petra , *Balkan Babel: The Disintegration of Yugoslavia from the Death of Tito to Ethnic War.* 2d ed. Boulder, Colo.: Westview Press, 1996.

Raskovich, Alexander, "Ye Shall Have No Other Gods before Me: A Legal-Economic Analysis of the Rise of Yahweh," *Journal of Institutional and Theoretical Economics* 152 (1996), 449–471.

Rasler, K., "Concession, Repression, and Political Protest in the Iranian Revolution," *American Sociological Review* 61 (1996), 132–152.

Ricolfi, Luca, "Palestinians, 1980–2001," in Diego Gambetta, ed., *Making Sense of Suicide Missions.* Oxford: Oxford University Press, 2005.

Rodrik, Dani, *Has Globalization Gone Too Far?* Washington, D.C.: Institute for International Economics, 1997.

Roll, Richard, "The Hubris Hypothesis of Corporate Takeovers," *Journal of Business,* 59 (1986), 197–216.

Root, Hilton, *The Fountain of Privilege.* Berkeley: University of California Press, 1994.

Rose, Richard, "Getting Things Done in an Anti Modern Society: Social Capital Networks in Russia," in P. Dasgupta and Ismail Serageldin, eds., *Social Capital: A Multifaceted Perspective.* Washington, D.C.: World Bank, 1999.

Rousseau, Jean-Jacques, *The Social Contract and Other Later Political Writings.* Edited and translated by Victor Gourevitch. Cambridge: Cambridge University Press, 1997.

Roy, Olivier, *Globalized Islam: The Search for a New Ummah.* New York: Columbia University Press, 2004.

Rubin, Paul H., *Darwinian Politics.* New Brunswick: Rutgers University Press, 2002.

Runciman, W. G., and Amartya Sen, "Games, Justice and the General Will," *Mind* 74 (1965), 554–562.

Ruthven, M., *Islam in the World.* 2d ed. London: Penguin, 2000.

Ruthven, M., *A Fury For God: The Islamist Attack on America.* London: Granta, 2002.

Sacerdote, Bruce, and Edward L. Glaeser, "Education and Religion," NBER Working Paper 8080, 2001.

Sachs, Jeffrey, "International Economics: Unlocking the Mysteries of Globalization," in Patrick O'Meary et al., eds., *Globalization and the Challenges of a New Century.* Bloomington: Indiana University Press, 1999.

Sachs, Jeffrey, and Steven Radelet, "The East Asia Financial Crisis: Diagnosis, Remedies, Prospects," *Brookings Papers on Economic Activity* 1 (1998), 1–90.

Salmon, Pierre, "Extremism and Monomania," in Albert Breton, Gianluigi Galeotti, Pierre Salmon, and Ronald Wintrobe, eds., *Political Extremism and Rationality.* Cambridge: Cambridge University Press, 2002.

Samuelsson, Kurt, *Religion and Economic Action: A Critique of Max Weber.* Translated from the Swedish and edited by E. Geoffrey French, with an introduction by D. C. Coleman. New York: Harper and Row, 1964.

Sandler, Todd, "Patterns of Transnational Terrorism, 1970–99: Alternative Time Series Estimates," *International Studies Quarterly* 46 (June 2002), 145–165.

Sandler, Todd, and Harvey E. Lapan, "The Calculus of Dissent: An Analysis of Terrorists' Choice of Targets," *Synthese* 76 (1988), 245–261.

Sawhill, Isabel V., "Income Inequality and the Underclass," in Dmitri B. Papadimitriou, ed., *Aspects of the Distribution of Wealth and Income.* London: Macmillan, 1994.

Schumpeter, Joseph, *Capitalism, Socialism and Democracy.* New York: Harper and Brothers, 1950.

Sears, David O., Leonie Huddy, and Robert Jervis, *Oxford Handbook of Political Psychology.* Oxford: Oxford University Press, 2003.

Shachar, Ron, and Barry Nalebuff, "Follow the Leader: Theory and Evidence on Political Participation," *American Economic Review* 89 (1999), 525–547.

Shapiro, Carl, and Joseph Stiglitz, "Equilibrium Unemployment as a Worker Discipline Device," *American Economic Review* 74 (1984), 433–444.

Shleifer, Andrei, and Lawrence Summers, "Breach of Trust in Hostile Takeovers," in Alan J. Auerbach, ed., *Corporate Takeovers: Causes and Consequences.* Chicago: University of Chicago Press, 1988.

Shleifer, Andrei, and Robert Vishny, "Corruption," *Quarterly Journal of Economics* 108 (1993), 599–617.

Sinn, Hans-Werner, "Germany ín the World Economy – Hope Springs Eternal," *Supplement to CESifo Forum* 3 (Summer 2002), 1–11.

Skocpol, Theda, *States and Social Revolutions.* Cambridge: Cambridge University Press, 1974.

Smith, Anthony D., "The Formation of Nationalist Movements," in Anthony D. Smith, *Nationalist Movements.* London: Macmillan 1976.

Smith, Anthony D., "The Ethnic Sources of Nationalism," *Survival* 35 (1993), 48–62.

Snyder, Jack, and Karen Ballantine, "Nationalism and the Marketplace for Ideas," in Michael E. Brown, Owen R. Coté Jr., Sean M. Lynn-Jones, and Steven E. Miller, eds. *Nationalism and Ethnic Conflict.* Cambridge: MIT Press, 1997.

Sontag, Susan, *The Observer* (April 1999).

Sprinzak, Ehud, "The Emergence of the Israeli Radical Right," *Comparative Politics* 21 (1989), 171–192.

Stiglitz, Joseph E., *Globalization and Its Discontents.* New York: Norton, 2002.

Sullivan, Stacy, "Milosevic's Willing Executioners," *New Republic,* May 10, 1999.

Sunstein, Cass R., *Why Societies Need Dissent.* Cambridge: Harvard University Press, 2003.

Sutherland, D. M. G., *The French Revolution and Empire.* Oxford: Blackwell, 2003.

Tanzi, Vito, "Corruption: Arms' Length Relationships and Markets," in G. Fiorentini and S. Peltzman, eds., *The Economics of Organized Crime,* 161–180. Cambridge: Cambridge University Press, 1995.

Taylor, A. J. P., *Revolutions and Revolutionaries.* New York: Atheneum, 1980.

Thomas, Mark, "Complete Control," *New Statesman and Society,* June 24, 1994.

Thomas, Robert, *Serbia under Milosevic: Politics in the 1990s.* London: C. Hurst, 1999.

Thompson, M. R., "Why and How the East Germans Rebelled," *Theory and Society* 25 (1996), 263–299.

Tocqueville, A., *The Old Regime and the French Revolution.* Edited and with an introduction and critical apparatus by Francois Furet and Francoise Melonio. Translated by Alan S. Kahn. Chicago: University of Chicago Press, 1998.

Tullock, G., "The Paradox of Revolution," *Public Choice* 11 (1971), 88–99.

Tullock, G., *Autocracy.* Boston: Kluwer Academic Publishers, 1987.

Uhlaner, Carol, "Rational Turnout: The Neglected Role of Groups," *American Journal of Political Science* 33 (1989), 390–422.

Uslaner, Eric, "Democracy and Social Capital," in Mark E. Warren, *Democracy and Trust.* Cambridge, 1999.

U.S. State Department, *Patterns of Global Terrorism.* 2004. Available at www.mipt.org/Patterns-of-Global-Terrorism.asp.

Van Belle, D., "Leadership and Collective Action: The Case of Revolution," *International Studies Quarterly* 40 (1996), 107–132.

Van Winden, Franz, "On the Economic Theory of Interest Groups: Towards a Group Frame of Reference in Political Economics" *Public Choice* (1999), 1–29.

Varian, H., ed., "Symposium on Takeovers," *Journal of Economic Perspectives* 2, no.1 (1988).

Vishwanath, T., and Daniel Kaufman, "Toward Transparency: New Approaches and Their Application to Financial Markets," *World Bank Research Observer* 16 (2001), 41–57.

Wade, Robert, *Governing the Market: Economic Theory and the Role of Government in East Asian Industrialization.* Princeton, N.J.: Princeton University Press, 1990.

Wade, Robert, and Frank Veneroso, "The Asian Financial Crisis: The High Debt Model versus the Wall Street-Treasury-IMF Complex," *New Left Review* 228 (March–April, 1998), 3–23.

Walder, Andrew, *Communist Neo Traditionalism: Work and Authority in Chinese Industry.* Berkeley: University of California Press, 1986.

Wang, Xiaoying, "The Post-Communist Personality: The Spectre of Chinas Capitalist Market Reforms," *China Journal,* (2002), 5–21.

Weber, Max, *The Protestant Ethic and the Spirit of Capitalism.* Translated by Talcott Parsons. London: G. Allen and Unwin, 1930.

Wei, Shang-Jin, "Domestic Crony Capitalism and International Fickle Capital: Is There a Connection?" *International Finance* 4 (Spring 2001), 15–45.

Williams, George C., *Adaptation and Natural Selection: A Critique of Some Current Evolutionary Thought.* Princeton, N.J.: Princeton University Press, 1966.

Williamson, John, "What Washington Means by Policy Reform," in John Williamson, ed., *Latin American Adjustment: How Much Has Happened?* Washington, D.C. Institute for International Economics, 1990.

Williamson, John, "What Should the World Bank Think about the Washington Consensus?" *World Bank Research Observer* 15 (2000), 251–264.

Wilson, William Julius, *The Truly Disadvantaged: The Inner City, the Underclass and Public Policy.* Chicago: University of Chicago Press, 1987.

Wintrobe, Ronald, "The Tinpot and the Totalitarian: An Economic Theory of Dictatorship," *American Political Science Review* 84 (September 1990), 849–872.

Wintrobe, Ronald, "Modern Bureaucratic Theory," in Dennis Mueller, ed., *Perspectives in Public Choice.* Cambridge: Cambridge University Press, 1997.

Wintrobe, Ronald, *The Political Economy of Dictatorship.* Cambridge: Cambridge University Press, 1998a.

Wintrobe, Ronald, "Privatization, the Market for Corporate Control and Capital Flight from Russia," *World Economy* 21 (1998b), 603–612.

Wintrobe, Ronald, "Downsizing Trust," in Gianluigi Galeotti, Pierre Salmon, and Ronald Wintrobe, eds., *Competition and Structure.* Cambridge: Cambridge, 2000.

Wintrobe, Ronald, "Slobodan Milosevic and the Fire of Nationalism," *World Economics* 3 (2002), 1–27.

Wintrobe, Ronald, "The Optimal Level of Solidarity," in Albert Breton, Gianluigi Galeotti, Pierre Salmon, and Ronald Wintrobe, eds., *Rational Foundations of Democratic Politics.* Cambridge: Cambridge University Press, 2003.

Wintrobe, Ronald, "Rational Revolutions," *Homo Oeconomicus* 21, no. 2 (2004), 171–197. Special issue on revolutions edited by Mario Ferrero.

Wintrobe, Ronald, *Extremism.* Two one-hour radio programs for the Canadian Broadcasting Corporation's *Ideas* series. First broadcast December 2004.

Wintrobe, Ronald, and Albert Breton, "Organizational Structure and Productivity," *American Economic Review* 76 (1986), 530–538.

Woodward, Susan L., *Balkan Tragedy: Chaos and Disillusion after the Cold War.* Washington, D.C.: The Brookings Institution, 1995.

Woodward, Susan L., "Intervention in Civil Wars – Bosnia and Herzegovina," Columbia University Institute of War and Peace Studies, February 1997.

Wydick, Bruce, "Can Social Cohesion Be Harnessed to Repair Market Failures? Evidence from Group Lending in Guatemala," *Economic Journal* 109 (1999), 463–475.

Xenophon, "Hiero or Tyrannicus." Reprinted in L. Strauss, *On Tyranny.* New York: Political Science Classics, 1948.

Zakaria, Fareed, *The Future of Freedom: Illiberal Democracy at Home and Abroad.* New York: W. W. Norton, 2003.

Zingales, Luigi, and R. Rajan, "The Tyranny of Inequality: An Inquiry into the Adverse Consequences of Power Struggles," *Journal of Public Economics* 76 (2000), 521–558.

Index

9/11, 220

afterlife, belief in. *See* religion, as motivation
   for suicide terrorists
*Age of Extremes, The: The Short Twentieth
   Century, 1914–1991* (Hobsbawm), 13
Akerlof, George A., 22, 25
   and gangs, 59
Al Qaeda, 3, 6, 8, 85, 113, 233
   organizational structure of, 14, 133–136,
      142
   recruitment and qualifications for, 116
   and use of Islam, 135–136
Albania, conflict in. *See* ethnic nationalism,
   in Yugoslavia; Milosevic, Slobodan
altruism, of suicide terrorists, 109–113, 128,
   248. *See also* suicide terrorism and
   terrorists
America in Peril (video, Koernke), 114
amoral familism, 41
Andreoni, James, 22, 59
Arendt, Hannah, 4, 185, 188, 210
   on Rousseau, 35–37
Armstrong, Karen, 146
army, solidarity in, 30–34, 42–43. *See also*
   solidarity
   and policy implications, 70
   and social interactions, 70
   table of social interactions and policy
      implications, 68
Arquilla, John, 133
Asia. *See also* Asian tigers, and corruption;
   specific country
   and corporate governance, 222–223
   financial crisis of, and crony capitalism,
      23, 64–66, 71

financial crisis of, and policy
   implications, 64–67, 71
financial crisis of, and social interactions,
   23, 64–67, 71
financial crisis of, table of social
   interactions and policy implications, 68
shareholder vs. stakeholder system in,
   221–222
stakeholder system, and corruption in,
   234–237
Asian tigers, and corruption. *See also* Asia;
   corruption, and economic growth;
   specific country
   and rent seeking, 234–237
asymmetric information, 43
   and contagion in financial markets, 64
Atta, Muhammad, 144
Aum Shinrikyu, 117
Autocracy (Tullock), 195
autocracy, and contractual exchange,
   148–150
Azzam, Jean-Paul, 110, 128

Baader-Meinhof Gang, 3, 260
Ba'athism, 11
Balkans, conflict in. *See* ethnic nationalism,
   in Yugoslavia; Milosevic, Slobodan
bandwagon effects, 12, 101. *See also*
   contagion; solidarity
   and East German Revolution, 172–173
   and French Revolution, 182, 184, 187
   in politics, 44–45
   and revolutions, 15, 95, 162–164, 172,
      189, 249
Banerjee, Abhijit V., 25, 44, 63
Banfield, Edward, 40–41

Bangladesh, poverty, and group lending in, 61–62
Barber, Benjamin, 16, 217, 218–219, 241
barriers to entry and exit, 232–233, 239, 246, 249, 253
and ethnic nationalism, 200
and McWorld, 225–228, 241, 250
and production of national solidarity, 187
Becker, Gary S., 23, 25, 42, 204
and criminal behavior, 54, 87, 105
model of addiction of, 53
theory of the family of, 27–30
Berman, Eli, 23, 25, 33, 35, 241
and suicide terrorists, 111–112, 128
Bernheim, B. Douglas, 25
and esteem, 26
Besley, Timothy, 62, 63
Bhagwati, Jagdish, 67
bin Laden, Osama, 3, 141, 254, 260. *See also* Al Qaeda; Islam; Islamic fundamentalism; September 11th, 2001; suicide terrorism and terrorists
hierarchical control by, 135
indivisible goals of, 85
rationality of, 78–79
Bokenkotter, Thomas, 145
Bonaparte, Napoleon, 184, 188
Borooah, Vani, 59
Bosnia, conflict in. *See* ethnic nationalism, in Yugoslavia; Milosevic, Slobodan
Bougarel, Xavier, 193
Bowling Alone (Putnam), 23, 39. *See also* *Making Democracy Work*; Putnam, Robert
Branch Davidians, 117
Bratton, William (New York City police commissioner), 56–58. *See also* New York City, broken-windows approach to crime in
Breton, Albert, 40–41, 42, 50
Buruma, Ian, 11, 233–234
Bush, George W. (U.S. president), 79, 232. *See also* United States

calculus of discontent, model of. *See* terrorism, model of choice of
Calvinist Protestantism, and lack of contractual exchange, 147. *See also* Christianity; religion
Campos, Edward, 236

Canada, approach to extremism policy, 105
Castro, Fidel, 167, 190. *See also* dictatorship, model of
Chen, Feng, 237–239
China, 190
economic growth and corruption in, 41, 217–226, 237–240
growth in, and liquidation of solidarity, 217, 239. *See also* solidarity, destruction of sources of, and McWorld's stimulation of *jihad*
and illegal asset stripping, 237–241
jihad in, 239, 240
"China's Descent into a Quagmire" (He), 238–239
Christian Identity movement, bizzare beliefs of, 113
Christianity. *See also* Calvinist Protestantism; religion
as contractual exchange with God, 145–147
Chua, Amy, 83
Coase, Ronald H., 183
Coate, Stephen, 62, 63
Cohen, Jean, 41
Coleman, James S., 25, 40–41, 43, 50
Coles, Catherine M., 55, 58
common beliefs, 187, 226–228, 233, 241, 248, 250
communism, 3, 4, 9, 79, 85, 99, 197, 257. *See also* China; Lenin, Vladimir; Marx, Karl; Milosevic, Slobodan; Russia
fall of. *See* ethnic nationalism, in Yugoslavia
indivisible goals of, 89, 104, 106
and solidarity, 37–38
conformity, 109. *See also* solidarity, trading of belief for
contagion. *See also* social capital
and asymmetric information in financial markets, 64
and crime. *See* crime, and social interactions
and drug addiction, 43, 53
and herd externality, 43–44
and the media, 208
and network externalities, 44
in politics, 44–45. *See also* bandwagon effects; ethnic nationalism, in Yugoslavia
and social capital, 43–45

contractual exchange, with God
  and autocracy, 148–150
  religion as, 145–152. *See also specific
    religion*
  and religious solidarity, 153–154,
    156–157
Corman, Hope, 58
corner solution, 43, 109, 141, 142
  implications for policy, 130
  and suicide terrorism, 125–128, 248
  and trading of beliefs for solidarity,
    125–128
corporate governance, shareholder vs.
  stakeholder systems, 222–223
corruption, and economic growth, 239–240
  in China, 41, 216–217, 237–240
  in Italy, 41, 235
  in shareholder vs. stakeholder systems,
    234–237
  in Singapore, 235
  in South Korea, 216–217, 235–237
cost and benefits, of terrorism, 110
Crenshaw, Martha, 113
crime, and social interactions, 21–23, 54–60
  and broken-windows approach to in New
    York City, 55–58
  in England, 59
  and gang behavior, 58–59
  and policy implications, 69–70
  and *Roe vs. Wade*, 58
  table of, and policy implications, 68
Croatia, conflict in. *See* ethnic nationalism,
  in Yugoslavia; Milosevic, Slobodan
crony capitalism, 65. *See also* corruption,
  and economic growth; social
  interactions
  and Asian financial crisis, 23, 64–66, 71
  in Indonesia, 64, 65
cults, solidarity in, 114, 131, 132, 142. *See
  also* extremism and extremist groups;
  extremist leaders
  and leaders, 117

Dallago, Bruno, 197
Darkness at Noon (Koestler), 114
Dawkins, Richard, 152
Declaration of the Rights of Man (France),
  183
Della Porta, Donatella, 41
democracy and democratic methods
  and attitude toward dictatorships, 214

as avenue to power by extremist groups,
  80–83
maintaining in extremism policy, 260
revolutions against, 162
and significance of September 11th for,
  256
and successful revolution, 183–184
and war with dictatorships, 210–213, 250
Diamond, Douglas, 25
Dictator's Dilemma. *See* dictatorship,
  model of
dictatorship, model of, 95, 166–167. *See also*
  East German Revolution; ethnic
  nationalism, in Yugoslavia; French
  Revolution; *individual dictator*; Iranian
  Revolution; Milosevic, Slobodan;
  revolutions
  equilibrium loyalty and repression,
    167–171, 176–178
  equilibrium power and budget, 173–178
  and French Revolution, 178–182
  and Iranian Revolution, 171
  and policy implications, 210–214
  and revolution, 176–178
  types of dictators, 167
  and upsurge in terrorism, 259
  and weakness of the state, 176–178,
    188–189
Divine Light Mission, 114, 117
divisible goals, of extremist groups, 14, 86
  and income inequality, 88, 106
  and policy implications for terrorism, 93
Division of Labour in Society (Durkheim),
  27
Djilas, Aleksa, 198, 199
Djilas, Milovan, 193
drug addiction, model of, and contagion,
  43, 53
Durkheim, Emil, 27, 153
Dybvig, Philip H., 25

East German Revolution, 165. *See also*
  Germany; dictatorship, model of;
  revolutions
  and bandwagon effects, 172–173
  and free-rider problem, 165
  and weakness of the state, 172–173
economic growth. *See* corruption, and
  economic growth
economic models of religious participation.
  See religious solidarity

economics of social relations. *See* social
  interactions
Enders, Walter, 7
enemies. *See* external enemy
England
  crime in, 59
  Glorious Revolution in, 148, 178
equality, 30, 225–227, 232–233, 240, 250. *See*
  also solidarity, destruction of sources
  of, and McWorld's stimulation of *jihad*
esteem, 26
ethnic capital. *See also* ethnic nationalism,
  in Yugoslavia
ethnic cleansing, 192, 259. *See also* ethnic
  nationalism, in Yugoslavia
  and social interactions, 209–210
ethnic nationalism, in Yugoslavia, 78, 131.
  See also ethnic cleansing
  as contagious, 201–210, 214
  explanations for, 192–195
  and the media, 208
  model of explosive rise of, 199–210
  and nationalist strategies of Milosevic,
    195–199
  and network externalities, 202–203
  and the security dilemma, 192–195, 201,
    204–210, 214, 249, 259
  table of social interactions and policy
    implications, 253
Europe. *See also specific country*
  convergence of poltical parties, and
    extremism, 80
  and corporate governance, 222–223
  history of extremism in, 3
  shareholder vs. stakeholder system in,
    221–222
  welfare programs and solidarity in, 226,
    232, 234
external enemy
  and creation of solidarity, 35, 131, 156,
    187, 226, 227, 232, 249, 255. *See also*
    solidarity
extremism and extremist groups. *See also*
  communism; dictatorship, model of;
  ethnic nationalism, in Yugoslavia;
  extremist leaders; East German
  Revolution; fascism; French
  Revolution; Iranian Revolution;
  McWorld, and stimulation of *jihad*;
  revolutions; suicide terrorism and
  terrorists; terrorism

  beliefs of, 109–113
  and coalitions, 81–83
  and convergence of political parties, 8, 80,
    250, 259–260
  and democratic avenues to power, 80–83
  and divisible goals, 14, 86, 88, 93, 106
  in Europe, 3, 80
  and globalization. *See* McWorld, and
    stimulation of *jihad*
  and a market-dominant minority, 83
  indivisible goals of, 14, 87–107, 247
  leaders of. *See* extremist leaders
  in North America, 3–4
  policy implications. *See* policy, on
    extremism and terrorism
  and political competition. *See* suicide
    terrorism and terrorists; terrorism
  and political pressure. *See* terrorism
  rational choice approach to, 6–9
  reasons for, 79–80
  and social interactions, 245–246
  and socioeconomic status, 110
  and solidarity, 9–12, 109–113, 245–246
  and the solidarity multiplier, 247–248
  and terrorist methods. *See* suicide
    terrorism and terrorists; terrorism,
    model of choice of
extremist leaders, 3, 75–79, 116. *See also*
  extremism and extremist groups;
  specific leaders; suicide terrorism and
  terrorists; terrorism
  of cults, 117
  and model of choice of extremism,
    87–100
  reasons for choosing extremism, 79–80
  and revolution, 164
  and violence, 75–79

Face of Battle (Keegan), 6, 30
family, solidarity in, 27–30, 42
  policy implications, 70
  and rotten-kid theorem, 28–29, 47–48,
    68, 246
  table of social interactions and policy
    implications, 68
Fanon, Franz, 4
fascism, 257
  in Germany, 38
  in Italy, 3, 38, 84
  and solidarity, 37–38
Fearon, James D., 194–195

Federalist Papers, 45
Fehr, Ernst, 25
Figueirdo, Ruij P., Jr., 194–195
financial markets. *See* Asia, financial crisis
    of; Asian tigers; corruption, and
    economic growth; crony capitalism;
    McWorld, and stimulation of *jihad*;
    microfinance, and poverty; poverty,
    group-oriented solutions for;
    shareholder vs. stakeholder systems;
    transparency, in economic systems
Finer, Samuel, 145, 146, 154, 155, 178, 180
    on Declaration of the Rights of Man, 185
Fixing Broken Windows (Kelling and Coles),
    55
Foundations of Social Theory (Coleman), 25
France. *See also* French Revolution
    industrial relations in, 221–222
    and the National Front, 3
free-rider problem, 10, 26, 29, 34, 44, 47, 48,
    111, 113, 115, 128, 225, 248. *See also*
    solidarity
    and the East German Revolution, 165
    and the French Revolution, 181
    and revolutions, 161–162, 177
French Revolution, 3
    and bandwagon effects, 182, 184, 187
    and Declaration of the Rights of Man, 185
    dynamics in, 184–188
    factors in, and the model of dictatorship,
       178–182
    and national solidarity, 35–187, 188
    and poverty, 187–188
    role of intermediary bodies in, 184–187
    social question in, 183
    and weakness of the French state, 178–182
Frey, Bruno S., 140, 141, 251
Friedman, Thomas, 219
Fukuyama, Francis, 41, 47, 50
    end of history argument of, 184, 256
Furet, F., 185, 186. *See also* French
    Revolution

Gagnon, V. P., 193
Galanter, Marc, 114, 117, 132
Galeotti, Gianluigi, 84
Gandhi, Mahatma, 4, 75, 76, 260
gangs, 22, 42, 54, 58–59, 85, 116, 129, 257.
    See also crime, and social interactions
    policy implications, 69–70
    positive view of, 59

Gandhi's Way (Juergensmeyer), 4
Geertz, Clifford, 4, 115
Germany, 3, 260. *See also* Baader Meinhof
    Gang; East German Revolution; Hitler,
    Adolf; Nazi Party
    fascism in, 38
    industrial relations in, 221–222
    and social capital, 44
Ghatak, Maitreesh, 61
Ginkel, John, 165
Giorgio (Italian terrorist), 116
Glaeser, Edward, 25, 58
Glazer, Nathan, 56
globalization, and extremism. *See* McWorld,
    and stimulation of *jihad*
Glorious Revolution (England), 148, 178
Goldstone, Jack, 177–178
Gordon, David, 222
Green Party
    divisible goals of, 86
    extremism of, 84
Guinnane, T. W., 61
Gunaratna, Robin, 116, 134, 135, 136

Hamas, 5, 6, 35, 133, 136. *See also* Palestine
    and Palestinians
Hardin, Russell, 115
He Qinglian, 238–239
Hechter, Michael, 27
herd externality, 25. *See also* contagion;
    crony capitalism; social capital; social
    interactions
    and contagion, 43–44
    and creditors, 24
    and international investors, 66, 67, 71
Hezbollah, determinants of participation in,
    110. *See also* extremism and extremist
    groups
History of Government (Finer), 44, 178
Hitchens, Christopher, 4
Hitler, Adolf, 135, 186
    and fascism, 38. *See also* Germany
    popularity of, 167. *See also* dictatorship,
       model of
Hobsbawm, Eric, 13
Hoffman, Bruce, 110, 113, 152
homeland, 80, 85, 87, 112, 142, 260
horizontal social capital, 24
horizontal trust. *See* social capital, and trust
human rights, 15, 37, 83, 183, 214, 233
    policy implications of, 102, 104, 255

Hussein, Saddam, 192, 213. *See also* Iraq
  popularity of, 167. *See also* dictatorship,
  model of; Iraq

Iannacconne, Lawrence R., 23, 25, 34, 111
  and economics of religion, 145
Ibn Khaldun, 11
Ignatieff, Michael, 191, 193
illegal asset stripping, in China, 237–241.
  See also China, economic growth and
  corruption in
individualistic, 154
individualistic approach, to social
  interactions, 12, 21, 54, 55–58, 64, 67,
  69, 71. *See also* social interactions
indivisible goals, of extremist groups, 14,
  247. *See also* communism, indivisible
  goals of; Palestine and Palestinians;
  policy, on extremism and terrorism;
  terrorism, model of choice of
  and choice of extremist methods, 87–107
Indonesia, and crony capitalism, 64, 65. *See
  also* Asia, financial crisis of
industrial relations, shareholder vs.
  stakeholder, 221–222
Inglehart, Ronald, 40–41
interdependent preferences, 25, 43
intermediary bodies, 184–187. *See also*
  social capital
international finance. *See* Asia, financial
  crisis of; Asian tigers; corruption, and
  economic growth; crony capitalism;
  McWorld, and stimulation of *jihad*;
  microfinance, and poverty; poverty,
  group-oriented solutions for;
  shareholder vs. stakeholder systems;
  transparency, in economic systems
Iran. *See* Iranian Revolution
Iranian Revolution. *See also* dictatorship,
  model of; revolutions
  and model of dictatorship, 171
  and repression, 165, 166, 171
  and social interactions, 164–165
Iraq, 152, 190, 254, 258
  and democracies waging war against
  dictatorships, 213
  ethnic groups in, 104
Irony of Absolutism, 14, 148, 178
Islam. *See also* Islamic fundamentalism;
  Muslim states
  and religious solidarity, 154–156

and suicide terrorism and terrorists,
  154–156
  as contractual exchange with God,
  145–147
  use of by Al Qaeda, 135–136
Islamic fundamentalism, 79, 260. *See also*
  bin Laden, Osama
  indivisible goals of, 106
  and McWorld's stimulation of *jihad*,
  230–231
  rise of, 80
  and threats to Islamic solidarity, 233–234
Israel, 6, 80, 81, 85, 87, 88, 98, 113, 145, 150
  Jewish fundamentalists in, 5
"It's All about State Structure" (Goldstone),
  177
Italy, 5–6, 102, 222, 260. *See also* Mussolini,
  Benito; Red Brigades
  corruption in, 41, 235
  extremist groups in, 3, 99, 250
  fascism in, 3, 38, 84
  social capital in, 38–39

Jankowski, Martin, 22, 59
jihad
  and globalization. *See* McWorld, and
  stimulation of *jihad*
  in China, 239, 240
Jihad vs. McWorld (Barber), 16, 217,
  218–219, 233. *See also* Barber,
  Benjamin; McWorld, and stimulation
  of *jihad*
Judaism, 87, 96. *See also* religion
  as contractual exchange with God, 145,
  146–147
  Jewish fundamentalists, 5
Juergensmeyer, Mark, 4

Kang, David, 235
Keefer, Phillip, 40–41, 47, 50
Keegan, John, 23, 30–34, 70. *See also* army,
  solidarity in
Kelling, George L., 55, 58
Key to the Fields (painting, Magritte), 216
King, Martin Luther, 76–77, 79, 260
Kirkpatrick, Jeanne (ambassador to the
  United Nations), 258
Kitschelt, Herbert, 80, 259
Knack, Stephen, 40–41, 47, 50
Knoke, David, 7
Koernke, Mark, 114

Koestler, Arthur, 114
Koresh, David (leader of Branch Davidians), 117
Krueger, Alan B., 110
Krugman, Paul, 66, 67
Kuran, Timur, 26

Laitin, David D., 194–195
  and suicide terrorists, 111–112, 128
Lenin, Vladimir, 37, 75. *See also* communism, and solidarity
Levitt, Steven D., 22, 57, 129
Lewis, Bernard, 156, 187
liberal theory, 79, 106
Linz, Juan J., 38
Lipset, Seymour, 11
Loong, Lee Hsien (deputy minister of Singapore), 235
Loury, Glenn, 25
loyalty, and repression. *See under* dictatorship, model of

Madison, James (U.S. president), 45
Mafia, 116
Magritte, Rene, 216
Making Democracy Work (Putnam), 23, 39. *See also Bowling Alone*; Putnam, Robert
Makiya, Kanin, 144
Maleckova, Jitka, 110
Mandela, Nelson, 4, 75, 78, 79
Margalit, Avishai, 11, 233–234
Margolis, Howard, 25
market-dominant minority, 83
markets, spread of. *See* McWorld, and stimulation of *jihad*
Marshall, Samuel L. A. (U.S. general), 31
Marx, Karl, 37, 88
McCauley, Clark, 155
McDonald's, and McWorld, 218–219
McWorld, and stimulation of *jihad*, 259
  and destruction of sources of solidarity, 224–234, 240–241, 250
  and effect on shareholder vs. stakeholder systems, 226–227, 241
  and Islamic fundamentalism, 230–231
  and September 11th, 68
  table of social interactions and policy implications, 253
  and transparency, 218–221

media, and contagious nationalism in Yugoslavia, 208
median voter, 80, 82, 94
Men against Fire (Marshall), 31
Menuhin, Yehudi, 13
microfinance, and poverty, 60–64
  in Bangladesh, 61–62
  table of social interactions and policy implications, 68
Microsoft, 53
Milgram, Stanley, 132
Miller, Geoffrey, 145
Milosevic, Slobodan, 75, 78–79, 189, 190–192, 260. *See also* ethnic nationalism, in Yugoslavia
  explanation of strategies of, 192–195
  and media, 208
  nationalist strategies of, 195–199, 214
  regime of, and model of dictatorship, 195–199
  and war with NATO, 191, 210–213, 214
Mneimneh, Hassan, 144
Mocan, Naci, 58
Mohammed, Khalid Shaikh (Al Qaeda operative), 134. *See also* Al Qaeda
monarchy, and contractual exchange, 148–150
MTV, and McWorld, 218–219
Muslim states. *See also* Islam; *specific country*
  failure of, and terrorism, 155–156
Mussolini, Benito, 186. *See also* dictatorship, model of; Italy
  and fascism, 38

National Front, 3
National Rifle Association (NRA), 4, 81, 86
national solidarity, 34. *See also* ethnic nationalism, in Yugoslavia; *individual country*; nationalism; solidarity
  and French Revolution, 35–187, 188
  sources of. *See* barriers to entry and exit; equality; external enemy; pensions; welfare
nationalism, 79. *See also* ethnic nationalism, in Yugoslavia; Israel; Judaism; Palestine and Palestinians
  defintion of, 199
  indivisible goals of, 106
NATO, and war with Slobodan Milosevic, 191, 210–213, 214

Nazi Party, 3. *See also* Germany; Hitler, Adolf
and intermediary bodies in, 184–187
reasons for rise of, 80
structural organization of, 135
network externalities, 43, 53, 225. *See also* social interactions
and contagion, 44. *See also* social capital; solidarity
and ethnic nationalism, 201, 202–203
definition of, 46–47
New York, broken-windows approach to crime in, 97–103. *See also* crime, and social interactions; United States
Norquist, Grover (U.S. conservative activist), 82
North Atlantic Treaty Organisation. *See* NATO
North, Douglass, 148, 178
NRA (National Rifle Association), 4, 81, 86

Occidentalism (Buruma and Margalit), 233–234
Olson, Mancur, 161, 195
"On Subway Graffiti in New York" (Glazer), 56
Opp, Karl-Dieter, 165
Oxford Companion to Politics of the World (Krieger), 4

Paldam, Martin, 39
Palestine and Palestinians, 5, 9, 88, 98, 110, 112. *See also* Hamas; homeland; terrorism, model of choice of
indivisible goals of, 87, 96, 98
and suicide terrorists, 144, 152
suicide terrorists and revenge, 125
Pape, Robert A., 110, 113, 140
Paxton, Robert O., 38
pensions, 221, 225, 232, 237, 239
Perrie, M., 163
Podhoretz, Norman, 256
policy, and social interactions, 12, 53–54, 67–71, 250–251. *See also under* army, solidarity in; Asia, financial crisis of; crime, and social interactions; extremism and extremist groups; ethnic solidarity, in Yugoslavia; family, solidarity in; gangs; McWorld, and stimulation of *jihad*; poverty,

group-oriented solutions for; revolutions; terrorism
table of, 68
policy, on extremism and terrorism, 251–256
carrot vs. stick, 140–142
in Canada, 105
and corner solution, 130
and dictators, 210–214
and divisible goals, 93
and human rights, 102, 104, 255
and indivisible goals, 14, 79, 87–107, 255
maintaining democratic values in, 260
table of, 252–253
and U.S. subsidizing of by supporting dictatorships, 258
and welfare, 102, 103, 104
political competition. *See* suicide terrorism and terrorists; terrorism, model of choice of
political loyalty, and revolution. *See* dictatorship, model of
politics
bandwagon effects in, 44–45
contagion in, 44–45. *See also* bandwagon effects; ethnic nationalism, in Yugoslavia
convergence in, and extremism, 8, 80, 250, 259–260
social capital in, 44–45
Posen, Barry R., 131, 151, 193
Post, Jerrold M., 113
poverty
in Bangladesh, 61–62
and French Revolution, 187–188
and national solidarity. *See* welfare
poverty, group-oriented solutions for, 60–64. *See also* social interactions
and microfinance, 60–64
and policy implications, 70–71
table of social interaction and policy implications, 68
preference falsification, 26
price solution. *See* individualistic approach, to social interactions; policy, and social interactions
Propaganda Due, 3
Protestant Ethic and the Spirit of Capitalism (Weber), 147
Protestantism. *See* Calvinist Protestantism
Przeworski, Adam, 172

Putnam, Robert, 23
  and horizontal social capital, 11, 24
  and social capital, 38–41, 44

Rabb, Earl, 11
Rabin, Yitzhak (prime minister of Israel), 6.
    See also Israel; Judaism
Radelet, Steven, 66
radical Islam. *See* Islamic fundamentalism
Raskovich, Alexander, 145
Rasler, K., 164–165, 171
rational choice, and extremism, 6–9
Red Brigades, 3, 85, 99, 116, 260. *See also*
    extremism and extremist groups; Italy
religion. *See also* Calvinist Protestantism;
    Christianity; Islam; Judaism; religious
    solidarity
  as contractual exchange with God,
    145–152, 156–157
  as motivation for suicide terrorists,
    109–113, 144–145, 150–152, 248–249.
    See also religious solidarity
religious solidarity, 34–35, 248. *See also*
    religion; solidarity
  as contractual exchange with God,
    153–154, 156–157
  and Islam, 154–156
  and suicide terrorism, 151–157,
    248–249
repression, and revolution, 165–166. *See
    also* dictatorship, model of; revolutions
  and Iranian Revolution, 165, 166, 171
  and loyalty. *See under* dictatorship, model
    of
revenge, and suicide terrorism, 125, 128
revolutions, 249. *See also* East German
    Revolution; Iranian Revolution; French
    Revolution; Glorious Revolution
  and bandwagon effects, 15, 95, 162–164,
    172, 189, 249
  collective rationality of, 182–184,
    188–189
  criteria for successful, 182–184
  against democracies, 162
  against dictatorships. *See* dictatorship,
    model of; Milosevic, Slobodan
  dynamics in, 184–188
  as improvements in society, 162–163
  leadership of, 164
  and political loyalty. *See under*
    dictatorship, model of

and repression, 165–166. *See also*
    dictatorship, model of
  and social interactions, 164–165
  success of, and democracy, 183–184
  table of social interactions and policy
    implications, 253
  and weakness of the state, 163, 166,
    172–173, 176–182, 188–189, 249. *See
    also* dictatorship, model of
Ricolfi, Luca, 113, 125
risk, and choosing terrorist methods, 86–87,
    247. *See also* extremist leaders, model
    of choice of extremist methods;
    terrorism, model of choice of
Robespierre, Maximilien, 188
Roe vs. Wade, and crime, 58. *See also* crime,
    and social interactions
Root, Hilton, 236
Rose, Richard, 45
rotten-kid theorem, 30, 68. *See also*
    solidarity
  and solidarity in the family, 28–29, 47–48,
    246
Rousseau, Jean-Jacques, 35–37, 187
Roy, Olivier, 230–231, 241
Rubin, Robert (U.S. treasury secretary),
    66
Ruehl, W., 165
Russia, 170, 201
  privatization process in, 238, 240
  social capital in, 45
Ruthven, M., 147

Sacerdote, Bruce, 25
Sachs, Jeffrey, 66, 67
Salmon, Pierre, 43, 81
Sandler, Todd, 7, 251
Sati' Husri, 11
Scheinkman, Jose A., 25, 58
Scientologists, 117
security dilemma, 16, 131, 232, 251, 253
  and ethnic nationalism, 192–195,
    204–210, 249, 259
selective incentives, 161, 162, 197, 225
September 11th, 2001, 3, 135, 234, 254. *See
    also* suicide terrorism and terrorists;
    United States
  as form of theatrical protest, 142
  and McWorld's stimulation of *jihad*, 220
  religious motivation of terrorists,
    144–145, 150

September 11th, 2001 (*cont.*)
  significance of for liberal democracy, 256
  and stick policy for terrorism, 140, 251
Serbia, conflict in. *See* ethnic nationalism, in
    Yugoslavia; Milosevic, Slobodan
shah, of Iran, 165, 171. *See also* dictatorship,
    model of; Iranian Revolution
shareholder, 226
shareholder vs. stakeholder systems, 69. *See
    also* China; Singapore; South Korea;
    United States
  and corporate governance, 222–223
  and economic transparency, 216–217, 224
  effect of McWorld on, 226–227, 241
  and industrial relations, 221–222
  and role of the government, 223
  solidarity and corruption in, 234–237
Singapore, corruption in, 235
Smith, Alistair, 165
Smith, Anthony D., 199
social capital. *See also* contagion;
    intermediary bodies; solidarity
  and trust, 38–43
  as contagious, 43–45
  definition of, 46–52
  in Germany, 44
  in Italy, 38–39
  production of, 41–43
  Putnam on, 38–41
  in Russia, 45
  in the United States, 39
  variations of, 38–41
social cohesion. *See* solidarity
social interactions. *See also under* army,
    solidarity in; Asia: financial crisis of;
    crime, and social interactions; ethnic
    nationalism, in Yugoslavia; family,
    solidarity in; McWorld, and
    stimulation of *jihad*; poverty,
    group-oriented solutions for;
    revolutions; terrorism. *See also*
    bandwagon effects; contagion;
    individualistic approach, to social
    interactions; network externalities;
    solidarity
  and crime. *See* crime, and social
    interactions
  and ethnic cleansing, 209–210
  and extremism, 245–246
  and policy implications of. *See* policy, and
    social interactions

and the Iranian Revolution,
    164–165
four types of, 24
in international finance. *See* Asia,
    financial crisis of; Asian tigers;
    corruption, and economic growth;
    crony capitalism; McWorld, and
    stimulation of *jihad*; microfinance, and
    poverty; poverty, group-oriented
    solutions for; shareholder vs.
    stakeholder systems; transparency, in
    economic systems
neglect of in social problems. *See*
    individualistic approach, to social
    interactions
theories of, 24–26
social programs, and solidarity. *See* barriers
    to entry and exit; equality, pensions,
    welfare
solidarity, 26–27. *See also* barriers to entry
    and exit; external enemy; ethnic
    nationalism, in Yugolslavia; national
    solidarity; religious solidarity; social
    capital; social interactions; solidarity
    multiplier
  in army. *See* army, solidarity in
  and communism, 37–38
  and corner equilibrium, 125–128
  in cults, 114, 117, 132, 142
  definiton of, 46–52
  destruction of sources of, and McWorld's
    stimulation of *jihad*, 224–234,
    240–241, 250. *See also* China, *jihad* in;
    China, growth in, and liquidation of
    solidarity; corruption, and economic
    growth
  and extremist groups, 9–12, 109–113,
    245–246
  in family. *See* family, solidarity in
  and fascism, 37–38. *See also* Germany;
    Italy
  liquidation of, in China, 217, 239. *See also*
    China, *jihad* in; solidarity, destruction
    of sources of, and McWorld's
    stimulation of *jihad*
  and revenge, 125
  and rotten-kid theorem, 28–29, 47–48
  and solidarity systems. *See* shareholder vs.
    stakeholder systems
  in stakeholder systems, and corruption,
    234–237

and suicide terrorism, 128–131
threats to Islamic, 233–234
trading of belief for, 114–121. *See also*
  solidarity multiplier
solidarity multiplier, 109, 121–125. *See also*
  solidarity, trading of beliefs for
in academia, 124
and economists, 124
and extremism, 247–248
Sontag, Susan, 191, 192
South Korea, economic growth and
  corruption in, 216–217, 235–237
stationary bandit, 195, 213
suicide martyrdom. *See* suicide terrorism
  and terrorists
suicide terrorism and terrorists, 108–109,
  111–113. *See also* Al Qaeda; extremism
  and extremist groups; policy, on
  extremism and terrorism; September
  11th, 2001; terrorism
72 virgins explanation for, 14, 150, 151,
  152
altruism of, 109–113, 128, 248
and corner solution, 125–128, 248
income and education of, 110, 130,
  248
and Islam, 154–156
Palestinian, and revenge, 125
religious motivation of, 111–113,
  144–145, 150–152, 248–249. *See also* Al
  Qaeda; Islam; religion; religious
  solidarity; September 11th, 2001
and religious solidarity, 151–157,
  248–249
and revenge, 125, 128
and solidarity, 128–131
and trading of beliefs for solidarity,
  125–128
Sutherland, D. M. G., 180–181

Tamil Tigers, 152. *See also* suicide terrorism
  and terrorists
Tanzi, Vito, 234
terrorism. *See also* extremism and extremist
  groups; policy, on extremism and
  terrorism; suicide terrorism and
  terrorists
choosing, and risk, 86–87, 247
costs and benefits of, 110
and failure of Muslim states, 155–156
model of choice of, 87–103

policy on. *See* policy, on extremism and
  terrorism
upsurge in from dictatorships, 259
use of, and indivisible goals of group,
  87–107, 247
Theory of Group Solidarity (Hechter), 27
Thomas, Robert, 191, 196
Thompson, M. R., 172
Thompson, Mark, 198
tipping, of system markets, 44
Tocqueville, Alexis de, 184, 186. *See also*
  French Revolution
transparency, in economic systems, 65,
  217–218
illusion of, 216
and McWorld, 218–221
in shareholder vs. stakeholder systems,
  216–217, 224
trust. *See* social capital, and trust
Tudjman, Franco (Croatian leader), 194
Tullock, G., 161, 195
tyrannies. *See* dictatorship, model of

United States. *See also* September 11th, 2001
and 2004 election in, 81–83
corporate accounting scandals in, 216
decline of social capital in, 39, 45
downsizing in, 240–241
and external enemy created solidarity,
  232
shareholder system in, 69
shareholder system in, and corporate
  governance, 222–223
shareholder system in, and industrial
  relations, 221–222
and subsidizing of dictatorships and
  terrorism, 258
Uslaner, Eric M., 42
Uvalic, Milica, 197

Van Belle, D., 164
Veneroso, Frank, 67
Venkatesh, Alladi, 129

Wade, Robert, 67
war. *See* NATO, and war with Slobodan
  Milosevic
Washington Consensus, and transparency
  in economic systems, 219, 237, 246
Weber, Max, 147
Wei, Shang-Jin, 66

Weingast, Barry R., 148, 178, 194–195
welfare, 187, 221, 239, 241, 246, 257
    and European solidarity, 226, 232, 234
    and policy implications of, 102, 103, 104
Williamson, John, 219
Wintrobe, Ronald, 40–41, 42, 50
World on Fire (Chua), 83
"World War IV" (Podhoretz), 256
Wretched of the Earth (Fanon), 4

Wydick, Bruce, 63

Yellen, Janet, 22
    and gangs, 59
Yew, Lee Kwan (prime minister of
    Singapore), 235
Yunus, Muhammad, 61

Zanini, Michele, 133